ATLANTIS
DISCOVERED

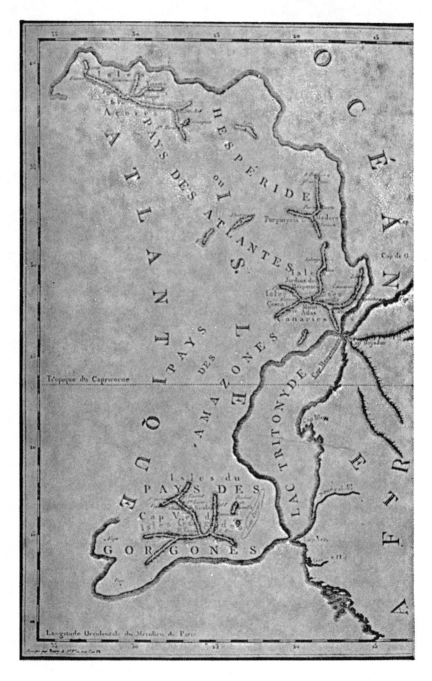

Conjectural Map of Atlantis.

(After Bory de St Vincent.)

ATLANTIS DISCOVERED

by LEWIS SPENCE

with sixteen full-page plates

INTRODUCTION TO THE CAUSEWAY
EDITION BY MICHAEL LORD

CAUSEWAY BOOKS

Causeway: A bridge from here to there

Published by Causeway Books
95 Madison Avenue, New York, N.Y. 10016
Copyright © 1974 by Causeway Books
Library of Congress Catalog Card No.: 73-92310
ISBN: 0-88356-023-2
Printed in the United States of America

Was there really a great lost continent of Atlantis?

The romantic tradition of a mighty civilization that perished beneath the waves of the Atlantic Ocean thousands of years ago was known in the time of Plato, about 600 B.C. Arabian geographers carried the story into medieval times, when it became entangled with all those legendary territories of myth and romance—the Isles of the Blest, the Fortunate Islands, the Blessed Isle of Avalon, and other-worldly paradises of the mind. Columbus knew Plato's story, and it may have influenced his quest for a New World. The legend of lost Atlantis was debated in seventeenth and eighteenth century France by Montaigne, Buffon and others. Even Voltaire conducted an interesting correspondence on the question with Bailly, then Mayor of Paris, and their letters have been preserved in a rare volume, *Lettres sur Atlantis*. In 1793, William Blake's *America: A Prophecy* used Atlantis as a symbol of the visionary ideal of liberty.

In the nineteenth century, serious study on the Atlantis question was stimulated by Ignatius Donnelly's amazing book *Atlantis: The Antediluvian World*. Donnelly was a unique personality who studied law, worked as a farmer, and became a prominent Republican Congressman as well as a brilliant and daring author. In the ninety years since Donnelly's trail-blazing book there have been more than five thousand publications on the Atlantis theme, in many different languages. Many scholars came to accept that there was good evidence that the legend of Atlantis was substantially true.

One of the greatest of these scholars was Lewis Spence. In this present book he gives a skilful analysis of the evidence for the reality of the Atlantis tradition.

James Lewis Thomas Chalmers Spence, to give him his full name, was a great-hearted Scotsman with sufficient down-to-earth realism to run a newspaper and enough romance to write poetry and study the occult. He was born in Scotland on November 25, 1874, and attended Edinburgh University. He became Sub-Editor of the influential newspaper *The Scotsman* from 1899 to 1904, and also edited *The Edinburgh Magazine*. He was a Fellow of the Royal Anthropological Institute of Great Britain and Ireland, and Vice-President of the Scottish Anthropological and Folklore Society. He held the degree of D.Litt. and was awarded a Royal Pension for his services to literature.

He wrote nearly fifty books, many concerned with the occult. He specialized in the Atlantis story, and a number of his books are devoted to this theme. In 1932, together with fellow poet Charles Richard Cammell, he founded and edited *The Atlantis Quarterly*, a journal devoted to Atlantean and occult studies.

The present book, originally published in 1924, is one of the best introductions to the Atlantis story ever written. It surveys the whole background of Plato's story and other accounts which corroborate it. It is sometimes said that Plato intended his story as fiction, but this is not true. Plato stated that the tale 'though strange, is perfectly true' and that he received the data from Critias (who inherited it in manuscript form from his grandfather). The great philosopher Proclus, in his discussions of the writings of Plato, also insisted that the story was true.

The great contribution of Lewis Spence, in modern times, was to assemble reliable evidences from many disciplines—archaeology, anthropology, geology, and folklore. He showed that a definite Atlantean culture-complex existed on both sides of the Atlantic, and that the submerged continent must have been the means of dissemination from east to west.

He discusses the myths and legends of the North American Indians, the Indians of Brazil and the Aztecs of Mexico, all bearing witness to the reality of the Atlantis culture. He examines themes echoed in the little-known *Popul Vuh*, the unique sacred book of the ancient Mayans, written in the Quiche language. He traces images and inscriptions which link the iconography of the Southern Mexicans with Egyptian and European themes, showing their connection with a common cultural source. He compares traditions of a great deluge from many countries. Like pieces of a great jigsaw puzzle, folk memories, traditions, and artifacts are assembled to create a picture of the great lost land mass and its marvelous culture.

In his final summing-up, Spence suggests that visionaries might be able to strengthen the scholarly evidence for the reality of Atlantis. So far, regretfully, psychic revelations have added little but wildly improbable stories of flying saucers and hidden occult masters. Such unreliable sources have no evidential value and only confuse the issue, but as to the creative force of Spence's own imaginative vision in stimulating reliable study and research there can be no doubt. Spence's poetic intuition gave an insight, strengthened by his scholarly disciplines. It is to be regretted that this is such a rare combination of talents.

Lewis Spence died on March 3, 1955, after devoting many years of patient research to his Atlantean studies. In one of his later books, published in 1942, he had foretold that Europe might one day follow Atlantis and itself become a dimly remembered legend to future generations.

There is, of course, something profoundly romantic and nostalgic about legends of old gods and lost cities, vanished civilizations and ancient wisdom. In the marvelous story of Atlantis, Lewis Spence is undoubtedly our best guide, combining scholarship with intuition.

This book was highly praised on first publication in 1924, and the influential *Times Literary Supplement,* London, stated:

> Mr. Spence has certainly put forward the most levelheaded work which has yet appeared in support of the Atlantis theory.

The original title of this book, *The Problem of Atlantis,* is inappropriate today in view of the many supporting works which have removed the subject from the realm of speculation and legend. Today, this fascinating subject is hardly a problem, but rather a challenge. Many details still need to be filled in. One major riddle is the date of the cataclysm. Plato's story placed the Atlantean deluge about 9,600 B.C., but it might equally have been some fifteen thousand years earlier in the days of Cro-Magnon man. It is to be hoped that this new Causeway edition will stimulate further research into civilized man's mysterious past. It should certainly introduce many modern readers to a real-life mystery stranger than any science-fiction.

London   Michael Lord
November 1973

PREFACE

THE purpose of this book is not so much to demonstrate the former existence of an Atlantean continent as to place the study of the whole problem on a more accurate basis than has yet been attempted in recent times. Where the weight of proof has seemed to me to justify such a course I have not hesitated to speak plainly and perhaps dogmatically, and have even in places adopted the attitude of the ardent protagonist. But it is not my intention to leave the reader with the impression that I am absolutely convinced of the infallibility of every consideration I have brought forward. Many of my arguments may be traversed, but I hasten to say that that will not in any way alter my belief in the basic truth of my contention that the wreck of Atlantis sleeps beneath the sea. A hypothesis must, in any case, stand or fall by the nature of the proof brought to its support, and this I have sought to make of a character as unimpeachable as the very difficult circumstances admit of.

What I have written regarding the evidence for the Atlantean origin of the civilisations of Central America and Peru is the outcome of prolonged study of the problems presented by the archæology of these areas. My predecessors in this portion of the task, the Abbé Brasseur de Bourbourg, and Dr Augustus le Plongeon, were certainly precipitate, and I may have fallen into the same error. But even when farthest astray, there is considerable method in their madness. Brasseur tells us that " a city named

Atlan existed, when the continent was discovered by
Columbus, at the entrance to the Gulf of Uraba, in Darien,
with a good harbour : it is now reduced to an unimportant
pueblo named Acla."

What I have said regarding the movement of early civilisation from West to East may arouse opposition from the
upholders of that still unofficial theory that all culture
emanated from the Egypt of the Pyramid era. I do not
deny that during that era Egyptian civilisation progressed
slowly Westwards. But it was, as I believe, retracing its
steps towards regions whence it had originally come. So
far as is known, the earth's earliest civilisation appeared in
the Biscayan and Pyrenean area, centuries before it took root
in Egypt, and all the arguments in the world cannot discredit
that fact. Nor can they alter the equally salient fact that
the Crô-Magnon civilisation alluded to contained the germs
of early Nilotic culture, and that it continued to flourish in
the Canary Islands until their discovery by the Spaniards.
These are, indeed, the most damaging arguments which the
opponents of the Atlantean hypothesis have to confront.

I have not, like some of my predecessors, attempted to
show that Atlantis must have flourished in the " Bronze
Age." The whole circumstances render such a theory
untenable. The possession of metal implements is, in my
view, not essential to a high standard of human culture.
The ancient Maya, Mexicans, and Peruvians were without
metal tools or weapons, but they were more truly " civilised "
than many peoples with higher pretensions existing at the
present time, who could not approach them in the spheres
of architecture or social polity.

I have left untouched the question of the Sargasso Sea,
as the result of recent researches by skilled investigators in

that Atlantic area has convinced me that most of the former conclusions as to the possibility of its indicating the site of a sunken land were based on mistaken and insufficient data. On the other hand, I think I have brought cogent arguments against the now widely accepted theory that the idea of Atlantis arose out of a memory of the former civilisation of Crete.

LEWIS SPENCE.

CONTENTS

LIST OF ILLUSTRATIONS

CHAPTER I

THE ATLANTIS OF PLATO

THE student of tradition will not readily encounter in the annals of his science a legend so persistent or so powerful in the appeal it makes to human imagination as that which tells of a great island-continent sunk fathoms deep beneath the waves of the Atlantic Ocean. With the passing of generations credence in the former existence of such a region, instead of dwindling into a shadowy and inchoate myth, has assumed an appearance of scientific probability which compels the respectful attention of the serious geologist and folklorist. Within the past half-century a great and growing body of proof has by degrees gathered round a nucleus of conjecture. Expeditions fitted out by successive governments, American and European, have dragged the ocean-bed in search of the relics of a submerged land. Learned biologists have assured us that it is impossible to account for the similarities of certain forms of life in Western Europe and Eastern America otherwise than by assuming the existence of a former terrestrial connection between these regions. The folklores of the opposing European and American littorals are rich in memories of an ancient cataclysm, which precipitated the wreck of an oceanic culture from which their peoples believed themselves to have drawn the elements of progress. Indeed the testimony

1

in favour of the existence of an Atlantean continent has now assumed proportions so formidable as to give pause to even the most dogmatic of those who once flatly rejected it as fabulous.

The gradual growth of certainty in relation to the Atlantean theory closely resembles the process by which the existence of an American continent became increasingly clear to European men of science. The opponents of the belief in a western hemisphere laid stress upon the circumstance that the whole fabric of proof concerning it rested upon a traditional basis. They laughed to scorn the notion that the tales of the Island of Brasil, or of St Brandan's Isle might have some foundation in fact. But with the passage of time, and the gradual accumulation of evidence, actual and analogical, a strong impression took hold upon the imagination of scientific Europe that these venerable and picturesque tales were not altogether mythical. Enlightened and independent thinkers and geographers boldly announced their belief in a new world across the ocean, and at last the greatest of these, inspired as much by intuition as by his perusal of the Icelandic sagas and the classics, and the growth during his own lifetime of the geographical proof, put his convictions to the test and demonstrated to the astonishment of humanity that tradition is often but the truth fossilised, the skeleton beneath the superincumbent strata of history.

Just as a world-intuition regarding the existence of a transatlantic continent prevailed in the time of Columbus, so a similar instinct, overwhelming and ineradicable, is being manifested in our own day regarding the existence of a great continent in the Atlantic Ocean in times past. This belief unquestionably has its origin in folk-memory, and is thus safe from the assaults of that description of science which has ever held tradition in disesteem. The triumphant vindication of the Atlantean hypothesis is merely a matter of time and opportunity. That hypothesis, I maintain, rests not on Plato's account alone, or indeed, on any one class of evidence, but on the great mass of testimony, tradition, and scientific argument which has accumulated throughout the ages on its behalf.

But only one account which can be classed as strictly of the nature of documentary evidence has come down to us concerning Atlantis. This is the narrative of Plato alluded to above, which has been retold so frequently of late years that it must be fairly familiar to everyone in the least interested in the problem of the drowned continent. A brief summary, then, from which no salient fact has been omitted, is all that space can admit of in these pages.

In the dialogue known as *The Timæus* Plato makes a certain Critias tell Timæus and Socrates that Dropidas, his great-grandfather, had handed down writings and traditions concerning the Athenians of the early world. These he had received from Solon, one of the wisest of the Greeks, who had himself been apprised of them by an Egyptian priest of the goddess Neith, or Net, at Saïs, in Egypt. This priest identified the goddess in question with the Greek divinity Pallas Athene, and assured Solon that she had founded Athens " nine thousand years ago," which, as this conversation must have taken place about 600 B.C., throws back the date of Athenian origin to 9600 years before the Christian era. A thousand years later, added Solon's informant, Neith or Athene founded Saïs itself, as was recorded in the sacred registers of the temple.

The Egyptian then proceeded to impart to Solon an outline of early Athenian history. He told him that at a date unspecified in this particular dialogue the Greek city was attacked by a mighty power which had tried to fix the yoke of empire upon the whole of Europe and Asia. This power came forth out of the Atlantic Ocean, from an island situated in front of the Pillars of Hercules, otherwise the

Straits of Gibraltar. The island in question was greater than Libya or Northern Africa and Asia (Asia Minor) put together, " and was the way to other islands, and through the islands you might pass through the whole of the opposite continent which surrounded the true ocean." The largest body of land in this archipelago was, we gather, called Atlantis, and sustained a great and wonderful empire, " which had rule over the whole island and several others, as well as over parts of the (opposite) continent." But its inhabitants, not content with the territory which already belonged to them, subjected the parts of Libya within the Pillars of Hercules as far as Egypt, and those of Europe as far as Tyrrhenia (Italy). Pressing eastward, they attacked Greece itself. But through the courage and address of the Athenians the invading Atlanteans were beaten off and finally expelled from the whole of their possessions within the Mediterranean area.

At a later period, continued Solon's priestly informant, violent earthquakes and floods occurred. In a single day and night of heavy rains all the warlike men of Athens sank into the earth, and the island of Atlantis " in like manner " disappeared beneath the sea, " and this is the reason why the sea in those parts is impassable and impenetrable, because there is such a quantity of shallow mud in the way, and this was caused by the subsidence of the island."

Further details of the story of Atlantis as told to Solon by the priests of Saïs are furnished by Plato in the dialogue known as *The Critias*. From these we gather that the date of the invasion of the Mediterranean basin by the Atlantean kings took place about 9600 B.C. Many great convulsions of nature had occurred since then. Dropidas, the great-grandfather of Critias, who preserved the tale, had received the facts in writing from Solon, who in turn had them from the Egyptian priests of Saïs. The manuscript at the time the dialogue took place was still in the possession of Critias.

Plato makes Critias say that the names of the Atlanteans referred to in the account had been " Egyptianised " by the priests, and later Hellenised by Solon himself.

The gods, remarks Critias paraphrasing this account, in dividing the regions of the earth among themselves, apportioned the island of Atlantis to Poseidon or Neptune. On the side of it nearest the sea (the Atlantic Ocean) and in the centre of the island was a fertile plain, at a distance of fifty stadia [1] from which stood a low mountain where dwelt one of the aborigines of the country, Evenor, who had a wife Leucippe, and a daughter Cleito. Poseidon fell in love with Cleito, and enclosed the hill where she dwelt with alternate zones of sea and land encircling one another, so that no man might reach this Eden. In this insular labyrinth he begat and brought up five pairs of male twins, and divided the island among them, the eldest, Atlas, receiving as his portion his mother's dwelling, the largest allotment, and the kingship. The others became rulers of the contiguous islands, but the branch founded by Atlas always retained the central or imperial power. From foreign countries much rich merchandise was brought, and the Atlanteans, or the tribes who owed their origin to Atlas, dug precious metals out of the earth, including orichalcum, or copper. They had abundance of timber for carpenter-work, and the animals they made use of included the elephant. The fruits of the island-continent, both wild and cultivated, were very numerous. Vegetables, chestnuts, and a fruit with a hard rind " affording drinks, and meats, and ointments " flourished exceedingly.

The Atlanteans, we are informed, employed themselves in constructing temples, palaces, and harbours. They laid out the country in the following manner : they threw bridges over the zones of sea which surrounded the central height, and made a passage into the royal palace, which they

---

[1] The Greek stadium was equal to 602⅔ English feet.

increased in size and beauty with each successive reign.
They drove a canal through the zones of land three hundred
feet wide and about one hundred deep, and fifty stadia,
or about six miles in length, constructing a harbour at
the landward end of this waterway which was capable
of sheltering the largest vessels. " They also divided
the zones of land which parted the zones of sea, erecting
bridges of such a width as would leave a passage for a
single trireme (or galley with three banks of oars) to pass
out of one into another, and roofed them over. Now the
largest of the zones into which a passage was cut from the
sea was three stadia in breadth, and the zone of land which
came next of equal breadth. But the next two zones, the
one of water, the other of land, were two stadia, and the one
which surrounded the central island was a stadium only in
width. The island in which the palace was situated had a
diameter of five stadia. All this, including the zones and the
bridge, which was the sixth part of a stadium in width, they
surrounded by a stone wall on all sides, placing towers and
gates on the bridges where the sea passed in."

The stones of which the Atlanteans constructed their
buildings were quarried from the native rocks, and were
white, black, and red in colour. In many of their houses
and temples these were intermingled for purposes of ornament. The walls of the city were faced with brass, tin, and
orichalcum, which emitted a red light. In the centre of the
citadel was a temple dedicated to Cleito and Poseidon,
inaccessible and surrounded by a golden enclosure, as well
as another fane solely dedicated to Poseidon and built in
a style of " barbaric splendour." Its walls were covered with
silver, and its pinnacles with gold. The interior was roofed
with ivory, gold, silver, and the brilliant orichalcum. Here
stood a golden statue of Poseidon erect in his chariot, to
which were harnessed six winged steeds. Golden statues of
his ten sons and their wives were placed at intervals around

this glowing edifice. Fountains and baths leading from hot and cold springs surrounded the temple site, and between the Acropolis and the densely packed houses of the city lay a racecourse which encircled the whole island. The great docks sheltered numerous large ships and were frequented by merchants from all parts, and the hum of human voices and the din of commerce rose in the streets from sunrise to sunset.

The country itself was lofty and precipitous " on the side of the sea," but the city was built on a level plain, oblong in shape, and surrounded by mountains. The whole region of the island was open toward the south, but sheltered on the northern side. The surrounding mountains were celebrated for their height and beauty, and contained many large villages, rivers, lakes, and woods. The plain was encompassed by a mighty ditch or fosse, which received the mountain streams and the outflow of the canals. The island was divided into sixty thousand lots, each of which was ten stadia square. The owner of a lot was bound to furnish the sixth part of a war-chariot, so as to make up ten thousand chariots, two horses and riders upon them, a light chariot without a seat, and an attendant and charioteer, two heavily armed infantry-men, two archers, two slingers, three stone-shooters, three javelin-men, and four sailors, to make up the complement of twelve hundred ships.

Each of the twelve kings was absolute in his own island. The laws of Poseidon governed the relations between the various insular states, and these laws had been inscribed by the first men on a pillar of orichalcum in the temple of Poseidon, where the people were gathered together and held festival every fifth and every sixth year. Near the temple grazed the sacred bulls of Poseidon, and these the ten kings of the islands periodically offered up in sacrifice, shedding the blood of the victim over the inscription, and vowing not to transgress the laws of Poseidon. When night fell they put on azure robes and judged offenders. Their laws did not permit them to take up arms against one another, instructed them to deliberate together, and gave no power of life and death to the monarch over his kinsmen, unless he had the assent of the majority.

For many generations the polity of Atlantis was undisturbed; the people were gentle and obedient to the laws and to the gods, and wise in their intercourse with one another. Nor were they attracted by wealth. But gradually the blood of the gods which flowed in their veins was diluted with the mortal admixture, and they became degenerate. Zeus regarded them with disfavour, and convening a council of the gods, spoke as follows :—

Here Plato's account ends abruptly. But, even so, it has succeeded in awakening the imagination of successive generations of readers as perhaps few passages in Hellenic literature have done.

Other notices in classical authors which refer to Atlantis are, for the most part, probably based on Plato's account. A fragment from a lost work of Theopompus of Chios, a historian of the fourth century B.C., which is to be found in the *Varia Historia* of Ælian, a compiler of the third century A.D., purports to be told by the satyr Silenus to Midas, king of Phrygia, and as here given is taken from the English translation of Abraham Fleming, published in London in 1576.

" Silenus tolde Midas of certaine Islands, named Europa, Asia, and Libia, which the Ocean Sea circumscribeth and compasseth round about. And that without this worlde there is a continent or percell of dry lande, which in greatnesse (as hee reported) was infinite and unmeasurable, that it nourished and maintained by the benefite of the greene medowes and pasture plots sundrye bigge and mighty beastes ; that the men which inhabite the same climats exceede the stature of us twise, and yet the length of their life is not equale to ours."

He related many other wonders of the two cities, Machimus the warlike and Euseues the peaceful, and how the inhabitants of the former to the number of ten millions once made an attack on Europe, coming first to the land of the Hyperboreans. When they learnt that these were people of peculiar sanctity, they abhorred them and held them in contempt, and withdrew, supposing it to be a worthless enterprise to annex their country. The concluding passage relates to the strange land of the Meropes, from whose name later writers have called the country Meropian.

An account of the great continent of Saturnia from the dialogue attributed to Plutarch, " On the Face appearing in the Orb of the Moon," and printed with his *Morals*, tells us that " an isle, Ogygia, lies in Ocean's arms, about five days' sail west from Britain, and before it are three others of about equal distance from one another, and also from that, bearing north-west, where the sun sets in summer. In one of these the barbarians feign that Saturn is detained in prison by Zeus." The neighbouring sea was known as the Saturnian, and the continent by which the great sea was circularly environed was distant from Ogygia about five thousand stadia, but from the other islands not so far. A bay of this continent in the latitude of the Caspian Sea, was inhabited by Greeks, who once in thirty years sent certain of their number to minister to the imprisoned Saturn. One of these paid a visit to the great island, as they called Europe, and from him the narrator learned many strange things, especially regarding the state of the soul after death.

Proclus reports that Marcellus, a writer of whom nothing else is known, in a work entitled *The Ethiopic History*, speaks of ten islands situated in the Atlantic Ocean, close to Europe. He says that the inhabitants of these islands preserved the memory of a much larger Atlantic island, Atlantis, which had for long exercised dominion over the other islands of that ocean.

Strabo says that Poseidonius (151–135 B.C.) remarked that as the land was known to have changed in elevation the account of Plato ought not to be regarded as fiction, and that such a continent as Atlantis might well have existed and disappeared.[1]

Such are the principal classical allusions to Atlantis. If we direct the light of modern criticism upon them they may not appear so destitute of probability as some authorities believe them to be.

[1] Didot-Müller, *Fragmenta Historium Græcorum*, tom. iii, p. 281.

CHAPTER II

PLATO'S ACCOUNT EXAMINED

BEFORE proceeding further, it will be necessary to make a careful and critical examination of Plato's account of Atlantis. This has, of course, been essayed by many writers, but, unfortunately, much of the scrutiny was undertaken at a period in literary history when it was a generally accepted axiom that legend was seldom, if ever, founded on probability. Half a century ago the tale of Troy and the epic of Arthur were regarded as so purely mythical in essence that any writer who ventured to assert their historicity was regarded with tolerant amusement. To-day no serious student of these problems denies that Troy actually existed, or that the Arthurian legend is based on the facts of Romano-British history. The historical portions of the Old Testament itself were in the days of our grandfathers by no means exempt from the suspicion of legendary connections. But archæological proof from excavation in Egypt, Assyria, and elsewhere has been forthcoming for the vindication of such passages as that, for example, which deals with the episode of Chedorlaomer, long declared by Biblical critics to be legendary. Broadly speaking, it is now generally accepted by critics of insight—the others do not matter much—that when a large body of myth crystallises round one central figure, race, or locality, it is almost certain to enshrine a certain proportion of historical truth capable of extraction from the mass of fabulous material which surrounds it, and when so refined, is worthy of acceptance by the most meticulous of historical purists.

Plato, it seems to me, set down the story of Atlantis much in the same spirit as Geoffrey of Monmouth set down the tale of Arthur, or Homer that of Troy. For a long time Geoffrey, as students of the Arthurian epic will recall, was branded as the perpetrator of " the greatest fraud in literary history," and the " British book " from which he stated he had drawn his material was regarded as a mere figment of his fraudulent imagination. But recent careful investigation has made it evident that he undoubtedly drew upon Welsh, and perhaps Breton manuscripts now lost to us. Unless I err greatly, Plato in his *Critias* and *Timæus* drew upon similar sources. He makes Critias say that his great-grandfather Dropidas " had the original writing," which Solon had set down after his conversation with the priests of Saïs, and a long experience in dealing with traditional material leads me to the conclusion that the sneer of Jowett in his commentaries on the *Timæus* and *Critias* [1] that Plato invented " a noble lie," is much more in keeping with the fearful spirit of Victorian scholarship than with the more liberal propensities of that of our own day, which are all in favour of regarding the writers of antiquity as equally worthy of credence with those of modern times, if ordinary critical care be exercised in dealing with the material they have handed down to us.

Nor do I believe that Plato in these extraordinary dialogues intended to allegorise as did Sir Thomas More in his *Utopia*, or Mr Wells in his *Men Like Gods*. He points no moral to adorn his tale, but draws a fairly complete picture of a civilisation which had as few points of resemblance with the Greece of his day as it is possible to imagine. That he did not invent Atlantis is obvious from the following considerations :—

He makes Socrates declare that the tale is " suitable to

[1] See the Introductions to his *Dialogues of Plato*, and especially vol. iii, p. 684.

the festival of the goddess " (Pallas Athene), and that it has the very great advantage of being fact and not fiction. Critias asserts that " the sacred Egyptian record has rescued from oblivion " the circumstances of the story.[1] He further states that it had made a wonderful impression on his mind as a child, that he had heard it time and again, and that it had been " branded into his mind in ineffaceable letters."

It is obvious that, as several commentators have admitted, the Egyptian origin of the story is not far to seek. It is now known that Neith, the goddess of Saïs, or the city of Het-byati, " the House of the Bee-man " (*i.e.* the king of Lower Egypt), was, as the priest averred, no other than the goddess Pallas Athene, the patroness of Athens, in another form. The names have a similar provenance : both goddesses were virgins and presided over war. The arrow with which Neith is invariably represented is but the spear of Athene in another form. Neith was of Libyan origin, and her worship was prevalent in that part of Egypt where the majority of the population was of Libyan blood. Her worship had almost certainly been introduced into the Nile Valley by Iberians from the west, who also carried it to Greece. It is without the bounds of possibility that a Greek of Plato's period and opportunities should have been aware of the resemblance between the Egyptian and Hellenic forms of Neith-Athene unless he had received the information through an Egyptian source. He draws parallels between the castes who served the goddess in Egypt and Greece which have been substantiated by modern research, resemblances which must

---

[1] Proclus (*fl.* A.D. 412–485) reports that Crantor, the first commentator on Plato (*c.* 300 B.C.), asserts that the Egyptian priests told Solon that the story was written on pillars which were still preserved. This appears to me as not at all improbable, and was certainly an Egyptian custom. See *The Commentaries of Proclus on the Timæus of Plato*, translated by Thomas Taylor, London, 1820. Martin, who was hostile to the Atlantean theory, expresses his belief in his work on *The Timæus of Plato* (Paris, 1841) that Solon received his account of it from Egyptian priests at first hand.

have remained unknown to any Greek unless he had them
at first or second-hand from a Nilotic source.

Plato's statement that the Atlantic was not, in his time,
regarded as navigable is, as will be shown, strictly in accordance with what is known of the maritime history of his day.
Had his account been of an allegorical character, like More's
or Mr Wells's, its fictional atmosphere would have been
obvious. He would have transported us as these masters
of fiction have done to the allegorical region and atmosphere,
to Atlantis itself, and would surely have feigned its contemporary existence. But he tells us that it has been sunken
in ocean these nine thousand years, and this at once differen-
tiates his story from all of those which speak of supernatural
lands. These, as all students of folklore are aware, are
invariably spoken of as still existing.

I will preserve the geological justification of Plato's
account for the chapter in which it is dealt with in detail,
and will pass on to consider his chronology. Nine thousand
years, he tells us, had in his day elapsed since Atlantis
invaded the Mediterranean basin and was valiantly with-
stood by the Athenians. This places the date of that
invasion roughly at 9600 B.C. Here we are met by what at
first sight seems an insuperable obstacle to credence. We
are asked to believe that thousands of years prior to the
institution of the First Dynasty in Egypt the Athenian state
already existed in a condition of comparative enlightenment.
It is now generally admitted that Egypt had for many
centuries prior to the dynastic period enjoyed a certain
measure of civilisation. But is there reason for the inference
that Hellenic culture had at that period yet emerged from
barbarism ? The First Dynasty in Egypt is now known to
be coeval with the beginning of the Bronze Age in Crete
and the First Early Minoan civilisation there (c. 3500 B.C.),
and with the Early Helladic culture discovered by Wace
on the mainland of Greece. All that has been found at

Athens of a prior date is a little Neolithic pottery. The date 9600 B.C. takes us back to the early Neolithic or New Stone Age in Europe, when metals were not as yet used by any race, and were not to be for another six thousand years, when agriculture was as yet almost unknown, and even Egypt was in a condition of utter barbarism.

There is, of course, not the slightest incumbency upon the most meticulous or most irresponsible protagonist of the Atlantean hypothesis to accept Plato's chronology. He evidently received it from Egyptian sources, and the Egyptians, like the Chinese, were prone to refer great events to an antiquity which connected them with the deities of the national religion and appealed to their national pride. And can we upbraid Plato for a lack of knowledge of the circumstances of Hellenic prehistory ? If so, we must arraign every historian who ever wielded pen for the crime of dealing with such material as he had to his hand. History is the art of arranging the writings and traditions which refer to a nation or period in a consecutive narrative. The older historians are too often called to account for embroidering that narrative. But it is only from the modern viewpoint that they can be accused of so doing. If they introduce occurrences or episodes which appear to us as marvellous or exaggerated, we must reflect that these did not so appear to them. The same applies to their chronology. Only fifty years ago many British historians were still employing the chronological system of Archbishop Usher, which fixed the commencement of the world about 4004 B.C. That chronology was part of the theological belief of the generation immediately preceding our own, and those who first infringed its principles were regarded as desperate atheists. What then can we expect from a writer of twenty-three centuries ago but a strict compliance with a chronology which was part of the religious belief of his time ?

But this notwithstanding, I am prepared to show later that

Plato's chronology is substantially correct, so far at least as that part of it which deals with the date of the Atlantean invasion is concerned. For the present I must confine myself to the criticism of the details of his narrative, which constitutes the only strictly " documentary " evidence of the existence of Atlantis. That part of his account which makes the Athenian state the successful upholder of European freedom against the invading hordes of Atlantis must, it is clear, go by the board, instigated as it probably was by national pride or sheer ignorance. Solon, possessing as he probably did an account of an Atlantean reverse in the Ægean, concluded that it was inflicted by " Greeks," much as a historian of the future cut off from the history of the past by lack of documentary evidence might believe that the conquest of Britain by Cæsar had been effected by modern Italians.

Plato naturally treats of the " mythical " period of Atlantean history as a Greek writer of his period might be expected to do. Poseidon, its lord, is god of the sea, a suitable ruler in an oceanic area. It was the Greek custom to refer to Hellenic gods as the patrons or founders of foreign lands. Atlas, the son of Poseidon, is mentioned by several Greek writers as the founder of Mauretania, the land in the neighbourhood of the Pillars of Hercules, and this may have seemed to Plato good evidence of his Atlantean connection. Atlas had a fair territory in his island kingdom, which was provided with all the materials required for the growth of a civilised state. It had mines of silver, gold, and orichalcum, this last mysterious metal being nothing more nor less than the Greek word *oreichalkos*, " mountain copper." The word is used by Spenser to describe a gold-coloured alloy resembling brass, a kind of pinchbeck.

The disposal of the zones of sea and land in Atlantis might at first seem as reminiscent of the machinery of fable as once did the famous Labyrinth at Thebes, or the Hanging

PLATE I.

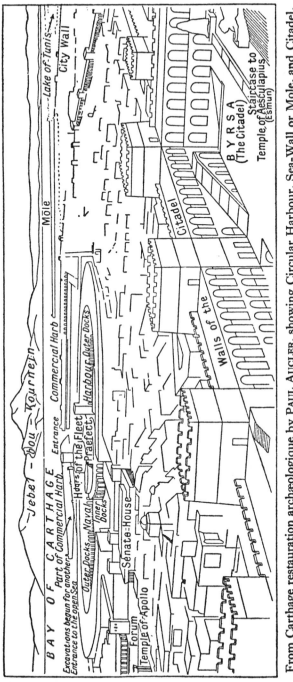

From Carthage restauration archæologique by PAUL AUCLER, showing Circular Harbour, Sea-Wall or Mole, and Citadel.

(By courtesy of the Librairie Delagrave.)

Gardens at Babylon, since identified.[1] But a perusal of a recent plan of Carthage reconstructed by M. Paul Aucler has led me to observe a marked resemblance between the plan of that city and Plato's description of Atlantis. Carthage resembled Atlantis in this, that her power lay to a great extent in her secret situation. The low, walled hill of the Byrsa or citadel on which stood the splendid temple of Æsculapius at Carthage was strengthened on the mainland side by three great ramparts which stretched across the breadth of the peninsula, and which were fortified at intervals by towers. Below the market-place and the Senate House a vast waterway, 1066 feet wide, had been constructed round a circular island on which stood the admiral's headquarters. The docks surrounding this waterway were roofed in by a great circular colonnade supported by Ionic pillars, and were capable of accommodating war-vessels of the largest size. The basin thus enclosed was known as the *cothon* or drinking-cup, and from this a narrow channel ran southward into a mercantile harbour 1396 feet long. The sea-entrance to this was only 76 feet broad, could be quickly closed by chains, and was the only entrance to both harbours. A great sea-wall masked this entrance and prevented attack by a hostile fleet. Marshes surrounded the landward side, and the water-supply was drawn from great cisterns on the neighbouring hills, which seem also to have been used as baths.

Both Atlantis and Carthage had thus a citadel hill encircled by zones of land and water, a canal to the sea, penetrating to the inmost zone, the zones were bridged over, and the connecting bridges were fortified by towers. Moreover in both cases the docks were roofed in, the cities were encircled by three walls, both had great cisterns for the supply of drinking-water and baths, and, finally, both were guarded by a great sea-wall, masking the entrance to their harbours.

[1] See the late Professor King's *Hist. of Babylon*, p. 46 ff.

I think that a comparison of these resemblances, which include most unusual features, will leave no doubt in any unbiassed mind that the plan of Carthage was substantially the same as that of Atlantis. The inevitable question of course arises, how is this to be accounted for ? We can only do so either by the assumption that Carthage was herself Atlantis, or that her plan was an architectural memory of that city. The first hypothesis is untenable, as the date at which Critias is said to have delivered his narrative was prior to the building of Carthage in its modern aspect as conceived by M. Aucler. I therefore incline to the view that when Plato described Atlantis as he did, he was naturally unaware that he was also practically describing the more modern Carthage that was yet to be, even though the general plan of that city had been laid down long before his time.

If these conclusions be accurate, we are left face to face with the assumption that Carthage was constructed in accordance with a traditional scheme of " town-planning " which had ancient local sanction, a plan not uncommon in the Atlantic area of Western Africa. Aristotle and Strabo state that the Phœnicians knew of a secret island in the Atlantic to which they intended to fly in the event of disaster overtaking them in Africa. I have, too, discovered proof that the plan of surrounding a town or settlement by zones of land and water was anciently in use in North-Western and Western Africa, that an island within an island was there regarded as a site of great natural strength, and this, as every archæologist is aware, is nothing more or less than the general idea carried out in many of the prehistoric island-forts of Britain, which were indubitably of Mediterranean origin, and are not to be distinguished in their architectural features from the *nuraghe* or dry-stone towers of Sardinia. But I will reserve this proof for future discussion, and will content myself by remarking here that Carthage was situated in the territory of Atlas, and that no consideration of Atlantean civilisation can, in my view, afford to dispense with the substantial degree of proof afforded by the existence of a city of this architectural character so close to the Atlantean scene.

To proceed with the task of criticism. We are told that the stones employed for the building of the city of Atlantis were quarried from underneath the central island, and the inner and outer zones. They were of three colours, white, black, and red—" ancient rocks," says M. Termier of the Geological Survey of France, in describing the site of Atlantis, " bearing with some fragments of whitish calcareous terranes, extinct volcanic mountains, and lava-flows, black and red, long since grown cold." [1]

The descriptions of the temples of Atlantis appear to me by no means fortuitous, or as efforts of the imagination. Nor do they approximate to any architectural style to be found in Greece in Plato's time. Indeed they are as unlike the stark purity of Hellenic architecture as could well be imagined, and much more resemble the buildings of Nineveh and Persepolis. Especially is this the case as regards the construction of the roofs or ceilings, which were of gold, silver, and bronze, like those of Assyria and early Persia.

I might also point out that the passage which speaks of the existence of twenty golden statues of the kings of Atlantis and their wives has a striking parallel in Peruvian history. When the conquering Spaniards entered the golden-walled Temple of the Sun, at Cuzco, they beheld the mummies of the Incas seated within in an imposing semicircle. A similar sight was encountered in the Temple of the Moon, where the embalmed queens of the Incas were seated in all the panoply of dead royalty.

---

[1] See his address to the Institut Océanographique of Paris, 30th Nov. 1912, translated in the annual report of the Smithsonian Institution.

The civil and religious details which conclude the *Critias* will, in spite of their vagueness, furnish us with interesting parallels at a later stage.

Enough has been said for the present to establish the fact that Plato's account of Atlantis was by no means an effort of the imagination. To summarise :—

1. Modern research has justified the contention that all legend is based on a substratum of truth.

2. Plato's account of Atlantis is of the same class as that of Geoffrey of Monmouth regarding Arthur, or that of Homer regarding Troy—an admixture of partially authentic tradition and facts drawn from documentary evidence. He lays stress on the strong impression the tale made upon Critias as a boy, and emphasises the fact that he deals not with fiction, but with reality.

3. Although the Atlantean hypothesis by no means rests upon the account of Plato alone, still, as proof already adduced and to be adduced shows and will show, there is no good reason to doubt the substantial and general accuracy and historicity of that account.

4. He could not have known of the resemblance of the goddess Neith to Pallas Athene unless through Egyptian sources, and this strengthens the assumption that documentary evidence regarding Atlantis existed in Ancient Egypt, as critics of standing admit.

5. Plato's statement regarding a prehistoric Athens was probably instigated by patriotic motives, and his statement that the Athenians repulsed the invading Atlanteans probably preserves the memory of a foreign defeat in the Ægean at an early date.

6. Plato gives the story of Atlantis an Hellenic setting as a Greek of his period would naturally do, but he affords reasons for his employment of Hellenic names for Atlantean personages. These, he states, were translated from Atlantean into Egyptian, and from Egyptian into Greek—a rather

involved process, which would scarcely have occurred even to the most imaginative of story-tellers.

7. His description of Atlantis bears a strong resemblance to a recent " restoration " of Carthage, the Atlantean connection of which has frequently been stressed. Plato could not have been aware that this description could apply to a future Carthage, therefore it seems probable from this and other considerations still to be brought forward that Carthage was planned in accordance with an ancient Atlantean design which had long been in vogue in North-Western Africa and Western Europe.

8. The character of the stone of which Atlantis is said to have been built has been recognised by a geologist of eminence as such as would have existed in an oceanic area where volcanic disturbances were of frequent occurrence.

It is manifest that these conclusions by no means exhaust the inferences to be drawn from Plato's account. But they have at least the merit of novelty, and, I venture to think, provide fresh material of considerable critical value worthy the attention of future investigators, and go far to confirm Plato's honesty of purpose. It has been the misfortune of the Atlantean hypothesis that in some quarters it has not hitherto been approached in any logical or tolerable manner. Analogies of the wildest description have all too often alienated serious investigators and great disservice has been done to the study by the wholesale manner in which ill-equipped writers have drawn upon false and absurd archæological and philological resemblances to support the theory of the Atlantean penetration of European and American regions. The quest has, indeed, no need of such meretricious aids. It rests on a foundation of scientific truth as well as upon a great and well-defined world-memory, and that its legend is capable of scientific demonstration I shall endeavour to make abundantly clear. If the problem of Atlantis is at present obscure, it is as the science of Egyptology, or the archæology of Central America was once obscure. Painful research, patient endurance, have worked miracles of enlightenment in these fields. So will they do in the field of Atlantean study. But the same cautious and scientific spirit of inquiry must prevail, the same critical attitude be maintained, if success is one day to be accomplished and the wonders of the island-continent which have haunted the dreams of mankind for so long are ever to be unveiled.

As has already been remarked, no hypothesis of the former existence of Atlantis can be built up on the Platonic account alone. This has been the grand error of many of the former protagonists of the theory. Plato's account but furnishes the clue. To attempt to justify every one of its assertions is as futile as to try to do so in the case of the Trojan or Arthurian legends, and that is one of the reasons why I have not attempted to draw from the *Critias* or the *Timæus* any proof which would not commend itself to strict literary or historical opinion.

Is it possible that the memory of a great world-catastrophe which caused vast and far-reaching changes in human history should persist for many thousands of years ? The reply, given out of a prolonged experience of the vitality of tradition, is unhesitatingly in the affirmative. No man with any real experience in dealing with traditional material can doubt that Plato's account of Atlantis is founded on sources much more ancient, and that these again owed their origin to a persistent folk-memory of a mighty series of upheavals, the geological proof concerning which will be found in the following chapter.

CHAPTER III

THE EVIDENCE FROM GEOLOGY

IN order that the non-scientific reader may better be able to follow the evidence placed before him in this chapter, I have prefaced its consideration by a brief and simple outline of geological time. The two great epochs of the earth's physical history which are connected with mankind are the Tertiary and the Quaternary. The first of these is divided into Early and Late Tertiary. The Early Tertiary period is again subdivided into Palæocene, Eocene, and Oligocene, the last of which is contemporary with the appearance of the anthropoid apes. The Late Tertiary is subdivided into Miocene and Pliocene, during the latter of which true man first makes his appearance.

The great Quaternary epoch is divided into the Pleistocene or Ice Age, and the Holocene or recent. The whole may be tabulated as follows :—

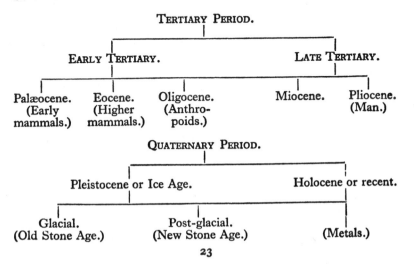

23

The problem before us is, then, with what stage of the earth's and man's history does the existence of such an island-continent as that which has come to be known as Atlantis coincide ? That is the crux of the whole matter from the geological point of view. Is it capable of proof that such a continent or region existed at such a period as would permit of its being peopled by the human species ?

It will be obvious from the foregoing that the only part of the above human-geological table which concerns us is that which deals with the Quaternary epoch as a whole.

Opinions differ considerably as to the length of time during which the Pleistocene or Ice Age, with its recurrent periods of inter-glacial warm conditions, lasted. Professor Sollas [1] has estimated it at 400,000 years, Penck [2] at 520,000 to 840,000, and Professor James Geikie [3] at a minimum of 620,000 years.

The beginning of the Pleistocene Age is, for practical purposes, generally reckoned at about 500,000 years ago, and is subdivided into four glacial epochs and one post-glacial epoch, and three inter-glacial stages.

Now it is only in the post-glacial or final stage, which, according to a consensus of the best opinion, commenced about 25,000 years ago, that any form approaching modern man is to be found in Europe. Before that time the conti-nent was inhabited by races of low physique and mentality, one of which, known as Neanderthal Man,[4] was by no means so far advanced on the road of evolution as present-day man. His ape-like hand was incapable of grasping the clumsy stone weapons he made use of in such a manner as to permit him to undertake any finer work. With the advent of newer races he seems to have vanished and no traces

[1] *Evolutional Geology*, 1900.
[2] *Die Alpen im Eiszeitalter*, 1909.
[3] *The Antiquity of Man in Europe*, 1914.
[4] See Osborn, *Men of the Old Stone Age*, p. 214 ff.

of him are to be found in the physiology of present-day humanity.

If, then, we are to search for a lost Atlantis peopled by types recognisable as modern, or semi-civilised, the period in which we must do so is narrowed down to Post-glacial time—that is, to the last 25,000 years of European history. What has geology to tell us of the probability of the existence of such a continent during this period ? We must remember that it is not by any means incumbent upon us to attempt to justify Plato's account word for word. That is the grand error that has been made by nearly every one of our predecessors in this quest. It is obvious that we are dealing with a great world-memory, of which Plato's story is merely one of the broken and distorted fragments, and we must seek to justify its broad contentions not by reference to any solitary and possibly fallible account, but by all other reasonable means as well.

Many of the older geologists were in favour of the idea of an Atlantean continent. Lyell confessed to its likelihood, though he could not see in the Atlantic islands traces of a mid-Atlantic ridge.[1] Buffon dated the separation of the New and the Old Worlds from the catastrophe of Atlantis. In 1846 Forbes declared his belief in the former existence of a bridge of islands in the North Atlantic, and in 1856 Heer attempted to show the necessity of a similar connection from the testimony of palæontological history. In 1860 Unger tried to explain the likeness between the fossil flora of Europe and the living flora of Asia by virtue of the Atlantean hypothesis, and Kuntze, who was struck with the case of the tropical seedless banana occurring at once in Asia and in America before the discovery of the latter continent, saw in this a strong evidence of the truth of the Atlantean theory.

I will summarise a number of recent accounts of the

[1] *Elements of Geology*, London, 1841, p. 141.

physiographical researches of geologists and others in the bed of the Atlantic Ocean, and will begin this survey of modern evidence for a sunken continent by a précis of the very important paper, entitled "Atlantis," read by M. Pierre Termier, Director of Science of the Geological Chart of France, a geologist of the highest standing and authority, before the Institut Océanographique of Paris on 30th November 1912.[1]

M. Termier first pictures the bed of the Atlantic as emptied of its waters. According to soundings, he tells us, we should, looking at it from above, behold two great depressions or valleys extending north and south parallel with the two shores, and separated one from the other by a middle zone elevated above them. The western valley, extending the length of the American coast, is the larger and deeper, stretching to more than 6000 metres below the level of the shore. The eastern, along the European coast, seems narrower and more shallow, yet more hilly, with numerous peaks resembling those of Madeira and the Canaries. The middle zone or height between these is S-shaped, like the valleys it divides. It commences at Greenland and ends at the 70th parallel of south latitude. The map of the Azores shows that the nine islands of which the group is composed cover a total length of about 500 miles, and this distance is probably prolonged very far beneath the waves.

Now the eastern region of the Atlantic, says M. Termier, is a great volcanic zone. In the European-African depression sea-volcanoes and insular volcanoes are abundant. Most of the islands in this portion are largely formed of lava. The same phenomenon occurs in the American or western region of the Atlantic. This would seem to indicate that in the bottom of the Atlantic Ocean there is a certain mobility. It is, indeed, *still in movement in the extreme*

---

[1] This will be found translated into English in the annual report of the Smithsonian Institute for 1915.

eastern zone for a space of about 1875 miles in breadth, which comprises Iceland, the Azores, Madeira, the Canaries, and the Cape Verde Islands. It is the most unstable zone on the earth's surface, where at any moment unrecorded submarine cataclysms may be taking place.

Great cataclysms certainly have occurred, and these, geologically speaking, date only as from yesterday. In the summer of 1898 a ship employed for the laying of the cable from Brest to Cape Cod was trying to fish up a broken strand at a point about 500 miles north of the Azores, and at a depth of about 1700 fathoms. The grappling-irons drew up soil and broken pieces of rock, which established the fact that the bottom of the sea at this latitude presents the characteristics of a mountainous country with high summits, steep slopes, and deep valleys. They were evidently being caught on hard rocks, and drew up coarse striæ and small mineral splinters, fragments of an actual outcropping, sharp and irregular, a vitreous lava or tachylyte, now preserved at the Musée de l'École des Mines at Paris. This species of lava, as is well known, could solidify into such a condition *only under atmospheric pressure.* If formed under 3000 metres of water it would have become crystallised. M. Termier then quotes M. Lacroix, who examined the lava of Mont Pelée in Martinique, which was vitreous when it congealed in the open air, but became crystallised when cooled under a mass of previously solidified rocks.[1] Further, he infers that the surface which to-day

[1] Dr Frederick Finch Strong, writing of the geological problems involved in the Atlantean theory, says : " It seems that geologists have learned much from the phenomena that followed the eruption of Mont Pelée in the island of Martinique, West Indies. It will be remembered that the lava stream divided, part flowing into the sea and solidifying suddenly, and part congealing slowly on land and requiring weeks to cool. Microscopic studies of thin sections of the two lavas showed a marked difference in their crystalline structure, and gave science the data from which a water-cooled lava could invariably be distinguished from one which cooled slowly on land. Some years ago on dragging

constitutes the bottom of the Atlantic 562 miles north of the
Azores was, therefore, covered with lava which was once
above water, and the ruggedness of this shows that the
sinking of the land to 3000 metres below the sea followed
suddenly upon the emission of lava.   Otherwise atmospheric
erosion would have levelled inequalities and planed down
the entire surface.   This region is set in the zone of Atlantic
instability, therefore it is a fair conclusion that it was recently
submerged, probably during the epoch which the geologists
call the present because it is so recent.

The Atlantic abyss, as a whole, seems to be of relatively
recent date.   Other collapses occurred there, the size of
which staggers the imagination.   Eduard Suess and Marcel
Bertrand have shown that an ancient continental band existed
between Northern Europe and North America, and another
between Africa and South America.

" There was," says M. Termier, "a North Atlantic continent comprising Russia, Scandinavia, Great Britain, Greenland, and Canada, to which was added later a southern band
made up of a large part of Central and Western Europe and
an immense portion of the United States.   There was also
a South Atlantic, or African-Brazilian, continent, extending
northward to the southern border of the Atlas, eastward to
the Persian Gulf and Mozambique Channel, westward to
the eastern border of the Andes and to the sierras of Colombia

the bed of the Atlantic for a lost cable, bits of rock, torn from jagged
submarine prominences, were brought to the surface. Microscopic
examination showed these to consist of lava. Now geologists have
learnt that lava exposed to sea-water will disintegrate to a known extent in about 15,000 years. This lava from the ocean bed proved
to be recent, i.e. undecomposed, and was evidently the result of an
eruption which occurred less than 15,000 years ago. But its microscopic structure proved that it had cooled slowly above the surface,
exactly like the lava that had flowed on the land near Mont Pelée. The
inference is obvious—the eruption which ejected the lava must have
occurred above the surface of the ocean, and, therefore, what is now the
bed of the Atlantic Ocean must have been above sea-level less than
15,000 years ago."—The Messenger, 1919.

and Venezuela. Between the two continents passed the Mediterranean depression, that ancient maritime furrow which has formed an escarp about the earth since the beginning of geologic times, and which we see so deeply marked in the present Mediterranean, the Caribbean Sea, and the Sunda or Flores Sea. A chain of mountains broader than the chain of the Alps, and perhaps in some parts as high as the majestic Himalaya, once lifted itself on the land-enclosed shore of the North Atlantic continent, embracing the Vosges, the Central Plateau of France, Brittany, the south of England and of Ireland, and also Newfoundland, Nova Scotia, and, in the United States, all the Appalachian region. The two coasts which front each other above the Atlantic waters, 1875 miles apart, that of Brittany, Cornwall, and the south of Ireland on one side, that of Newfoundland and Nova Scotia on the other side, are among the finest estuary shores in the world, and their estuaries are face to face. In the one, as in the other, the folds of the ancient chain are cut abruptly and often naturally by the shore, and the dirigent lines of the European chain are directly aligned with those of the American chain. Within a few years it will be one of the pleasures of oceanographers, by clearing up the detailed chart of the ocean beds between Ireland and Newfoundland, to establish the persistence of a fold, of oriented mountainous aspect, on the site of this old engulfed mountain chain."

The end of this continental era, thinks M. Termier, came during the Tertiary period, when the mass, bounded on the south by a chain of mountains, was submerged long before the collapse of those volcanic lands of which the Azores are the last vestiges. The South Atlantic Ocean was likewise occupied for many thousands of centuries by a great continent now engulfed beneath the sea. These movements of depression probably occurred at several periods. In the Europe of the Tertiary era the movement was developing which gave rise to the Alpine mountain chain. How far did this chain extend into the Atlantic region ? Did some fragments of it rise high enough to lift themselves for some centuries above the waters ? The West Indies, too, are but a prolongation of the Andes chain. Was there a tectonic or structural bond between these systems, as there is certainly a stratigraphic bond ? Louis Gentil has followed the Western Atlas Mountains in Africa, a branch of the great Tertiary chain, into the ocean, so to speak, and this prolongation would lead us to the Canaries.

" Summing up," says M. Termier, " there are strong reasons for believing in the Atlantic prolongation of the Tertiary folds, those of the Atlas Mountains towards the Canaries, those of the Alps towards the southern islands of the Azores, but nothing yet permits of either extending very far or limiting very narrowly this prolongation. The sediments of Santa Maria prove only this, that at the Miocene epoch—that is, when the great Alpine movements were terminated in Europe—a Mediterranean shore extended not far from this region of the Azores, the shore of a continent or of a large island. Another shore of the same Miocene sea passed near the Canaries."

The geology of the Atlantic region, remarks M. Termier, has singularly changed in the course of the later periods of the earth's history. During the secondary period there were numerous depressions, the Tertiary period saw the annihilation of the continental areas, and subsequently there appeared a new design the general direction of which was north and south. Near the African continent there have certainly been important movements during Quaternary times, when other changes undoubtedly took place in the true oceanic region.

" *Geologically speaking, the Platonian history of the Atlantic is highly probable. . . . It is entirely reasonable to believe that long after the opening of the Strait of Gibraltar certain of these emerged lands still existed, and among them a marvellous island, separated from the African continent by a chain of other smaller islands.* One thing alone remains to be proved— that the cataclysm which caused this island to disappear was subsequent to the appearance of man in Western Europe. The cataclysm is undoubted. Did men then live who could withstand the reaction and transmit the memory of it ? That is the whole question. I do not believe it at all insoluble, though it seems to me that neither geology nor zoology will solve it. These two sciences appear to have told all that they can tell, and it is from anthropology, from ethnography, and, lastly, from oceanography, that I am now awaiting the final answer."

Professor J. W. Gregory, Professor of Geology in the University of Glasgow, in his valuable treatise *Geography : Structural, Physical, and Comparative* (1908), makes it clear in several passages that he does not reject the hypothesis of a former Atlantean continent. In speaking of the islands of the Atlantic, he observes that they " are of the oceanic type, are irregularly scattered, and are mostly piles of volcanic rocks that have been raised above sea-level by volcanic eruptions, such as the island of Teneriffe ; but others are fragments of the ancient land known as Atlantis, and the St Paul's Rocks are reefs of ancient continental rocks that once belonged to a land which has foundered beneath the sea. The Azores are a group of volcanoes built upon a foundation of limestones, similar to those of the Mediterranean countries." Again, on pages 59–60, he states that " the islands of the Atlantic are irregularly arranged with the exception of those on the Faroes ridge, which forms the northern boundary of the Atlantic, and the islands of the West Indies. The sinuous shape of the Atlantic, moreover, has no relation to the mountains or the geographical grain of the adjacent lands. Thus it cuts abruptly across the old mountain line which runs across southern Ireland, southern England, and northern France, and also across the Cantabrian Mountains, which reach the Atlantic at the north-western corner of Spain. There can be little doubt that both these mountain lines once continued into the present site of the Atlantic. On the coast of North America the Atlantic cuts with equal abruptness across the remains of mountain lines in Nova Scotia and Newfoundland, which must once have extended eastward into the present ocean. They probably represent the former continuation in America of the ancient mountain chains of Europe. Similarly there are striking resemblances in structure between Equatorial Africa and Brazil. The intermediate basin of the Atlantic has probably been formed by the foundering of the plateau land which once connected South America and Africa."

Professor Gregory also points out that the old highlands of Brazil must once have extended eastward into the Atlantic, and were built largely of materials derived from the destruction of an old Atlantic land.

The famous geologist, Sir J. William Dawson, who did so much for the elucidation of Canadian geology, in his delightful book, *Salient Points in the Science of the Earth* (1893), includes a chapter on the " History of the North Atlantic." He writes of the great Pleistocene or Ice Age submergence in an arresting manner. He remarks (p. 77) : " It was one of the most remarkable of all : one in which nearly the whole northern hemisphere participated, and which was probably separated from the present time by *only a few thousands of years. . . .* The recent surveys of the Falls of Niagara coincide with a great many evidences to which I have elsewhere referred in proving that the Pleistocene submergence of America and Europe came to an end *not more than ten thousand years ago.*" He further states that all continents have been " many times submerged." In his presidential address to the Geological Section of the American Association in 1876, he asserted that " the Hyrcanian Ocean had dried up, and Atlantis had gone down."

" Subsidence," says Professor H. F. Osborn, " was the great feature of closing glacial times, both in Europe and America." [1]

One of the most important contributions to the literature of Atlantean research from the geological and biological points of view is the exhaustive paper of Professor R. F. Scharff of Dublin, " Some Remarks on the Atlantis Problem," read before the Royal Irish Academy in November 1902, and published in the *Proceedings* of that body (vol. xxiv, 1902). I must content myself with a summary of this valuable paper, giving here the geological findings of this brilliant scientist, and dealing with the evidence he adduces regarding animal and plant life in the chapter on that subject. Professor Scharff summarises the history of the geological culture-war which has raged round the subject of Atlantis, and as this information is of value to students of the question, I will include it in my précis of his excellent paper.

" Edward Forbes," [2] he says, " maintained that at the close of the Miocene epoch a vast continent extended far into the Atlantic from the coast of Portugal, past the Azores, and bounded on the north by Ireland. While adopting Forbes's hypothesis, Murray [3] enlarged the area of this continent as far as Newfoundland, Greenland, and Spitzbergen."

Dr Alfred Russel Wallace,[4] believing in the permanence of the great ocean basins, founded his view on three important statements. " He pointed out, in the first instance, that the Atlantic islands were entirely composed of volcanic rocks ; secondly, that they were surrounded by great depths of water ; and, lastly, that they possessed no indigenous land mammalia. As regards the fact that the Atlantic islands are composed of volcanic rocks, it does not necessarily

---

[1] *Men of the Old Stone Age*, p. 36.
[2] *Geological Memoirs*, 1846, vol. i.
[3] *Geographical Distribution of Mammals*, 1866, p. 37.
[4] *Studies Scientific and Social*, 1900, vol. i, p. 250.

imply that they could not, therefore, have formed part of the continent of Europe in former times, for even Hartung, who made a special study of the geology of Madeira, looked upon the Atlantic islands as the summits of submerged mountain chains, while two other geologists, Guppy and Neumayr, maintain that these islands are the remnants of a great continent which united the Old World with the New. Lyell, on the other hand, arguing from the supposed great depths separating the Atlantic islands from the Continent, does not consider it possible that they could have been connected with Europe. However, as Dr Blandford reminds us in his interesting address to the Geological Society of London,[1] 'the occurrence of volcanic islands does not prove that the area in which they occur is not a sunken continent.' ' If,' he continues, ' Africa south of the Atlas subsided two thousand fathoms, what would remain above water ? So far as our present knowledge goes, the remaining islands would consist of four volcanic peaks— the Cameroons, Mount Kenia, Kilimanjaro, and Stanley's last discovery, Ruwenzori, together with an island, or more than one, which, like the others, would be entirely composed of volcanic rocks.'

" Dr Wallace's second statement, that the Atlantic islands were surrounded by great depths, is only partially correct. On the little map he published in 1900 Dr Wallace indicated a depth of 12,000 feet between Madeira and Europe, though it is now twenty-five years since Commander Gorringe of the United States Navy discovered the Gettysburg Bank, and demonstrated the undoubted fact that there are shallow banks only a couple of hundred feet below the surface of the sea in that area. He also suggested that a submarine ridge probably connected the island of Madeira with the coast of Portugal.

" The Azores seem to be separated by much greater

[1] London, 1890.

depths from the continent ; and Dr Wallace is so convinced of the permanence of the great ocean basins that he will not allow that any very great changes of level have taken place in former times. But that Dr Wallace's views are not generally accepted may be gathered by the remark made by Dr Blandford that ' not only is there clear proof that some land-areas lying within continental limits have within a comparatively recent date been submerged over a thousand fathoms, whilst sea-bottoms now over a thousand fathoms deep must have been land in part of the Tertiary era, but there are a mass of facts, both geological and biological, in favour of land connection having formerly existed in certain cases across what are now broad and deep oceans.' Moreover, when asked to give his opinion on this important question of ' permanence of ocean basins,' Professor Suess [1] remarked that the geological evidence did not prove, nor even point to, a permanence of the great depths—at least, in oceans of the Atlantic type—and that he believed some kind of a coast-line stretched across the present Atlantic Ocean during part of Tertiary times."

Teneriffe, says Professor Scharff, covered as it is by immense masses of recent lava, exhibits no ostensible traces of older or fossiliferous rocks, but in the islands of Palma, Fuerteventura, and Gomera, an older mountain chain consisting of diabase—an eruptive rock—has been shown to exist. On Grand Canary and Palma an upheaval of from 600–1000 feet can be demonstrated, and in Madeira one up to nearly 1400 feet. Professor de Lapparent [2] favours the view of the existence of a coast-line, or at least that of an island-chain, during the Miocene period, connecting the West Indies with southern Europe. The end of the Pliocene and the whole of the Pleistocene period, he believes, were dis-

---

[1] " Are Great Ocean Depths Permanent ? " *Natural Science*, 1893, vol. ii, pp. 185, 186.

[2] *Traité de Géologie*, Paris, 1893, p. 193.

tinguished by a series of subsidences which resulted in finally opening up the northern depression of the Atlantic Ocean. Mr Haug,[1] too, has recently come to the conclusion that the convex arch formed by the Antilles and the one found along the western border of the Mediterranean were connected in the Tertiary era by tangential chains of land. According to his view, a coast-line stretched across the Atlantic from Venezuela to Morocco, and another between the Lesser Antilles and Portugal, the intervening space being covered by the sea.

" From the facts quoted," remarks Professor Scharff, " I conclude that Madeira and the Azores up to Miocene times were connected with Portugal, and that from Morocco to the Canary Islands, and from them to South America, stretched a vast land which extended southward certainly as far as St Helena. This great continent may have existed already in Secondary times, as Dr Ihering suggested ; and it probably began to subside in early Tertiary times. But I think its northern portions persisted until the Miocene Epoch, when the southern and northern Atlantic became joined, and the Azores and Madeira became isolated from Europe. This, however, does not explain the whole history of the Atlantic islands. To account for the extraordinary predominance of the Mediterranean element in their fauna, they must have again united with the Old World in more recent times. This took place, no doubt, in a precisely similar manner as before, and I believe that they were still connected in early Pleistocene times with the continents of Europe and Africa, at a time when man had already made his appearance in Western Europe, and was able to reach the islands by land."

Among those modern geologists who uphold the Atlantean theory is Professor Edward Hull,[2] whose investigations have

[1] *Bull. Soc. Géol. de France*, 1900, vol. xxviii, p. 635.
[2] *The Sub-Oceanic Physiography of the North Atlantic.*

PLATE II.

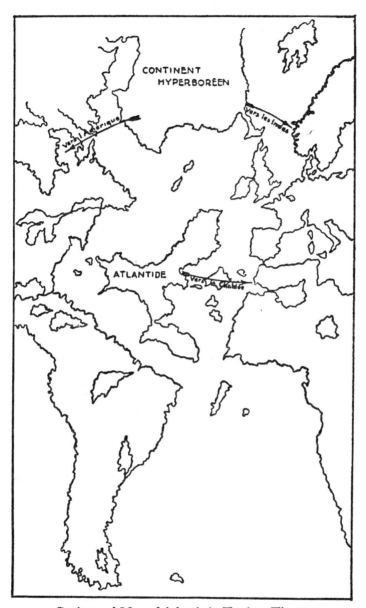

Conjectural Map of Atlantis in Tertiary Times.

(After R. M. Gattefossé.)

led him to conclude that the Azores are the peaks of a sub-merged continent which flourished in the Pleistocene period. At this epoch the British and continental rivers flowed out many miles beyond their present outlets, and this mid-Atlantic island enjoyed an equable climate when the temperature of the British Isles was, apparently, of a semi-polar nature. "The flora and fauna of the two hemispheres," says Professor Hull, "support the geological theory that there was a common centre in the Atlantic where life began, and that during and prior to the glacial epoch great land-bridges north and south spanned the Atlantic Ocean." He adds: "I have made this deduction by a careful study of the soundings as recorded on the Admiralty charts." Dr Hull also holds the view that at the time this Atlantic continent existed there was also a great Antillean continent or ridge shutting off the Caribbean Sea and the Gulf of Mexico from what is called the Gulf Stream.

Last century more than one Admiralty authority took deep-sea soundings of the Atlantic, notably the British, who dispatched the *Hydra*, *Porcupine*, and *Challenger*; the American, the *Dolphin* and *Gettysburg*; and the German, who commissioned the *Gazelle* for this especial purpose. These expeditions resulted in the entire ocean-bed of the Atlantic being carefully mapped out, and this process revealed the existence of a great bank or elevation com-mencing at a point not far from the coast of Ireland, traversed by the 53rd parallel, and stretching in a southerly direction, embracing the Azores, to the coast-line of South America near French Guiana and the mouths of the Amazon and Para Rivers. Thence this bank stretches in a south-easterly direction towards the African coast, taking in the rocky islands of St Paul. Changing its course again just north of the island of Ascension, it stretches due south to the island of Tristan d'Acunha, where it ends. The general

level of this great ridge or plateau is some 9000 feet above
that of the Atlantic bed, and the islands connected with it
are obviously the mountain-peaks of this sunken continent.
The soundings of the United States expedition showed
that that part of the bank situated in the North Atlantic
between the 26th and 45th parallels of latitude measured at
its base a distance from east to west of about 1000 nautical
miles.

The results of the *Challenger* expedition brought to
light the fact that the ridge, throughout its entire length,
is covered with volcanic detritus, and there is every
evidence that the ocean-bed, particularly in the neighbourhood of the Azores, has been the scene of volcanic disturbances on a large scale.   Nor could the inequalities,
the mountains and valleys, so to speak, have been produced by submarine agencies such as deposit, but must
have received their present contour whilst still above
water.   The commander of the *Gettysburg* found that
when about 150 miles from the Straits of Gibraltar the
soundings decreased from 2700 fathoms to 1600 in the
course of a few miles.

But, as will be shown later on, these conclusions have been
surpassed in an extraordinary manner by fresh and surprising
evidence collected by the agents of the Western Telegraph
Company and others, which proves that the entire bed of
the Eastern Atlantic has altered greatly during the last
twenty-five years.   This would seem to sustain the contention of certain geologists that the contour of the bed of
the Atlantic has undergone constant change, and that,
indeed, it may have risen and sunk many times since the
Pleistocene epoch.   New and more reliable apparatus has
recently been available for purposes of sounding, and in
the course of the next few years the utilisation of this will
undoubtedly bring about a better comprehension of Atlantic
oceanography.

If we summarise the salient points of the evidence we find :—

1. Termier believes the Atlantic to be a great volcanic zone, an unstable portion of the earth, the eastern part of which is still in movement, the bed of which resembles a mountainous country. The lava with which it is covered must have solidified under atmospheric pressure, and not under water. The conclusion is, therefore, that it was recently submerged.

2. Land-connection between the Old and New Worlds is agreed upon by all geologists of standing, the only variation of opinion being as to the epoch to which this connection must be assigned. Land depression appears to have commenced in Tertiary times and to have continued to a comparatively recent epoch. Important movements took place in Quaternary times near the African continent. Long after the opening of the strait of Gibraltar an island existed, opposite the strait, but connected with the continent by a chain of lesser islands.

3. Professor Gregory believes the Atlantic islands to be fragments of the Atlantean continent, and that certain European mountain chains were once prolonged into the present site of the Atlantic. The South Atlantic, he says, was formed by the foundering of the plateau land between South America and Africa.

4. Sir William Dawson believed that extensive submergences took place at the end of the Great Ice Age, " not more than ten thousand years ago." He was a firm believer in the former existence and final submersion of the Atlantean continent.

5. Professor Scharff, summarising the culture-war which raged round the question of Atlantis, showed that because the Atlantic islands are formed of volcanic rocks, that does not imply that they could not once have formed part of the continent of Europe. Hartung, Guppy, and Neumayr,

believed them to be the remains of a continent which united the New and the Old Worlds. Wallace's statement that the Atlantic islands were surrounded by great depths of sea is only partly correct, some shallow banks existing at a depth of only two hundred feet. Blandford stated that some land-areas lying within continental limits have within a comparatively recent date been submerged over a thousand fathoms. Suess credits the existence of an Atlantean continent in Tertiary, and Lapparent that of a coast-line or insular chain in Miocene times, and the latter also believes that the end of the Pliocene and the whole of the Pleistocene era were distinguished by subsidences which resulted in opening up the northern portion of the Atlantic Ocean. Scharff concludes that the Azores and Madeira were connected with Portugal up to Miocene times, and that from Morocco to the Canaries a vast land stretched which extended southward to South America. Its northern portion persisted until the Miocene epoch, when the South and Northern Atlantic became joined, and the Azores and Madeira became isolated from Europe. He also believes that the Atlantic islands must have been again united with the Old World in more recent times, and that the connection still existed in early Pleistocene times, when man had made his appearance in Western Europe, and was able to reach the islands by land.

6. Professor Hull believes the Azores to be the peaks of a submerged continent which flourished in the Pleistocene period. He states that the flora and fauna of the two hemispheres support the geological theory that there was a common centre in the Atlantic where life began, and that at the time this Atlantic continent existed there was also a great Antillean continent or ridge in the neighbourhood of the West Indies.

7. The soundings taken by the vessels dispatched by the various European and American Admiralties served to map

out the ocean-bed of the Atlantic, and revealed the existence of a great bank occupying the major portion of the whole Atlantic basin. This is covered with volcanic detritus. The irregularities of its surface could not have been produced by submarine agencies, but must have received their present contour while still above water.

From such an array of geological evidence I think it will be conceded that we are justified in concluding that the hypothesis of a formerly existing land-mass in the Atlantic Ocean is by no means based on mere surmise. The fact that geologists of distinction have risked their reputations by testifying in no uncertain manner to the reality of a former Atlantean continent should surely give pause to those who impatiently refuse even to examine the probabilities of the arguments they so ably uphold. But the most significant consideration which emerges is that this expert evidence is almost entirely in favour of the existence of a *comparatively recent* land-mass, or masses, in the Atlantic, and taking into consideration the whole of the evidence and the nature of its sources, I fail to see how it can reasonably be disputed that at a period probably no earlier than that mentioned by Plato this ancient continent was still in existence, but in process of disintegration — that an island of considerable size, the remnant, perhaps, of the African " shelf," still lay opposite the entrance to the Mediterranean, and that lesser islands connected it with Europe, Africa, and another similar island-continent which occupied the present site of the West Indian Islands, the whole forming a continuous archipelagic chain such as is described by Plato.

As I hope to prove, the evidences from ethnology, tradition, and history strongly support such a view. The persistent legends of a series of cataclysms, from the horrors of which the inhabitants of this archipelago took refuge in Europe and America, have, in my opinion, an indubitable basis of certainty. The sudden appearance in

Spain and France at an early period of races of comparatively high culture whose original homes, as we shall see later, cannot be traced even by the ingenuity of modern anthropologists, the undoubted and now partially admitted "Atlantic" origin of civilisation, and its spread from west to east rather than from east to west, as was formerly held, all assist the conclusion that the Atlantean hypothesis is based on evidence of the most irrefragable character.

If modern thought refuses to entertain the idea of an Atlantean continent as the early home of civilisation, it does so at the risk of casting aside evidence which undoubtedly throws a gleam of intelligence on the question of human advancement, which at present it sadly needs. I venture, then, to present my own conclusions, based on the geological evidence, as follows :—

1. That a great continent formerly occupied the whole or major part of the North Atlantic region, and a considerable portion of its southern basin. Of early geological origin, it must in the course of successive ages have experienced many changes in contour and mass, probably undergoing frequent submergence and emergence.

2. That in Miocene (late Tertiary) times it still retained its continental character, but towards the end of that period it began to disintegrate, owing to successive volcanic and other causes.

3. That this disintegration resulted in the formation of greater and lesser insular masses. Two of these, considerably larger in area than any of the others, were situated (a) at a relatively short distance from the entrance to the Mediterranean ; and (b) in the region of the West Indian Islands. These may be called respectively Atlantis and Antilia. Communication was possible between them by an insular chain.

4. That these two island-continents and the connecting

chain of islands persisted until late Pleistocene times, at which epoch (about 25,000 years ago, or the beginning of the Post-glacial epoch) Atlantis seems to have experienced further disintegration. Final disaster seems to have overtaken Atlantis about 10,000 B.C. Antilia, on the other hand, seems to have survived until a much more recent period, and still persists fragmentally in the Antillean group, or West Indian Islands.

A theory which may, perhaps, be regarded as having a bearing on the Atlantean hypothesis may briefly be alluded to here. A certain school of geologists is of the opinion that the Old and New Worlds have actually drifted more or less slowly apart, and still continue to do so. The student of geology will recognise in this argument an old theory the recent consideration of which has had surprising developments as regards the internal constitution and condition of our globe. The earth, as most of us know, is 8000 miles thick, so that the nature of its inner constituents must naturally remain matter of conjecture. But its weight shows that it is at least twice as heavy as it ought to be if it consisted throughout of matter of the same ponderability as the rocks of its outer crust. The nucleus must, therefore, be of much weightier matter than the crust, and good reasons exist for the belief that it consists of nickel and iron.

Many scientists believe that the earth is composed of three concentric zones—the nucleus of nickel and iron alluded to, and called, from the chemical symbols of these two elements (Fe and Ni), the Nife. Regarding this nucleus little can be posited, and whether it is solid, liquid, or gaseous is unknown. The stratum superimposed upon it is, however, in a liquid condition, and is thought to be composed of silica and magnesia, the symbols of which confer upon it the artificial name Sima. Above all is the outer crust, which is made up of silica and aluminium, and is consequently named the Sal.

The more conservative school of geologists believe the Sal to be a true crust, but unequal in thickness. In those places where it is thick continents exist, while in the thinner parts we have ocean basins. But more daring speculators believe that beneath the ocean spaces no solid Sal exists at all, and that the continental masses float in the liquid Sima much as icebergs in the ocean. If, for any reason, a fissure develops in these floating masses the break may grow until at last two separate bodies appear, which will naturally drift away from each other by degrees. Such a condition, it is thought, accounts for the separation of the American Continent from the Old World. To commence with, the degree of separation may have been comparatively rapid, but careful observations made during the past forty years show that, after all possible errors in longitude have been eliminated, the mass of Greenland is farther from Europe by 2500 yards than it was at the beginning of that period.

Now, by means of a very simple calculation, we find that the yearly rate of separation of the two continents averages, roughly, about 60 feet, that is about 6000 feet in a century, or 30 miles in a thousand years. In ten thousand years, then, the land-masses would drift no less than 300 miles apart. The theory has been advanced that Atlantis may thus have been much closer to the European and American coasts at the date of its submergence than the present distance between these coasts would seem to imply, but it does not appear to me that the Atlantean hypothesis has anything to gain from such an admission. Professor W. de Sitter, of the University of Leyden, has recently put forward the suggestion that the earth is not rotating as a rigid body, but that some parts of its surface are moving relatively to other parts. It is, in fact, behaving as though composed of viscous elements.   Wireless time-signals exchanged between various observatories having shown discrepancies, reaching on occasion several tenths of a second.   Similar fluctuations in recent years, says Professor de Sitter, have been observed on the surface of the moon.   See for this latter theory, *Nature*, July 1923.

CHAPTER IV

THE BIOLOGICAL EVIDENCE

IN this chapter I intend to use only such of the evidence from biological sources as appears to me to afford actual justification of the Atlantean hypothesis. I am aware that a mass of material exists which purports to be evidence of this kind. But I must frankly admit that much of it seems to me of far too general and far-fetched a character to permit of its acceptance by the serious student. The prolonged controversy which raged round the question of the Atlantean origin of the seedless banana, for example, seems to me worse than futile considering the present stage of our knowledge, so I propose to adhere to the conclusions of tried modern scientists, and to disregard the gropings of the older school as no longer of much avail in our quest.

As I indicated in the last chapter, the Atlantean hypothesis has no more powerful advocate than Professor R. F. Scharff, of Dublin, whose paper, " Some Remarks on the Atlantis Problem," contains a wealth of reference to the biological evidence of a sunken continent in the Atlantic. Criticising the views of Dr A. R. Wallace on the theories of Heer, Forbes, and Murray, which were favourable to the Atlantean theory, he meets them with some trenchant arguments.

" Dr Wallace's address," he says, " deals only with the beetles of Madeira, one of the Atlantic islands ; but he maintains that the opinion he enunciates, and which is founded on a study of these insects, explains the origin of the Madeiran and of other insular faunas."

Dr Wallace asks, if Madeira were the remains of a continent

with a connection with Europe, how we are to explain the absence of certain genera of beetles abundant in Southern Europe, the wingless nature of which admirably suits them for island life ?   If Madeira had been connected with Europe, replies Scharff, it must have been joined with Southern Spain or Portugal, and Wallace should have drawn his comparisons with these regions, and not with Southern Europe as a whole.   The insects Wallace speaks of are far more numerous in the east of Europe than in the west. In Spain and Portugal their presence is negligible, so that even had these countries been joined to a now sunken continent, not one of the species alluded to would probably have reached Madeira.

As for Dr Wallace's statement that the Atlantic islands possess no indigenous land mammalia, and that such animals as are found there have been introduced since the discovery, Professor Scharff can find no record of their artificial introduction. " The results of my endeavours," he says, " to trace the history of their origin on the islands point rather to some of them, at any rate, having reached the latter in the normal way, which is by a land-connection with Europe."

In the case of the rabbit, for instance, the presence of large hawks or buzzards observed by the discoverers of the Azores in 1439 led to the islands receiving the name of Açores, or Hawk Islands, and such birds usually live on mice, rats, and young rabbits. Indeed it seems to be substantiated that the existence of the Azores had already been known to earlier navigators, for in a book published in 1345 by a Spanish friar the Azores are referred to, and the names of the several islands given.   On the atlas dated 1385, and published at Venice, some of the islands are indicated by name, as Capraria, or Isle of Goats, now San Miguel ; Columbia, or Isle of Doves, now Pico ; Li Congi, Rabbit Island, now Flores ; and Corvi Marini, or Isle of Sea Crows, now Corvo. Drouet [1] has directed attention to the goat of San Miguel, with its antelope-like horns. This nomenclature given prior to the discovery—the " official " discovery, that is—seems to justify the assumption that mammals such as the wild goat and rabbit reached the islands from Europe by a land-connection.

The rabbit may, indeed, have reached the Azores and Europe from America by way of the ancient land-connection. Professor Osborn [2] suggests the American origin of the rabbit and hare. " I am not," says Professor Scharff, " advocating a direct land-connection between Southern Europe and America by way of the Atlantic islands. I think there was only one land-bridge in southern latitudes between the Old World and the New, which joined Africa and South America. This must have lain farther south than the Atlantic islands. But from North Africa there was frequent intercourse with southern Europe—with which the Atlantic islands, I believe, were connected ; and South American species would then have been able to reach Madeira and the Azores indirectly." Dr Forsyth Major and Lydekker have shown the connection between the rabbit-forms of Africa and America, and that animal migration between these continents must have taken place. Professor Howes has also indicated the presence in the Argentine of a fossil mole like the golden mole of South Africa.

The carnivores of Tertiary times show a marked affinity with those of the New World. " Some of these cases, no doubt, can be accounted for by the supposition that the mammals migrated from or to Europe across Asia, where they may have found a land-connection joining that continent to America across the Bering Strait; but others seem to me to have used a more direct route between our continent and the New World. Messrs Sclater [3] recognise a distinct

[1] *Eléments de la faune açoréanne*, Paris, 1861, p. 15.
[2] *Ann. New York Acad. Science*, 1900, vol. xiii, p. 58.
[3] *The Geography of Mammals*, London, 1899, p. 208.

division of the marine area of the globe as consisting of the middle portion of the Atlantic which they call " Mesatlantic." Two genera of mammals are assigned as characteristic of this region — viz. Monachus, the Monk Seal, and the Sirenian Manatus. Now, neither of these animals frequent the open ocean, being bound to the proximity of land. *Monachus albiventer* inhabits the Mediterranean, and the closely allied *M. tropicalis*, the West Indies, separated by the enormous expanse of the Atlantic Ocean, where no Monachus is known to exist. Manatus is still more permanently attached to the coast. One species, *Manatus inunguis*, has even forsaken the sea, and now lives only in fresh water. Of the two other species, *M. senegalensis* inhabits the coasts and estuaries of West Africa, *M. americanus* being found along the South American coast and among the West Indian Islands. The range of these marine mammals appears to Messrs Sclater to imply that their ancestors have spread along some coast-line which probably united the Old World and the New at no very distant period."

" The reptilian fauna of the Atlantic islands," continues Professor Scharff, " is almost altogether European in its character." Among the Geckotidæ, a lizard family, the North African and Chilian species are allied. " One species inhabits the borders of the Mediterranean, while a closely related one is found not only in South America, but also in Madagascar and South Africa."

Interesting from a geographical point of view are the burrowing Amphisbænidæ, which, generally limbless, often spend their entire existence underground in ants' nests. " That such species," says Scharff, " are not likely to be conveyed across an ocean by accidental causes in the manner described by Wallace and others is evident. Now this large family of sixty-five species is quite confined to America, Africa, and the Mediterranean region. As very few species range into North America, while not a single one has been discovered in Asia, the hypothesis of a land-connection across the Atlantic explains the geographical distribution of this family better than any other theory."

In his monograph of the mollusca of the Atlantic islands Mr T. V. Wollaston [1] drew attention to the fact that the Mediterranean element is much more traceable in the Canaries than in the other groups of islands. "Altogether he believes that the Atlantic islands have originated from the breaking up of a land which was once more or less continuous, and which had been intercolonised along ridges and tracts (now lost beneath the ocean), thus bringing into comparatively intimate connection many of its parts; whilst others were separated by channels which served practically to keep them very decidedly asunder."

Professor Simroth,[2] writing on the similarity between the slugs of Spain, Portugal, North Africa, and the Canaries, concludes that there was probably a broad land-connection between these four countries, and that it must have persisted until comparatively recent times.

Dr W. Kobelt, who formerly adhered to Wallace's ideas and ridiculed the Atlantean theory, after having independently worked out the same problem more recently, altered his views. Comparing the European with the West Indian and Central American faunas, he points out that the land-shells on the two opposite sides of the Atlantic certainly imply an ancient connection having subsisted between the Old World and the New, which only became ruptured towards the close of the Miocene epoch of the Tertiary period.[3] Dr von Ihering [4] states that no malacologist nowadays could explain the presence of these continental molluscs on the islands in any other way but

[1] *Testacea Atlantica*, London, 1878.
[2] *Nova Acta d. d. Akad. d. Naturf*, 1891, vol. lvi, p. 223.
[3] *Nachrichtsbl. d. d. malakozool. Gesellsch.*, 1887, p. 53.
[4] Englen's *Botanische Jahrbucher*, 1893, vol. xvii, p. 51.

by their progression on land. He is also strongly in favour of the theory, on biological grounds, of a former land-connection between Brazil and Africa.

As regards insect life, certain ants occur both in the Azores and America. A species of the family Dorylidæ, which is of African origin, is also found in South America. Sixty per cent. of the butterflies and moths found in the Canaries are of Mediterranean origin, and 20 per cent. of these are to be found in America.

Some crustaceans afford excellent proof of the justice of Professor Scharff's hypothesis. The genus Platyarthus is represented by three species in Western Europe and North Africa, one in the Canaries, and one in Venezuela. Porcellio is also found in all three regions, and other allied forms occur widely in them. " There is, however, another group of crustacea which yields such decisive indications of the former land-connection between Africa and South America that scarcely anything else is needed to put that theory on a firm basis. The group referred to is that of the fresh-water decapods, the species on both sides of the Atlantic showing a most remarkable affinity."

The occurrence of earth-worms is a peculiarly reliable datum in fixing the former geographical relationship of any given region. The ocean is an insuperable barrier to earth-worms, and when it is found that those of the Atlantic islands are identical with European and North African forms, little more remains to be said as regards a former land-connection.

Certain species, concludes Professor Scharff, are liable to be accidentally carried away from their homes to distant lands, but they have difficulty in maintaining a foothold in their new quarters, and do not, as a rule, become established. Experiments with certain snails seemed to show that it was possible for those to withstand prolonged immersion in sea-water. " In order to find out whether animals could traverse oceans and thus populate islands, Darwin and others have attempted to determine experimentally how long certain snails could stand immersion in sea-water. For one of their experiments *Cyclostoma elegans* was taken, a snail provided with a lid or operculum, which can be closed over the mouth of the shell. This provision of nature enabled the creature to withstand a fortnight's immersion in sea-water; and one would imagine such a species to be easily transported by sea to distant islands in that time. *C. elegans* is common on the western border of France and England; but though dead shells of the species have been cast upon the shores of Ireland repeatedly, and probably living ones as well, it has never become established on this island. If a species so particularly favoured by nature to resist the deleterious influences of sea-water is unable to establish itself in a neighbouring island, what chances are there for less suitably endowed forms to cross the ocean ? "

Sir William Dawson remarks in his *Salient Points in the Science of the Earth*, p. 86 : " The late Mr Gywn Jeffreys, in one of his latest communications on this subject, stated that 54 per cent. of the shallow-water molluscs of New England and Canada are also European, and of the deep-sea forms, 30 out of 35 ; these last, of course, enjoying greater facilities for migration than those which have to travel slowly along the shallows of the coast in order to cross the ocean and settle themselves on both sides. Many of these animals, like the common mussel and sand-clam, are old settlers, which came over in the Pleistocene period, or even earlier. . . . The older immigrants may possibly have taken advantage of lines of coast now submerged."

M. Louis Germain, a French naturalist, was convinced of the continental origin of the fauna of the Atlantic isles by a study of its existing conditions. He even observed numerous indications of an adaptation to desert life, a close resemblance between the insular mollusca and those of the Mediterranean, and the existence in the Canaries of a fern found in Pliocene strata in Portugal. He states that the Pulmonata Mollusca called Oleacinidæ have a peculiar distribution, living only in Central America, the West Indies, the Mediterranean basin, and the Atlantic isles. In America they have preserved the large size that they had in Europe in the Miocene epoch. In the Mediterranean and the Atlantic islands they have become much smaller. This geographic distribution of these molluscs implies the extension at the beginning of Miocene times of the Atlantic continent to the West Indies, and a separation during the Miocene, or toward its close, between the West Indies and that continent.

" Two facts," says M. Termier, writing *à propos* of M. Germain's deductions, " remain relative to the marine animals, and both seem impossible of explanation, except by the persistence up to very nearly the present times, of a maritime shore extending from the West Indies to Senegal, and even binding together Florida, the Bermudas, and the bottom of the Gulf of Guinea. Fifteen species of marine mollusca lived at the same time, both in the West Indies and on the coast of Senegal, and nowhere else, unless this co-existence can be explained by the transportation of the embryos. On the other hand, the Madreporaria fauna of the island of St Thomas, studied by M. Gravier, includes six species—one does not live outside of St Thomas, except in the Florida reefs, and four others are known only from the Bermudas. As the duration of the pelagic life of the Madreporaria is only a few days, it is impossible to attribute this surprising reappearance to the action of marine currents. In taking all this into account, M. Germain is led to admit the existence of an Atlantic continent connected with the Iberian peninsula, and with Mauritania, and prolonging itself far towards the south, so as to include some regions of desert climate. During the Miocene period, again, this continent extends as far as the West Indies. It is then portioned off, at first in the direction of the West Indies, then in the south, by the establishment of a marine shore, which extends as far as Senegal and to the depths of the Gulf of Guinea, then at length in the east, probably during the Pliocene epoch, along the coast of Africa. The last great fragment, finally engulfed, and no longer having left any other vestiges than the four archipelagoes, would be the Atlantis of Plato."

M. R. M. Gattefossé of Lyons, well known as mystic, chemist, botanist, archæologist, and stout upholder of the theory that an Atlantean civilisation flourished in the Tertiary period, has made a special study of the botanical aspect of the question. He tells us that the Canaries, Azores, and Madeira have an existing flora comparable with that of Western Europe in Tertiary times, and that from the moment of rupture between these islands and the European continent this flora has undergone a special and localised evolution. It has also explicit relations with American flora.[1] Several species of orchids flourish only in the Canaries, Madeira, and America. Professor Hull has also enlarged upon these and other floral and faunal resemblances.

The evidence from animal and plant life in support of the Atlantean theory is in consonance with that drawn from geological sources, and assuredly defeats the well-worn contention that no land-connection ever existed between Europe, Africa, and America. But in dealing with this evidence, it seems to me that the main point has been missed. Most floral and much faunal life unquestionably dates from Tertiary times, and if the evidence capable of being adduced from it does not, for this reason, much assist us in our argument for the existence of a now submerged Atlantic continent in late Quaternary times, on the other hand it does not aid the presumption that this continent

---

[1] See his *Adam, Homme Tertiaire*, Lyons, 1919.

became submerged in Tertiary times. Quaternary forms which are not of recent importation appear to-day in its vestigial islands, as has been shown above. Thus the comparatively recent existence of an Atlantean continent is borne out by the biological evidence as well as by that of geology.

It is extraordinary that men who will cheerfully admit the fact of the subsidence of inhabited land in other regions, whether in Japan, the West Indies, the English Channel, or elsewhere, who will even support the hypothesis of a Lemurian continent in the Pacific Ocean, the original home of humanity, according to many, look askance at the theory of lost Atlantis simply because it has a traditional background. Such a standpoint is not only weak; it is thoroughly unscientific, for, by a consensus of opinion among the most advanced of living archæologists, tradition is now regarded as supplying a horizon to the archæologist, a clue, the proper apprehension of which has resulted in the justification of scores of local legends, and the enrichment of antiquarian science to a degree formerly undreamt of. Happily the Victorian assumption that tradition, and all it stood for, was of the nature of gibberish is now itself so much discredited that he who still affects it is usually regarded as a relic of an age when the credulity of incredulity and the crude denial of all facts not capable of instant and material proof were in fashion.

More than one acute observer of animal life has made allusion to a strange and fatal habit of the lemmings of Norway. The lemming, a small rodent, occasionally receives a migratory impulse which sends it southward in great numbers. Hosts of these animals annually leave the Norwegian coast, and swim far out into the Atlantic. On reaching the spot to which the migratory instinct has so unerringly called them, they circle round for some considerable time, as if in search of land, but, failing in their quest, gradually sink exhausted into the depths. Similarly it is well known that large flocks of birds annually fly to a part of the Atlantic where no land is now visible, and after fluttering about in dismay for some considerable time, fall exhausted into the water.

CHAPTER V

THE EVIDENCE FROM PRE-HISTORY

IF we imagine the continental mass of Atlantis slowly disintegrating during the Ice Age, we must admit that its gradual break-up would have given rise to repeated immigrations, or to invasions of Europe during a prolonged period of time. Plato gives the date of the destruction of Atlantis at 9000 years before Solon's day, or about 9600 B.C., but it is probable that men were making their way from the partially wrecked continent into Europe many thousands of years before that date, although they also did so almost precisely at the period he mentions.

But I shall try to adduce evidence that the first of these migrations did not reach Europe by sea, but by dry land, and that Europe at the time of its entrance was still in places joined to the now sunken continent of Atlantis. The migrating race I speak of is that known to archæologists as the Crô-Magnon, or Aurignacian, from the circumstance that one of the earliest discoveries of its peculiar culture was made by M. E. Lartet, a French anthropologist, in a grotto hard by the little hamlet of Crô-Magnon, near Les Eyzies, on the Vezère, where he found five skeletons which have come to be regarded as the type of the great Crô-Magnon race. Prior to this, similar remains were discovered in 1852 in the sepulchral grotto of Aurignac, from which locality the especial culture of this people came to be known as Aurignacian. Attempts have been made to differentiate between the racial character of these finds, but without success.[1]

Anthropologists at once remarked upon the extraordinary height and brain-capacity of the newly found Crô-Magnon race. Broca noted that the brain-content of the skull of a Crô-Magnon woman surpassed that of the average male of to-day. The average height of the men of this race was 6 feet 1½ inches. The shoulders were exceedingly broad, and the arms short as compared with the legs, an indication of high racial development. The nose was thin, but prominent, the cheek-bones high, the chin massive. Sir Arthur Keith remarks that this race was one of the finest mentally and physically the world has ever seen.[2]

When the Crô-Magnon race arrived in the Biscay region of Europe at the close of the Ice Age (which came to an end about 25,000 years ago), they found the continent sparsely inhabited by a sub-variety of the human species which did not at all approach it in physique or ability. This was Neanderthal man, a creature almost human, who had developed the art of making rough stone tools. But he was of a low and plantigrade type, scarcely differentiated in some ways from the higher apes, unable to grasp the tools or weapons he fashioned as might modern man. Also he was hampered by a relatively small brain capacity. He speedily retreated before the superior skill and strength of the Crô-Magnons, who, little by little, dispossessed him of the soil of Europe, so that in the end he became extinct.

Now such burying-places of the Crô-Magnons as have been discovered reveal new and extraordinary conditions. The graves of this race are full of flints, pebbles, perforated shells, teeth, and other charms, and amulets. Shells are particu-

---

[1] That both names are employed interchangeably by all anthropologists of standing proves that the peoples of the two settlements had a common origin, but " Crô-Magnon " is usually applied to the race and " Aurignacian " to the culture it developed.

[2] *Ancient Types of Man*, New York, 1911, p. 71.

larly numerous, and some of them seem to have been made into mantles or gorgets, which had covered the whole or part of the body. On the walls of the caverns where those burials took place are imprints of human hands which had been laid on the rock and then dusted round with coloured earth. In many cases it is plain that one or more finger-joints of the left hand had been cut off. The practice was analogous to that of some present-day African Bushmen, Australian Blackfellows, and some American-Indian tribes who practice finger-mutilation. This is done on the death of a relative, the intention being to " cut off deaths "; that is, to sacrifice a part of the body to save the whole. We shall see later that the Aztecs of Mexico left the imprints of the hands of their sacrificial victims on the door-jambs of the heroes who had taken them prisoners in battle. In some cases traces of red paint are found on the bones of the Crô-Magnon remains, and this implies that red ochre, ruddle, or some other red earth was rubbed on the body after death to give it the colour of blood, that is of life, to restore to it the hues of life, to bestow these hues in abundance, in the hope that one day it might resume existence, and shake off the heavy sleep into which it seemed to have fallen, or enjoy a healthy and natural life in another sphere.

The industry and art of this primitive people who settled on the Biscay coast, and in the Pyrenean region and Dordogne were much more highly advanced than anything the world has to show prior to their appearance in Europe. Indeed their art has been lauded by competent critics as in many respects equal to that of modern times. The technique of their flint work is far superior to that seen in the clumsy tools of Neanderthal man, and the great variety of graving-tools or burins which they used for engraving on stone are masterpieces of the flint-maker's art. They also, unlike the Neanderthals, used tools of bone and horn. Moreover, the inventive genius of the Crô-Magnons is well displayed in the flint implements they fashioned for use in fishing.

The distribution of this race in Europe extended by degrees along the Riviera into the Pyrenees, the Cantabrian Alps, and along the Dordogne, and the Somme, the Meuse, the Rhine, and the Danube. " The strongest proof," says Professor H. F. Osborn,[1] " of the unity of heredity as displayed in the dominant Crô-Magnon race in Europe from early Aurignacian until the close of Magdalenian times is the unity of their art impulse. . . . These people were the Palæolithic (Old Stone Age) Greeks ; artistic observation and representation and a true sense of proportion and of beauty were instinctive with them from the beginning. Their stone and bone industry may show vicissitudes and the influence of invasion and of trade and the bringing in of new inventions, but their art shows a continuous evolution and development from the first, animated by a single motive, namely, the appreciation of the beauty of form and the realistic representation of it." Elsewhere he says :[2] " Decorative art has now become a passion [with the Crô-Magnons], and graving-tools of great variety and shape, curved, straight, convex or concave—diversified both in size and in style of technique—are very numerous. We may imagine that the long periods of cold and inclement weather were employed in these occupations. . . . Strong and very sharp graving-tools were also needed for the sculpture out of ivory and soapstone of such human figures and figurines as the statuettes found in the Grottes de Grimaldi, and at Willendorf, and still more powerful tools for such work as the large stone bas-reliefs at Laussel. . . . As this industrial evolution widens, it is apparent that we witness not the local evolution of a single people but rather the influence and collaboration of numerous colonies reacting more or less

[1] *Men of the Old Stone Age*, 1915, pp. 315, 316.
[2] *Ibid.*, pp. 311, 312.

PLATE III.

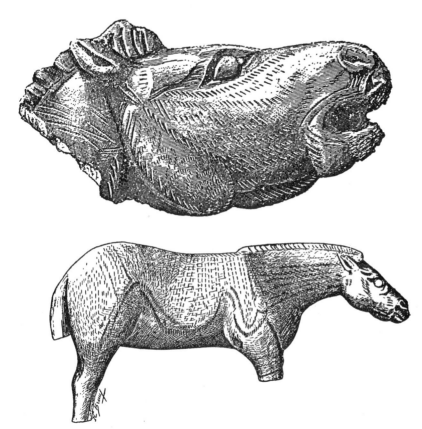

Figures of horses from Les Espélungues and Le Mas d'Azil.

(From *L'Anthropologie*, vols. x, xvii.)

Aurignacian Art.

one upon the other and spreading their inventions and discoveries."

The wonderful art of the Crô-Magnons has been brought to the gaze of an astonished world out of the caves which they formerly inhabited in the Biscayan regions of France and Spain. It consists chiefly of paintings, engravings, and sculptures of animals, bears, mammoths, horses, deer, and particularly the bison or aurochs, and not infrequent carvings, bas-reliefs, or figurines of the human form. These are chiefly female, and display an advanced knowledge of anatomy. The smaller figures in the round are almost certainly idols of goddesses, and, says Osborn, " resemble the work of modern Cubists." This Aurignacian art had many phases over a period of about 15,000 years, or during the period 25,000 to 10,000 years ago.

The Abbé Breuil, than whom no one has done so much for the elucidation of the Aurignacian period, sees in this art a certain similarity to that of North Africa. He believes that the Crô-Magnons followed the southern shores of the Mediterranean, and that the statuettes they made bear a resemblance to those of baked clay found in the Nile Valley. The head-dresses of some of them, he points out, bear a marked likeness to those seen in the Egyptian figurines. These statuettes of females represent the Great Mother, the fertile, productive Goddess of Nature, as may be observed from the exaggeration of the breasts and hips.

A glance at the accompanying reproductions of Crô-Magnon pictures and sculptures will do more than pages of description to demonstrate to the reader that the people who painted and carved them cannot be classed as savages. The horse's head, from Mas d'Azil, is, it will readily be conceded, worthy of an Athenian frieze, the reindeer engraved on a piece of antler has all the flair and technical completeness of modern French draughtsmanship, and the bison from the ceiling of Altmira gives a marvellous impression of life and force. Here is a masterly perfection to which the art of Egypt is as the angular scratchings of a child with slate and pencil. Such an art was not developed in a few decades. As has been said, it persisted in early South-Western Europe for many thousands of years before it was ultimately destroyed, and *it must have persisted elsewhere for nearly as many thousands of years*—for as long, at least, as it took for Egyptian art to develop, before it entered Europe at all. But where ? The race who carved and painted so wonderfully possessed a highly-strung æsthetic sense, a cultivated taste, a sure touch. They were unquestionably the parents of European civilisation. Whence did they come ?

The Abbé Breuil, who occupies a position in prehistoric studies at which none dare cavil, is strongly of opinion that successive invasions of culture took place either from the south or Mediterranean region, or from that part of Europe, the Biscayan coasts of Spain and France, which he calls the " Atlantic." " Certainly," adds Professor Osborn,[1] " the archæologic testimony strongly supports this culture-invasion hypothesis, and it appears to be strengthened in a measure by the study of the human types." " We can hardly contemplate an origin from the east," says Breuil,[2] " because these earlier phases of the Aurignacian industry have not as yet been met with in Central or Eastern Europe. " A southerly origin," says Osborn, " seems more probable, because the Aurignacian colónies appear to surround the entire periphery of the Mediterranean, being found in Northern Africa, Sicily, and the Italian and Iberian peninsulas, from which they extended over the larger part of southern France. In Tunis we find a very primitive Aurignacian, like that of the Abri Audit of Dordogne,

[1] *Op. cit.*, p. 277, and pp. 305, 306.
[2] " Les subdivisions du palæolithic supérieur," *Cong. Intern. d'Anthrop. Prehist.*, XIV session, Geneva, 1912, p. 175.

with implements undoubtedly similar to those of Chatel-
perron in France. Even far to the east, in the cave of
Antelias in Syria, as well as in certain stations of Phœnicia,
culture - deposits are found which are characteristically
Aurignacian "; but " the pure *early Aurignacian* industry is
seen in the regions of Dordogne and the Pyrenees."

The undoubted fact, then, is that Crô-Magnon man first
appeared in South-Western Europe at an epoch which is
universally dated at about 25,000 years ago, the end of the
Pleistocene or Ice Age, when widespread subsidences were
taking place in Europe and the Atlantic area. He brought
with him an art of high development, an art which had been
evolved elsewhere. That he came from the East is highly
improbable, as the finds of Aurignacian culture in that
region are obviously of much later date than those of France
and Spain ; nor does the art preserved in them at all approach
that of the Biscayan or Pyrenean type. As for the contention that Aurignacian art is of African origin, it is certainly
found in Tunis in a primitive (or debased ?) form, probably
derived from that of Spain.[1]   But it is noteworthy that those
Aurignacian stations which have so far been discovered in
Spain and southern France are, without exception, situated
*in the Biscayan district, and not on the southern coasts of the
peninsula.*

But another and even stronger proof of the Atlantic origin
of the Crô-Magnon race is forthcoming in the circumstance
that the culture of the Guanche aborigines of the Canary
Islands was undoubtedly of the Aurignacian type. Says
Professor Osborn (*op. cit.*, pp. 454, 455) : " Our interest in
the fate of the Crô-Magnons is so great that the Guanche
theory may also be considered ; it is known to be favoured

[1] Professor J. L. Myres draws a close parallel between the European
and African forms, and believes the latter to be older. It is a nice point,
and, even so, does not invalidate the Atlantean hypothesis, which regards
an African or Biscayan secondary origin for Aurignacian culture with
equal placidity. See *Cambridge Ancient History*, vol. i, p. 36.

by many anthropologists : von Behr, von Luschan, Mehlis, and especially by Verneau. The Guanches were a race of people who formerly spread all over the Canary Islands, and who preserved their primitive characteristics even after their conquest by Spain in the fifteenth century. The differences from the supposed modern Crô-Magnon type may be mentioned first. The skin of the Guanches is described by the poet Viana as light coloured, and Verneau considers that the hair was blond or light chestnut and the eyes blue ; the colouring, however, is somewhat conjectural. The features of resemblance to the ancient Crô-Magnons are numerous. The minimum stature of the men was 5 feet 7 inches, and the maximum 6 feet 7 inches ; in one locality the average male stature was over 6 feet. The women were comparatively small.[1] The most striking characters of the head were the fine forehead, the extremely long skull, and the pentagonal form of the cranium, when seen from above, caused by the prominence of the parietals—a Crô-Magnon characteristic. . . . The offensive weapons in warfare consisted of three stones, a club, and several knives of obsidian ; the defensive weapon was a simple lance. The Guanches used wooden swords with great skill. The habitation of all the people was in large, well-sheltered caverns, which honeycombed the sides of the mountains ; all the walls of these caverns were decorated, the ceilings were covered with a uniform coat of red ochre, while the walls were decorated with various geometric designs in red, black, grey, and white. Hollowed-out stones served as lamps. We may conclude with Verneau that there is evidence, although not of a very convincing kind, that the Guanches were related to the Crô-Magnons."

Dr René Verneau, a French anthropologist of large experience, who spent five years in the Canaries, says :[2]

---

[1] So were the Crô-Magnon women.
[2] *Cinq années de séjour \aux iles Canaries*, p. 47.

" The Guanches were above all troglodytes—that is to say they lived in caves. There is no lack of large, well-sheltered caves in the Canary Islands. . . . Here is a description of one of these caves, the Grotto of Goldar : The interior is almost square, 16 feet 4 inches along the left side, 18 feet along the right. The width at the back is 15 feet 6 inches. A second cave, much smaller, opens from the right wall. All these walls are *decorated with paintings*. The ceiling is covered with a uniform coat of red ochre, while the walls are decorated with various geometric designs in red, black, grey, or white. High up runs a sort of cornice painted red," which is decorated with white concentric circles.

Lord Abercromby, a most trustworthy authority on everything pertaining to archæology, writes : [1] " In the museums of the Grand Canary, Teneriffe, and Palma a considerable number of prehistoric vessels are preserved. Anthropologists are agreed that the natives of the archipelago, at the time of its conquest in the fifteenth century, were a composite people, made up of at least three stocks : a Crô-Magnon type, a Hamitic or Berber type, and a brachycephalic type (*i.e.* round skulled). These natives were in a Neolithic stage of civilisation. . . . Even the painted wares of the Grand Canary appear to be of local origin and not due to external influence ; although undoubted Lybian inscriptions in the Grand Canary and lava querns of Iron Age type prove that the archipelago was visited before its conquest by the Spaniards without affecting the general civilisation of its inhabitants."

All this proves, to my mind, that the Crô-Magnon race was indigenous to the Canary Islands, the remnants of Atlantis, and did not drift there from Europe. If it is implied that they did, how, it may be asked, did they make their way to the Canaries ? My contention is that they made their

[1] " The Prehistoric Pottery of the Canary Islands," *Nature*, 3rd Dec. 1914.

way from Atlantis to Europe by way of an existing land-connection, before the invention of boats. As I have observed, we can scarcely credit that part of Plato's narrative which speaks of Atlantis as a port frequented by the world's shipping—at the date 9600 B.C., and *a fortiori*, not at 25,000 B.C. That a third wave from Atlantis invaded Europe by sea 10,000 years ago I will later endeavour to prove. But that Crô-Magnon man came to Europe by water is out of the question. Equally absurd is the notion that he reached the Canaries by sea. *Like many of the animals and plants of these vestigial islands, he was cut off and marooned on them by some great natural cataclysm.* Reason and fact strongly buttress this opinion. Indeed, I can see no alternative to it that has any chance of acceptance by unbiassed minds. Not a single boat or drawing of a boat of the Aurignacian period has been found, and it is a mere truism that not even the humblest kind of craft was known to man for many thousands of years subsequent to the arrival of the Crô-Magnon race in Europe. We find this race in the Canaries, whence passage to or from Europe by sea was impossible during Aurignacian times. In what other way than by the hypothesis of the breaking down of a former land-connection can the mystery of the isolation of Crô-Magnon man on the Canaries be solved ?

But can we light upon any further evidence that the Crô-Magnons were of Atlantic origin ? The celebrated ethnologist, Ripley, in his *Races of Europe* (p. 38), gives it as his considered opinion that the Basque people of the Pyrenees speak a language inherited from the Crô-Magnons. " This hypothesis," remarks Osborn, " is well worth considering, for it is not inconceivable that the ancestors of the Basques conquered the Crô-Magnons and subsequently acquired their language." Now the Basque language has no linguistic affinities with any European tongue, but it has strong resemblances to certain American languages. " The fact is indisputable," says Dr Farrar, in his *Families of Speech* (p. 132), "and is eminently noteworthy, that while the affinities of the Basque roots have never been conclusively elucidated, there has never been any doubt that this isolated language, preserving its identity in a western corner of Europe between two mighty kingdoms, resembles in its grammatical structure the aboriginal languages of the vast opposite continent, and those alone." Says Professor J. L. Myres in *The Cambridge Ancient History* (p. 48): "The similarity between Aurignacian skulls in Europe and the pre-historic skulls in Lagoa Santa in Brazil and other remote localities round the margins of South America, suggests that this type had once almost as wide a distribution as that of the older types of implements."[1]

It has been noted, too, that the Crô-Magnons, as befitted a people of oceanic origin, practised fishing. Like the people of Plato's Atlantis, they seem to have had an especial reverence for the bull, the figure of which is so frequently depicted on the walls of their caverns. Sea-shells, too, appear to have entered in some manner into the ritual of their faith. Probably these symbolised the "god-body," or divine essence, as in Japan, but in any case they are employed by more than one sea-people (or by a race like the Mexicans, who conserved a strong memory of the sea) as a species of life-giving fetish.

Briefly, official anthropology has not as yet arrived at any definite conclusion as to the place of origin of Crô-Magnon man. He did not come from the East or the North, nor can his first home be placed in the South with any degree of

---

[1] The *Cambridge Ancient History*, which has only come into my hands while writing the above pages, and which, indeed, has just been published, contains some passages corroborative of my conclusions. It presumes the south-western origin of the Crô-Magnons, and speaks of their culture (p. 50) as "a well-marked regional culture of the Atlantic coast plain." It also corroborates other of my conclusions, as I will show at a later stage.

certainty. There is only one supposition left. The map shows that the greater number of his stations, especially those of early date, were situated in the Biscay country and in Dordogne. Does any good reason exist for believing that he did not come from the Atlantic region ? I can perceive none, but I do not expect to carry with me the great body of official archæological opinion. The archæologist is rightly cautious regarding his acceptance of what he would probably describe as a daring hypothesis, but my charge against him is that the mere habit of caution has bred within him the " credulity of incredulity." I behold an art full-fledged and having behind it many centuries of development suddenly imported into a region to which it has hitherto been foreign. I ask myself whence did it come ? The facts adduced before prove that the Aurignacian art of Crô-Magnon man arrived in Biscay neither from the North nor the East, nor did it originate in Africa. Only the West is left as the place of its provenance. " Ah, but you must not look in that direction," cries the official archæologist. I reply that I look in the direction to which the facts point—to the Atlantic region, where the Spaniards found the Crô-Magnon race still in possession of the remnant of Atlantis. If Crô-Magnon man did not hail from that region, whence, I ask, did he enter Europe ? I consult the oracles, but, alas ! " the oracles are dumb." They cannot answer me, and that for the most excellent of reasons—because they do not know themselves, or, if they do know, fear to speak.[1]

It seems to me that the geological as well as the archæological evidence makes it more than clear that Crô-Magnon man was the first of those immigrant waves which surged over Europe as the great continent in the Atlantic experienced cataclysm after cataclysm, partial submergence or volcanic upheaval. In my view these catastrophes forced him east-

---

[1] Excepting those I have quoted, who are among the few with first-hand knowledge of Crô-Magnon archæology.

PLATE IV.

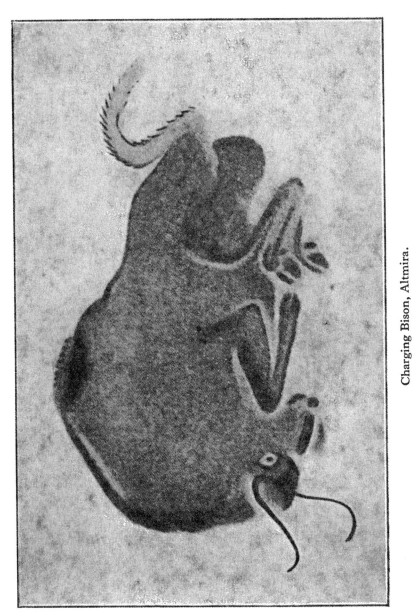

Charging Bison, Altmira.

(Drawn by M. l'Abbé Breuil; from *La Caverne d'Altmira*.)

Aurignacian Art.

ward over a still existing land-connection into northern Spain and southern France. I am well aware that this view has been expressed in past years with more or less cogency, but not, I think, with such an array of modern evidence as I have brought to its support, and with only fragmentary knowledge of the whole circumstances of Aurignacian culture as recently brought to light.

After many thousands of years Crô-Magnon man adopted the later Solutrean flint culture, in which we find the flint chipped by pressure in fine, thin flakes from the core. This beautiful technique originally came from the East, probably from Libya or Somaliland, but it never penetrated to the south of the great barrier of the Pyrenees, and the Crô-Magnons southward of that mountain chain were not affected by it. This seems to me to prove conclusively that it was of extraneous origin. Nor did it penetrate Italy. Who its " carriers " were is at present unknown. Although it affected Crô-Magnon tool-making, it had no influence on Aurignacian art, which, however, languished somewhat at this period. Soon, notwithstanding these new influences, it underwent a renascence, which is generally described by archæologists as the Magdalenian epoch. This Magdalenian phase of Aurignacian art seems to have had its rise about 16,000 years ago, and exhibits the genius of the Crô-Magnon race at its apogee, preceding its sudden decline and disappearance as the dominant type in Europe. The Crô-Magnons of this time, says Osborn, are commonly known as Magdalenians, " taking their name from the type station of La Madeleine, as the Greeks in their highest stage took their name from Athens and were known as Athenians." He shows elsewhere that the ultimate origin of this Magdalenian culture is, like that of its predecessor, unknown. " It seems," he remarks, " *like a technical invasion in the history of Western Europe* and not an inherent part of the main line of cultural development." Breuil observes that " it appears as if the fundamental elements of the superior Aurignacian culture had been contributed *by some unknown route* to constitute the kernel of the Magdalenian civilisation while the Solutrean episode was going on elsewhere."

This can only mean that the older Aurignacian art received impetus and stimulation from its original and parent source. " These Magdalenians *were newcomers in western France,*" *but undoubtedly of Crô-Magnon race.* " Breuil himself," says Osborn, " has positively stated that the whole Upper Palæolithic art development of Europe was *the work of one race ; if so, this race can be none other than the Crô-Magnon.*" I gather from this that at what is called the Magdalenian period a further immigration set into Europe from disintegrating Atlantis. Naturally these immigrants would bring with them, coming from the hub and centre of the ancient civilisation they represented, a higher culture than the older settlers of their race had introduced into Europe. They appear as from nowhere. Naturally it occurs to many archæologists to refer their origin to the East. The East has probably served official archæology much better as an imaginary *oficina gentium* than it ever did the world of reality. It is a handy place from which to conjure up any race or people the precise home of which is in any way conjectural. Why the provenance of practically all the civilised peoples who have ever contributed to the sum of human culture should be located in the Orient has, I must say, been to me an abiding mystery. This extraordinary bias in favour of an Eastern origin for everything is a capital example of the manner in which traditions may be abused. The golfer gives an absurd waggle to his club simply because all other golfers do ; the smith clinks on his anvil, between the heavier strokes of his hammer, simply because all other smiths from the beginning of time have done the same. The barber keeps snipping his scissors when he is not cutting your hair ; similarly the antiquary, quite as unthinkingly, or instinctively,

keeps looking eastward, because it is in his professional blood
to do so.

Archæologists of experience who have studied the Aurignacian culture deny an Eastern origin to its early phases.
They assert that Magdalenian culture is but a later phase
of Aurignacian—and then go on to look for an Eastern origin
for Magdalenian !

It would seem then, so comparatively sudden is the change
in artistic standards of excellence, that at the Magdalenian
epoch the Crô-Magnons of France and Spain were reinforced
by a second wave of immigrants from the old Atlantean home,
who had perfected the ancient and common art of both in a
different sphere. The climate of Europe was changing, and
the ice-cap was once more creeping southward, so that
France and Spain were cold and damp, and later experienced
tundra conditions. Nevertheless, prehistoric art was never
at such a height of excellence. The cave-shelters were once
more adorned with masterly representations of wild animals.
The use of colour became more complex, and was employed
with increasing skill and taste. Paint was mixed on palettes,
and placed on cavern walls by lamplight. The rich and
varied art of this period, its sculpture and carving, compares
well with those of Egypt and Babylon, says Osborn, who
continues (p. 358) : " There can be little doubt that such
diversities of temperament, of talent, and of predisposition
as obtain to-day also obtained then, and that they tended
to differentiate society into chieftains, priests, and medicine-
men, hunters of large game and fishermen, fashioners of
flints and dressers of hides, makers of clothing and footwear,
makers of ornaments, engravers, sculptors in wood, bone,
ivory, and stone, and artists with colour and brush. In their
artistic work at least these people were animated with a com-
pelling sense of truth, and we cannot deny them a strong
appreciation of beauty."

It is significant that these later Aurignacians introduced

the harpoon of bone, which proves conclusively that they were a fishing people. The Magdalenian culture, like its predecessor, still centred round the Biscay-Pyrenean region and the Dordogne, although it branched out later to Germany and Austria and to Britain by way of the land-bridge which connected our island with the European continent until as late as about 3000 B.C. But it never reached southern Spain or Italy. Crô-Magnon man at this period travelled far and wide ; there was an extensive system of barter, and his progress north and south can readily be traced.

But this culture declined. The dry cold with its tundra conditions, in which flourished the antelope and the mammoth, turned once more to moistness, and these animals disappeared. New conditions of life obtained, and the Crô-Magnons lived mostly by fishing. Stagnation set in. Another race was knocking at the door.

CHAPTER VI

THE THIRD ATLANTEAN INVASION

THE race which now challenged the supremacy of the Crô-Magnons, and which appears in Spain and France at a date generally fixed by archæologists at about 10,000 years ago, was the Azilian-Tardenoisian, so called from the Pyrenean locality in which their remains were first found. Once again we have to look to the Pyrenees and Biscay for the first traces in Europe of an invading race arriving at a period long before that in which European history begins. This people brought with them a flint culture of their own. They worked surprisingly small flints, especially in the form of fish-hooks, of surprising smoothness and delicacy, and possessed a geometric art which was undoubtedly the parent of the arabesque. They painted strange symbols, which have been described as alphabetic, on pebbles, and introduced the bow and arrow. They spread round the Mediterranean basin, pressing northward. The men were dressed in short trousers and wore feather head-dresses ; the women in short skirts and caps, and both were lavishly covered with ornament.

Whence came this people ? " The Azilian bone-harpoon industry, like the Tardenoisian microlithic flint industry, was largely pursued by fisher-folk," says Osborn. Breuil believes the Azilian-Tardenoisians to be of Mediterranean origin, and sees the gradual introduction of Azilian culture in that area gradually mingling with the Aurignacian. Similar industrial centres have been discovered in Tunis, Portugal, and southern Spain. That is, the Azilian culture is found in its earliest known stages in North Africa and South-Western Europe.

The question which confronts us is : Did it develop in these regions, or was it introduced there ? Azilian burials invariably show the face turned to the west. The body was smothered in ochre. These Azilian-Tardenoisian people were undoubtedly the parents of the great Mediterranean or Iberian race, who spread over southern Europe and penetrated to Britain and Norway on the north and Egypt on the east. They certainly introduced the Neolithic or New Stone Age civilisation. " So striking," says Professor Elliot Smith, " is the family likeness between the early Neolithic peoples of the British Isles and the Mediterranean and the bulk of the population, both ancient and modern, of Egypt and East Africa, that a description of the bones of an early Briton of that remote epoch might apply in all essential details to an inhabitant of Somaliland." In passing, I may mention as regards the view of the wide diffusion of the Iberian people, that Professor Gregory of Glasgow suggests that the Incas of Peru may have been of Iberian or Berber stock, and crossed from Africa " by the Canaries and the Azores, and possibly other islands now non-existent."

But much difference of opinion exists regarding the origin of the Azilian-Tardenoisian stock and culture. It invaded Europe and the Mediterranean basin at a date which, broadly speaking, can well be collated with that given by Plato in his *Critias* and *Timæus*. If the statements made in these works arise out of a genuine folk-memory of such an event (as, indeed, I am convinced is the case), we then have before us one of the most remarkable survivals in the records of folk-history. The modern world possesses no such records, because these are no longer handed down from parent to child in the sanctity of a hushed wonder. But that less sophisticated races cherish the memory of such events over very long spaces of time we have excellent proof. Moreover, it is not improbable that, as has been shown, Egyptian records may have helped to bridge the gulf over several centuries. The Babylonians in the Gilgamesh epic undoubtedly preserved the confused memory of events which greatly antedated their own heyday, and the Maya of Central America had folk-tales, oral and literary, like the Popol Vuh, telling of early migrations which have been proved by subsequent research to have taken place at least fifteen to eighteen centuries before the Spanish conquest. Chinese tradition covers a lapse of time which must be counted in thousands rather than hundreds of years. But I will not stress this point, weak as it must undoubtedly seem to many, because, as I have already said, I do not rest my hypothesis of the former existence of an Atlantic continent on the tale of Plato alone. The fact that the date of the coming of the Azilian-Tardenoisians, as given by the best authorities, synchronises generally with the date Plato gives for the destruction of Atlantis may be purely coincidental. I will leave this phase of my argument with the observation that some coincidences are more extraordinary than proven facts.

To return to the origin of the Azilian-Tardenoisian race and culture. The Abbé Breuil believes them to have come from " circum-Mediterranean sources." Schmidt inclines to the view that Azilian-Tardenoisian is merely a later development of the Magdalenian. But both are vague regarding origins, and disinclined to commit themselves in view of what appears to them scanty evidence. It is significant to the student of Atlantean archæology that official archæologists should be unable or unwilling to venture more than a passing expression of opinion regarding the origins of the several races which entered Western Europe and the Mediterranean area in prehistoric times. Why, it may well be asked, should all these races *appear suddenly in the same area* ? And why should men of science hold such extremely vague views regarding their provenance ?

The Azilian-Tardenoisians were merely the first wave of a better-known stock, the Iberian, or so-called Mediterranean race. An equal difference of opinion on the part of authorities is to be encountered as regards the original home of this people. Sergi, than whom none made a closer study of the problem, held at least three different points of view at three different periods of his life on this thorny subject. He says (*Mediterranean Race*, p. 39 ff.) : " But that original stock could not have its cradle in the basin of the Mediterranean, a basin more fitted for the confluence of peoples and for their active development ; the cradle whence they dispersed in many directions was more probably in Africa. The study of the fauna and flora of the Mediterranean exhibits the same phenomenon and becomes another argument in favour of the African origin of the Mediterranean peoples."

He proceeds to say that a study of the Hamitic race has assisted him in arriving at a conclusion. In the description " Hamitic " he includes ancient and modern Egyptians, Nubians, Abyssinians, Gallas, Somalis, Berbers, Fulahs, and the Guanches of the Canaries. The physical characteristics of all these peoples he finds to be essentially the same, and he looks for their place of origin in Africa. At first he did so in East Africa, in the region of the great lakes, near the sources of the Nile and in Somaliland, chiefly encouraged to do so by the fact that the race was so frequently and anciently portrayed on the Egyptian monuments, and by the presence of flint implements of the Palæolithic Age in the Nile valley. But extensive finds of worked flints are also found in North Africa and the Sahara. " The idea has thus arisen that Western rather than Eastern Africa was the original home of these peoples." Later still, it seemed to him more reasonable to look once more to the region of the great lakes as being more favourable to human existence. All the same, he " will not deny to the Sahara the possibility of being the cradle " of the Mediterranean race.

There is thus very good reason to suppose that the Iberian race had a very early connection with the Atlas region of North Africa. The Iberians of the Roman era were known to the Italians as Atlanteans. " The Atlanteans," says Dr Bodichon, who passed many years in Algeria, " among the ancients passed for the favourite children of Neptune. They made known the worship of this god to other nations —to the Egyptians, for example. In other words, the Atlanteans were the first known navigators."

That these Iberians of the Atlas, the descendants of the Azilian-Tardenoisians, were a people with maritime proclivities has now been well substantiated. Mr Donald A. Mackenzie, summing up the proof of Azilian-Tardenoisian and Iberian maritime knowledge in his interesting book, *Ancient Man in Britain* (p. 68 ff.), says that the easiest crossing to Britain from the continent was over the English Channel land-bridge. This was ultimately cut through by the sea, so that the Azilian-Tardenoisian people from Central and Western Europe must have used boats to cross with before polished stone implements came into use. " It is possible," he says, " that the Azilian, Tardenoisian, and Maglemosian peoples had made considerable progress in the art of navigation. . . . There were boats on the Mediterranean at a very early period. One of the Clyde canoes, found embedded in the Clyde silt twenty-five feet above the present sea-level, was found to have a plug of cork which could only have come from the area in which cork trees grow—Spain, Southern France, or Italy. It may have been manned by the Azilians of Spain." He proceeds to show that these Azilians were possibly the fathers of British maritime skill.

Where, it may be asked, did these Azilian-Tardenoisians

and their Iberian descendants learn the seaman's art ? Mr Mackenzie believes that the boat was invented on the calm waters of the Nile, where conditions were most favourable to its development. But no data exists to show that the Egyptians braved the terrors of the ocean prior to the period 5000 B.C. The flint fish-hooks of the early Azilians of 10,000 years ago or about 8000 B.C. must have undoubtedly been employed not to catch the lesser species of river fish, for which they would seem to be unfitted by their size, but for deep-sea fishing, which must naturally have been pursued from boats. The lesser fish in the rivers would, as in some savage parts of the world at the present day, be speared with harpoons or taken with nets. One must admit that the later voyages to Britain and elsewhere were made within the Egyptian maritime period. But that is not to say that Azilian sailors never put to sea at a time considerably before that period.

Osborn says that Tardenoisian stations are usually to be found situated on ocean inlets or river-courses. He calls this people " a population of fishermen." Many of the stations are situated on the Bay of Biscay. No population of any size could long subsist on the finny spoil of one or more rivers of ordinary size, which would speedily become fished out, especially as it was not habitual among early peoples to observe a close time. When a community of considerable advancement makes its dwelling on the seashore, it may safely be suggested that it is because it intends to live on the harvest of the ocean, of whose plenty it has had experience for generations, and this it can do with any degree of success only by the use of sea-going craft of a fairly reliable character. No remains of fish, so far as I can find, are to be discovered in Azilian-Tardenoisian deposits, but this is readily to be accounted for by the exceedingly perishable nature of such remains and the great age of the deposits.

I can see no reason to deny a knowledge of primitive

navigation to the late Azilian-Tardenoisians, and believe that
this was not derived from Egyptian sources. But, in any
case, proof of this is not strictly essential to our hypothesis,
as in all probability they reached Africa, and later, Europe,
from their ancient home in Atlantis, by a land-bridge, or
by a closely knit insular chain.

We must regard the Atlantis of the period as resembling
the Europe of the same epoch—that is, as still in the Stone
Age. This is self-evident from the fact that the colonists it
sent out were still in the Stone Age culture. We need not
conclude, however, that that culture was a low one. The
civilisations of the Maya and Nahua of Mexico and the Incas
of Peru were Neolithic, but they were in no wise inferior to
those of Egypt or Babylon, or even to those of Greece and
Rome, save that their people made use of stone implements
instead of metals.

M. D'Arbois de Jubainville, in his *Les premiers habitants
de l'Europe*, says (pp. 24, 25) : " The Iberians seem to be
the descendants of those ten millions of legendary warriors
who, according to Theopompus, came from a continent
separated from ours by the ocean, and established themselves in the country of the Hyperboreans. These were
their ancestors, who, leaving Atlantis nine thousand years
before Plato, had impressed their domination on Western
Europe, Italy, and North Africa to the frontiers of Egypt."
He concludes, too, that they entered Spain, Gaul, Britain,
Corsica, and Sardinia.

It is also not improbable that earlier human races
reached Europe from the Atlantean continent. Professor
Osborn, speaking of Chellean man, a type which entered
Europe about 100,000 years ago, says (*op. cit.*, p. 126) :
" So far as present evidence goes, it would appear that the
pre-Chellean culture did not enter Europe directly from
the East, or even along the northern coast of the Mediterranean, but rather along the northern coast of Africa, where

Chellean culture is recorded in association with mammalian remains belonging to the Middle Pleistocene epoch."

Summarising the ethnological evidence from pre-history, we find :—

1. That the Crô-Magnon or Aurignacian, one of the finest races mentally and physically the world has ever seen, entered South-Western Europe about 25,000 years ago, at or about the close of the Great Ice Age.

2. They brought with them a highly developed art, such, indeed, as has earned them the name of " the Palæolithic Greeks." They were, indeed, passionately devoted to art in all its forms, appear to have possessed a highly developed social polity, and were by no means savages, or even barbarians.

3. Their culture must have germinated and developed elsewhere. It appears suddenly in South-Western Europe, and there are no traces of its actual infancy in the known world.

4. The Abbé Breuil, the highest authority on this civilisation, believes that it originated in that part of Europe, Biscayan France and Spain, which he calls " Atlantic." It certainly first appeared in Europe in that region, but it is not possible that it originated there, as no early or evolutionary traces of its infancy are to be discovered either in Europe, Africa, or Asia. Moreover, all the early Aurignacian stations are situated around the Biscay-Pyrenean region, and not on the southern coasts of the peninsula.

5. The culture of the Guanches or pre-Spanish aborigines of the Canary Islands has been recognised by the highest authorities as Crô-Magnon. This conclusively proves that the race was indigenous to Atlantis, of which the Canaries are among the last remnants ; that it made its way thence to Europe by a land-connection formerly existing, and did not drift to the islands from Europe by sea, as communication by sea was utterly unknown at the period of the first Crô-

Magnon migration to Europe 25,000 years ago, and even at a very much later period.

6. Remains strongly resembling those of Crô-Magnon man have been discovered in Lagoa Santa in Brazil and in other parts of South America. His facial contours strongly resemble those of the Red Indian of North America, who seems to employ many of his religious and social practices.

7. The Crô-Magnons had a special reverence for the bull or bison, the salient animal in Atlantean worship according to Plato's account. Sea-shells entered largely into their religious ritual. These phases are also found in pre-Columbian America.

8. A second wave of the Crô-Magnon civilisation, the Magdalenian, reached Europe from Atlantis about 16,000 years ago. A great renascence of Aurignacian art supervened. New inventions, such as the bone harpoon, suddenly appear in the Biscay region.

9. Ten thousand years ago a third invasion of the Biscay region occurred—that of the Azilian-Tardenoisian peoples, the parents of the Iberian race. They were fishers, and buried the heads of their dead facing westwards. Their culture shows a connection with the Aurignacian, but judging from its presently known manifestations, it would seem as if art, and perhaps civilisation in general, had meanwhile experienced a decline in the Atlantean sub-continent whence they came.

10. The Iberians, or later Azilian-Tardenoisians, settled first in the Atlas region, and were known to the Romans as Atlanteans. They were a race with maritime proclivities, but it is not necessary to suppose that they reached Europe by sea.

NOTE.—In the chapter which deals with the Atlantean affinities of Egypt, I shall bring evidence to bear that so far from that country's having been the original mother of European culture, it actually received its early impetus to civilisation from the West, whatever later contributions it may have made to Occidental culture. Here I shall only draw attention to the remarks of Mr H. R. Hall in the *Cambridge Ancient History* which assist belief in the western origin of Egyptian culture of the earlier type. He says (vol. i, p. 264): " We see Egypt originally inhabited by a stone-using Hamitic race (the Iberians) related to the surrounding Semites, Libyans, and Mediterraneans. . . . In the Delta they (the Armenoids, a later invading race) probably found a civilisation of a primitive Mediterranean type much more advanced than in the Upper country. . . . The hieroglyphic system and all the accompanying culture that it implies may have been theirs, but was more likely Mediterranean."

CHAPTER VII

THE EVIDENCE FROM EUROPEAN TRADITION

EUROPEAN traditions relating to lands which once existed in the Atlantic are numerous. To include the whole body of evidence afforded by these is impossible in a work of this scope, and is, moreover, needless, as these tales and legends have already been collected by numerous hands, notably by Basset, Warren, D'Avezac, and others. Here I must confine myself to the more important of these legends, and attempt some criticism of their origins, and a justification of their existence.

The Greeks, the world's first true geographers, were strong believers in the existence of large land-masses in the Atlantic. There were situated the floating island of Æolus, Ogygia, the navel of the sea, and the Elysian Fields. How far these localities were the fruit of religious speculation it is not my purpose to inquire. It is possible that the ideas concerning them may have arisen out of some hazy knowledge of the Canaries, or the Cape Verde Islands. In subsequent chapters I shall deal with this part of the subject at greater length, but at present I am concerned with the evidence from tradition and nothing more.

In dealing with Plato's account I have already outlined that of Theopompus and the legend of Ogygia. The Thessalian story of Deucalion is equally important to our thesis. Zeus, displeased with the men of the Age of Bronze, sent a deluge upon them. But one Deucalion, the son of Prometheus, acting upon the advice of his father, constructed

83

a coffer in which he took refuge along with his wife Pyrrha. For nine days and nights the coffer floated on the waves until it finally grounded on Mount Parnassus. Emerging, the pair found the world uninhabited, and Zeus, desirous of replenishing the earth, commanded them to effect this by casting behind them " the bones of the earth," otherwise stones, which by this process were changed into men and women.

Now we shall find in the following chapter abundant evidence that this very myth was known to more than one of the American peoples. Every modern student of myth is aware that tales of this character do not arise independently or in a spontaneous manner, but that racial contact is necessary to their dissemination. Moreover, in more than one picture in the Mexican native paintings the story of Deucalion and Pyrrha is told, especially in that in which the goddess of water, Chalchihuitlicue, is shown precipitating a flood, down the tumbling waters of which float a man and woman, one of whom holds or tries to reach a large coffer bursting with treasure.

More replete with interest are the mediæval legends connected with Atlantic localities. One of the most celebrated of these is the legend of St Brandan's Isle. St Brandan (d. 577) was Abbot of Clauinfert, in Ireland, according to the legend, where he was visited by a friend, Barontus, who told him that far in ocean lay the promised land of the Saints. St Brandan, accompanied by seventy-five monks, sailed thither, and, according to the Book of Lismore, spent seven years upon the ocean in two separate voyages. Eventually he discovered the island of his search. One authority states that he travelled up and *down the coast of Kerry,* " *inquiring as he went for traditions of the Western Continent.*" One of his disciples, St Malo or Maclovius, Bishop of Aleth in Brittany, accompanied him, and it is said discovered still other islands. Philoponus, in his *Nova typis transacta navigatio* (1621), gives an account of the voyages of St Brandan, with a curious map, in which he places the Saint's island N.W. of Spain and N.E. of the Canaries. After the discovery of the Azores, expeditions were fitted out to search for it, and were continued till as late as 1721. The island was reported as having been seen in 1759.

Of more importance is the legend of Antilia or the Isle of Seven Cities, which is described as the largest of the islands of the mediæval geographers, and as rectangular in shape, extending from north to south, and lying in mid-Atlantic about lat. 35° N. It appears again and again on the maps of the fourteenth, fifteenth, and later centuries, and it was thought before the discovery of America that it might be found suitable as a kind of half-way house to the Indies. The legend states that it was found and settled by refugees from Spain in 714 after the defeat of King Roderick by the Moors. There is also a story that the island was rediscovered by a Portuguese mariner in 1447. Legends survive too, of islands called Danmar or Tanmar, Reillo or Rayllo, and Satanaxio. The latter is of special interest. Formaleoni, an Italian writer, coming upon this name in an ancient map of Bianco, dated 1436, saw it there described as " Y^d laman Satanaxio." The description perplexed him, until he chanced to stumble upon a reference to a similar name in an old Italian romance. In a certain part of India, ran the story, a great hand rose every day from the sea and carried off a number of the inhabitants into the ocean. Adapting this tale to the west, he translated the name " the hand of Satan"; but D'Avezac believed the words to be a corruption of Satanagio or St Atanaxio (Athanasius).

Strangely enough, " the Great Hand " is a god of the Mexicans and Maya. As Huemac (Great Hand) he was regarded as first King of the Toltecs, and among the Maya

as Hunab Ku, a kind of " god behind the gods," the first
cause of all being.   He is the only god among the Maya
who can boast of a beard, and may be identified with the
moon, childbirth, and the healing art, but his personality
has many facets.   To this venerable god human sacrifice
was rendered on a considerable scale.   At a certain season of
the year criminals were sacrificed to him by a method called
" grinding between the stones."

Now in one myth (found in the Codex Tellerio-Remensis)
this god, or his Mexican equivalent, is spoken of as having
" breathed and divided the waters of the heavens and the
earth."   That he possessed volcanic propensities is also
clear from many passages.

I think, then, that it is this god, or his Antilian equivalent,
the memory of which has survived in the name " Hand of
Satan," given to the island of the Antilian group mentioned
by Formaleoni.   The tale of the hand rising out of the
sea and dragging down a number of the inhabitants of the
island appears to me as an allegory descriptive of frequent
earthquakes, just as the Cretan story of the Minotaur who
devoured a yearly tribute of maidens is obviously allegorical
of the worship of some ancient bull-headed deity, resembling
Moloch, to whom maidens were occasionally sacrificed.
Formaleoni saw in Antilia a European foreknowledge of the
Antilles, which, indeed, were called after the " mythical "
continent, and to transfer the name to a new discovery was
easy and natural.   Yet Peter Martyr, in 1493, states that
the geographers were assured that Hispaniola and the adjacent
islands were *Antillæ insulæ*, that is, they recognised them as
islands a vague and general knowledge of which had been
handed down from time immemorial.

For these and other reasons, as I have said before, I am of
the opinion that the great continent of Atlantis, in the course
of its age-long disintegration, broke up into two considerable
land-masses, the eastern portion of which retained the

original name, while the western portion came to be known by some such name as Antilia. The traditions respecting these appear to me as perfectly distinct, and, as I have mentioned, I believe the island continent of Antilia, the remains of which are the modern Antilles, or West Indies, to have survived the submergence of Atlantis by many thousands of years. For an elaboration of this theory the reader is referred to the chapter on the Geography and Topography of Atlantis : but I will say here that I believe Antilia to have conserved the remains of Atlantean culture, and to have been connected with the more easterly mass by an insular chain until the final destruction of Atlantis. I am not the first to identify the Antilles with Atlantis. This has already been done by Brasseur de Bourbourg, Bancroft, and Le Plongeon.[1] But I differ from them in that I see in the Antilles the remains of a distinct and surviving western portion of that continent, which remained above ocean long subsequent to the submergence of Atlantis itself. That Atlantis in later times (say 9000 B.C.) could have stretched from Europe to America and have been destroyed by the agency of one single cataclysm, and that its inhabitants could have colonised and civilised the American continent at that early period, is opposed to all we know of Mexican and Central American history. Indeed this view, rash and unscientific in the extreme, has done more to discredit the whole Atlantean hypothesis than anything else could possibly have done, and the absurd contention of Le Plongeon that Central America was colonised by Atlanteans 11,500 years ago is only paralleled by the rhetorical rubbish Brasseur saw fit to publish, which, despite his great erudition and the manifest knowledge he possessed of Central American history and tradition, entirely stultified his labours. Apart from the chronological and linguistic vagaries of these writers,

---

[1] None of them authorities of any great weight, I fear, and all inclined to rashness : but so it is, and decency dictates acknowledgment.

however, their remarks are full of suggestion to the careful student.

The legendary island of Brazil is found on the Medicean map of 1351, on the Pizigani map of 1367, and the Catalan map of 1375, which is to say that traditions concerning its existence must have been current for a very long period. It also appears on many other maps and globes dating between this time and the epoch of the discovery of America. The island of Brazil, or O'Brasile, plays a part as a vanishing island in early Irish legend, although it cannot be traced to its origin. It was first mentioned in modern literature by William Bettover, called William of Worcester, who says that on 15th July 1480 his brother-in-law, John Jay, began a voyage from Bristol in search of the island, returning on 18th September without having found it. Pedro Ayala, the Spanish ambassador to England, mentions in a letter dated 1498 that the mariners of Bristol had made a series of voyages in search of the island, which goes to show that a persistent tradition regarding it must assuredly have existed. Extraordinary are the impulses which arise from tradition! When the first Spanish expedition reached Florida in a quest for the Fountain of Perpetual Youth, the Elixir of Life, they encountered a band of Indians searching in these regions for the self-same thing!

Hardiman, in his *Irish Minstrelsy or Bardic Remains of Ireland* (London, 1831, vol. i, p. 368), which was written about 1636, says that there is an " iland which lyeth far att sea, on the west of Connaught, and sometimes is perceived by the inhabitants of the Oules and Iris . . . and from Saint Helen's Head. Likewise several seamen have discovered it . . . one of whom, named Captain Rich, who lives about Dublin, of late years had a view of the land, and was so neare that he discovered a harbour . . . but could never make to land, because of a mist which fell upon him. Allsoe in many old mappes . . . you still find it by the

PLATE V.

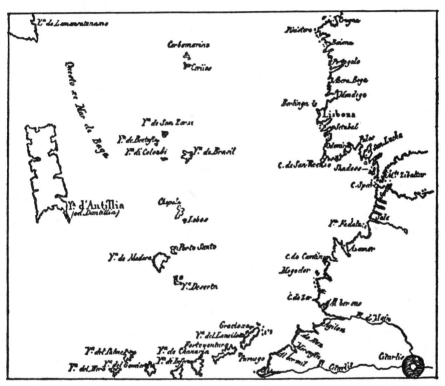

Part of the Map of Andreas Bianca showing the Islands of Antilia
and Brazil.

name of O'Brasile, under the longitude of 03° 00', and the latitude of 50° 20'." In 1675 a pretended account of a visit to this island was published in London, which is reprinted by Hardiman. The position he gives it is very nearly identical with that which it occupies in Dudley's *Arcano del Mare* (1646).

There are numerous other allusions to Brazil, as, for example, in O'Flaherty's *Ogygia* (London, 1685), in Jeremy Taylor's *Dissuasive from Popery* (1667), where it is mentioned familiarly, and elsewhere. The "conjectural map of Atlantis" which appears in his *Essais sur les Iles Fortunées* (1803), and which forms the frontispiece to this volume, illustrates the theory of Bory de St Vincent, that the Azores, Madeira, the Canaries, and the Cape Verde Islands were the remains of a great island-continent known to the ancients as the Hesperides, the country of Atlantis, the land of the Amazons, and the home of the Gorgons, containing each and all of these semi-fabulous regions.

If the reader desires to examine a map on which the islands of the Atlantic, real and imaginary, have been charted according to their most probable sites, he cannot do better than consult that of Gaffarel, " L'Océan Atlantique, et les restes de l'Atlantide," in the *Revue de Géographie*, vol. vi, p. 400. It shows all rocks and islets which have from time to time been reported as seen, or believed to have been seen, and these Gaffarel views as vestiges of the lost continent. But let us glance for a moment at some of the older maps with a view to discovering the frequency with which they charted the islands of which we have taken especial notice.

The map of Andreas Bianca (1436) shows Brazil as an island north of Madeira, Satanaxio on a parallel with the north of Spain, and Antilia as a large oblong mass opposite, but a considerable distance from, the opening to the Mediterranean. That of Benincasa (1476) shows these islands in almost the same position, while in the Laon globe

Antilia occupies the same latitude, and the others are not represented. In the interesting map of Ortelius (1587) a very large number of islands are charted. Brazil still occupies its traditional latitude, as does Satanaxio, which is here called " The Isle of Demons," but Antilia is not to be found.

Now I think that what I have written will suffice to show that a very ancient and widespread tradition existed on the western coasts of Europe regarding the former presence of insular masses of considerable size in the Atlantic. Considerations of space make it impossible for me to adduce the whole of the evidence for this tradition, which, indeed, is already to be found in several volumes of large content. It seems to me impossible to believe that this considerable body of legend was unsupported by earlier fact. Indeed, I am convinced that more than one of the islands which so plentifully besprinkle the maps of our ancestors remained in existence until comparatively late times. The question bristles with difficulties owing to the brief and meagre character of the references to these insular localities. But there seems to have been a consensus of opinion among the geographers of the thirteenth and fourteenth centuries that they actually existed, and, as I have shown, the latitudes in which they placed them on their charts are almost invariably the same. The fact that they were not so scrupulous in the indication of all localities assists the inference that they were incorrect with regard to the islands in question.

These by no means exhaust the store of traditional tales relative to lost islands and countries which were current on the western coasts of Europe. The Roman historian Timagenes, who flourished in the first century A.D., preserved traditions of the Gauls which spoke of invaders from a sunken island. Their descendants, especially those of Brittany, still speak of the submerged land of Ys, which lies deep-drowned beneath the cliffs of the Breton peninsula.

Giraldus Cambrensis tells us that similar beliefs were once current in Wales.

In this chapter I have merely tried to gather together a few of the most outstanding traditions obtaining in Western Europe regarding belief in former or actually existing island localities in the Atlantic Ocean. In a later chapter I will deal with those similarities between European and American lore and custom, which point to a common centre of origin for the early culture of the two continents. More than one of the legends here alluded to are dealt with at greater length in Chapter XVI.

CHAPTER VIII

THE EVIDENCE FROM AMERICAN TRADITION

IF the memory of the disintegration of an Atlantic continent by successive cataclysms of nature remained so strongly imbedded in the recollection and imagination of the peoples of Western Europe, it must have found a similar reminiscent echo among the tribes of America. Indeed, as we shall see, it gave rise to a much more extraordinary sequence of confirmatory traditions.

I have already said that I believe the lost continent to have broken up during the Pleistocene Age into two large land-masses—Atlantis, situated in close contiguity to Europe and Africa, and that which I shall call Antilia, which is represented by the Antilles group, just as Atlantis shows its last confirmatory peaks in the Canaries, Madeira, and the Cape Verde Islands. These two larger land-masses were, I believe, joined by an insular chain, of which the Azores and the Bermudas are the remaining vestiges. But I have always been of the opinion, and I think the geological and traditional evidence justifies the view, that Antilia did not finally disappear until long after Atlantis had finally sunk beneath the waves of the Atlantic Ocean. My chief reason for thinking so is that the American traditions of an oceanic cataclysm are manifestly much later than those of Europe, and this seems to be borne out by the fact that the civilisations of America themselves cannot by any process of reasoning be dated much before the beginning of the Christian era. This is the generally accepted chronology in the case of the Maya civilisation of Central America, but there is much more dubiety regarding the megalithic culture of pre-Incan Peru, which would seem to date from an earlier period. These questions I will deal with in their proper place, but at present I will content myself by saying that to the best of my belief no American civilisation greatly antedated 100 B.C., that is so far as its appearance on American soil is concerned.

Those American myths which preserve the memory of oceanic upheavals and Atlantean connections have not so far been collected in such a manner as to be accessible to the student of Atlantean research, and I have attempted to gather and describe them as succinctly and usefully as possible, in order that the evidence they bring to the subject may be readily available. This has entailed many years of research throughout the entire corpus of that literature which deals with American aboriginal tradition and history. I do not claim that the result is exhaustive—indeed it could scarcely be so ; but that it is representative, I certainly maintain. I will first of all summarise those traditions which deal with the creative legends of those American-Indian tribes which may be classed as uncivilised, retaining the more important testimony to be gleaned from the myths of Central America, Mexico, and Peru for later description.

Dealing first with the mythical and legendary tales of the Indians of North America, let us briefly review those of the Muskhogean stock, of which the Creeks, Choctaws, and Seminoles, are the chief representatives.

In the Muskhogean conception of creation we find that at the beginning the primeval waste of waters alone was visible. Over this two pigeons or doves flew hither and thither, and in time observed a single blade of grass spring above the surface. The solid earth followed gradually, and slowly took its present shape. A *great hill*, Nunne Chaha, rose in the midst, and *in the centre of this was the house of the deity Esaugetuh Emissee*, " Master of Breath." He made men from clay, and *built a great wall*, on which he set clay men to dry. Gradually the soft mud dried into bone and flesh. The god then *directed the waters into their proper channels*, reserving the dry land for the men he had made.

The hill alluded to in this myth has to my mind a suspicious resemblance to the Atlantean eminence on which we are told Poseidon built his dwelling. The encircling wall also appears to me to be an Atlantean reminiscence, as does the division of the sea and land into " zones."

The Iroquois tribes believe that their original female ancestress fell from heaven into the waste of primeval waters. But the land bubbled up beneath her feet, and quickly grew to the proportions of a continent. Some of the Iroquois tribes believe that the otter, beaver, and musk-rat, observing the fall of the original mother from heaven, hastened to break it by shovelling up the subaqueous mud so that she might fall softly thereon. They point to a mountain near the falls of the Oswego River as the locality where this took place.

The Aschochimi Indians of California have a myth which recounts the drowning of the world so that no man escaped. But by planting the feathers of divers birds, the Coyote grew a crop of men of various tribes.

The Algonquians relate that on one occasion Manibozho was hunting, and the wolves which he employed as hounds entered a great lake and disappeared. He entered the waters to effect their rescue, but they suddenly overflowed and submerged the entire habitable world. The musk-rat, however, supplied sufficient earth to recreate the terrestrial sphere. Manibozho married the musk-rat, and executed summary vengeance upon the demons, the perpetrators of the catastrophe. It is told of this god that *he carved and shaped the land and sea to his liking*, just as another Indian deity, Tawiscara, a god of the Hurons, " *guided the torrents into smooth seas and lakes*."

More important are the flood legends of the Indians of South America. The Antis Indians of the Bolivian Alps, north-western Brazil, the Ipurimas, Yurukares, etc., say that the world was overtaken by a great flood and men were imprisoned by this deluge in a large cave. Fiery cataclysms followed, and humanity perished. The Arawaks of the Guianas, northern Brazil, and Colombia say that the god Makonaima created a marvellous tree, each branch of which produced a different variety of fruit. A certain Sigu cut down this tree, the stump of which was found to be full of water, which began to flow, and a terrible flood ensued. Sigu led all the animals to an eminence, and succeeded in saving them during the period of submergence and darkness. The Macusi tribe of this family of Indians assert that the only people who survived the deluge *repeopled the earth by converting stones into human beings,* as did Deucalion and Pyrrha. The Tamanacs say that one man and one woman were saved by taking refuge on the lofty mountains of Tamancu, and *that they threw over their heads the fruits of the Mauritius palm, from the kernels of which sprang men and women.* The Arawaks of Guiana had a myth to the effect that Aimon Kondi, the Great Spirit, scourged the world with fire, from which the survivors sought refuge in underground caverns. A great flood followed, in which Marerewana and his followers saved themselves in a canoe.

A most striking myth is that of the Tupi-Guarani Indians of Brazil. Monan, the creator, they say, vexed with mankind, resolved to destroy the world by fire. But one, Irin Magé, a magician of might, extinguished the conflagration by a heavy rainstorm. This caused the rivers and lakes to overflow, and precipitated a flood. The Mundruku possess a myth to the effect that a god Raimi formed the world by *placing it in the shape of a flat stone on the head of another god.* (Compare this with the myth of Atlas and Hercules.) Another Tupi myth relates that the world was destroyed by a powerful supernatural agency called Maire, who sent upon it an inundation from which but a few were saved by climbing trees and hiding in caves.

The Tupuya or Ges Indians of eastern Brazil and Bolivia tell how the god Anatiwa originated the deluge, and that the water-hen fetched earth to the hills where those saved from the flood congregated, so that the area of safety might be enlarged. The Caribs believe that the ibis performed a like office for their ancestors. They believe also that their original ancestor *sowed the soil with stones, which grew up into men and women*, another variant of the Greek myth. The Chibchas of Colombia state that Bochica, a culture-hero, *carried the globe upon his shoulders like a second Atlas*, and that earthquakes were brought about by his changing it from one shoulder to the other.

Other North and South American myths are eloquent of Atlantean memories. Thus a legend of the Okanaguas states that a great medicine-woman named Scomalt *ruled over a " lost island "* (Bancroft's *Native Races*, vol. iii, p. 149) ; and the Delawares have legends telling of a mighty influx of rushing waters, and a hasty folk-migration in consequence (see Rafinesque, *The American Nations*, 1836).

Turning now to the more civilised nations of America, we may first examine certain traditions of the Aztecs of Mexico, which seem to conserve the memory of early convulsions of nature. The Aztecs believed that humanity had experienced a series of cataclysms or partial destructions of the earth. According to different authorities these had been four or five in number, and the periods or " suns " into which Mexican mythical history was divided were each thought to have concluded with the destruction of that luminary, which was again and again renewed.

The interpreter of the Codex Vaticanus, a manuscript-painting made by Aztec natives under Spanish priestly supervision, states that " in the first age (or sun) water reigned until at last it destroyed the world. . . . This age, according to their computation, lasted 4008 years, and on the occurrence of that great deluge they say that men were changed into fish, named Tlacamichin, which signifies men-fish." The second age, he tells us, lasted for 4010 years, and the world was ended by the force of violent winds, the catastrophe concluding by the transformation of men into apes. The third age endured for 4801 years, and ended in a universal fire; and in the fourth, which occupied 5042 years, the human race, which had never ceased to transmit survivors from one of these epochs to the next, was almost destroyed by famine.

The Mexican native historian, Ixtlilxochitl, in his *Historia Chichimeca*, or History of the Chichimecs (the Aztec race), alludes to the first of these ages or epochs as Atonatiuh, or "Water Sun," and states that during it all men perished in a great inundation. The second epoch, Tlachitonatiuh (Earth Sun), ended with violent earthquakes. In this age lived the giants or Quinames, the Aztec Titans, who, like the Greek or Scandinavian giants, appear to be connected with cataclysm. The third age, according to Ixtlilxochitl, was Ecatonatiuh, or Wind Sun, in which houses, trees, and men were nearly all destroyed by terrific hurricanes, those men who remained being changed into creatures of an in-telligence so low as to be almost indistinguishable from monkeys. Ixtlilxochitl in his *Relaciones* manages to trans-pose one of these ages, giving the second the third place. There is, indeed, considerable dubiety regarding the proper sequence of those epochs, some believing that five " suns " obtained.

It is probable that this cataclysmic theory was in vogue among the Aztecs for ages, and, indeed, Veytia and Ixtlilxochitl state that the number of suns was agreed upon at a meeting of native astronomers within traditional memory. We may rely, however, on the Calendar Stone of

Mexico, now in the National Museum there, to supply those capable of interpreting it with the " official " version of the myth.   According to this sculpture there were four epochs, the first " Four Jaguar," when the god Tezcatlipoca reigned as the sun, and at the end of which both men and giants were devoured by jaguars ; " Four Wind," presided over by the god Quetzalcoatl, ending in violent hurricanes and the transformation of men into monkeys ; " Four Rain," during which the god Tlaloc ruled, and the end of which was fire ; and " Four Water," the deity of which was the goddess Chalchihuitlicue, the catastrophe of which was deluge and the metamorphosis of men into fishes.[1]

Of late years my researches into the subject of Mexican mythology have led me to the especial consideration of several of those wonderful chronicles and annals which detail both the actual and legendary sides of Mexican history, and most of which were compiled by Europeanised natives subsequent to the conquest of Mexico.

One of the most important of these extraordinary books, and perhaps one of the richest in native lore, is the *Historia de los Mexicanos por sus Pinturas*, or History of the Mexicans according to their picture-manuscripts.   I have myself translated this work, but an excellent rendition of it by Mr T. Phillips will be found in vol. xxi of the *Proceedings of the American Philological Society*.   That it was written by a native, probably at the request of Europeans, as a kind of key to the Mexican symbolical and hieroglyphical paintings, is pretty clear. It commences with a description of the Creation, and then proceeds to recount such cataclysmic happenings as those to which we are presently confining our attention. It says (I quote from my own translation) " Tezcatlipoca became the sun-bearer.   And the gods created the giants, who were very great men and of much strength."   Quetzalcoatl then became the sun, and was followed in this office

---

[1] See my *Gods of Mexico*, 1923, chapter on " Cosmogony."

PLATE VI.

Quetzalcoatl as Atlas.

Small Figure of Atlas supporting the World on his
Shoulders, to compare with the above.

(From National Museum, Naples.)

by Tlaloc, who held it for 364 years, during which time
" Quetzalcoatl rained fire on the sun, and then created as
the sun his wife Chalchihuitlicue. In the last year in which
Chalchihuitlicue was the sun it rained so heavily that men
were turned into fishes. And when it had ceased to destroy,
the heavens fell upon the earth, and the great rain began.
And the gods ordered four roads to be made to the middle
of the earth for them."

Before I proceed farther I should like to indicate several
points of resemblance between this chronicle and Plato's narrative, which are, to say the least, remarkable as coincidences,
if nothing more. In the first place, the god Quetzalcoatl,
although he had many guises, can be equated with Atlas.
He is again and again, like the Greek god, represented in
architecture in caryatid form, as, for example, in a statuette
found in the Calle de Escalerillas in Mexico City in 1900,
and at Chichen Itza in Yucatan, and many other centres in
Mexico and Central America, and it is noteworthy that in
many of these he is represented as having a beard. These
figures Dr Herbert J. Spinden, a foremost authority on
Mexican and Central American archæology, calls " Atlantean," because of their likeness to the Greek caryatids of
Atlas. Quetzalcoatl, moreover, is one of the four Mexican
world-supporters. He is represented in this form in the
Codex Borgia (sheets 49–52, upper half), and in Codex
Vaticanus B (sheets 19–23), where he is shown upholding
the firmament. That he was an oceanic god, too, is clear
from the Popol Vuh, the sacred book of the Quiches of
Guatemala, where he is spoken of as " heart of the sea," and
as dwelling in the great waters. It is thus clear that he is
the American equivalent of Atlas. Chalchihuitlicue, his
wife, is goddess of water and of the sea. Like Atlas, too,
Quetzalcoatl, as his name implies, was a twin. The roads
he sets in the four corners of the earth remind one of the
division of Atlantis into zones. He is also an earthquake

god. The interpreter of the Codex Telleriano-Remensis says of him : " They celebrated a festival on the sign of four earthquakes to the destroyer with reference to the fate which again waited the world. For they said that it had undergone four destructions, and would again be destroyed."

Now I would submit that these similarities can scarcely be regarded as of the nature of coincidence. They are much too exact for anything of the kind. Moreover, the account in the *Historia de los Mexicanos* has a reference to the Mexican time-cycle or chronology, and is undoubtedly an attempt to date these cataclysmic occurrences. I will not here venture an opinion as to the exactitude of this attempt. But it seems to me to refer to a very explicit folk-memory to which the writer was trying to give expression. That it has a mythical colouring does not, in my opinion, detract from the substantial basis of fact which it seems to enshrine, for, as I have already shown, it is now generally agreed that most mythical writings embody a certain amount of historical fact, verifiable or otherwise. It would, however, be not a little difficult to try to construct out of these conflicting details something approaching an historical outline bearing upon the circumstances of the Antilian-Atlantean overthrow. For the present, I would point to the illustrations of Quetzalcoatl in his Atlantean form, and ask the unbiassed reader if the likeness of this god to the Greek Atlas is not in itself sufficient to dispel any doubts as to their ancient identity.

Let us now examine those Mexican legends which speak of a great flood. These are fairly numerous, and quite within the sphere of our researches. The first of those to which I will draw attention is that taken from the Codex Chimalpopoca, also known as the *Anales de Quahtitlan*.

" And this year was that of Ce-calli, and on the first day *all was lost*. The *mountain* itself was submerged in the water and the water remained tranquil for fifty-two springs. Now towards the end of the year Tezcatlipoca had forewarned the man Nata and his wife Nena, saying : ' Make no more pulque, but straightway hollow out a large cypress and enter it when in the month of Tozoztli the water shall approach the sky.' They entered it, and when Tezcatlipoca had closed the door, he said : ' Thou shalt eat but a single ear of maize, and thy wife but one also.' As soon as they had finished eating they went forth and the water was tranquil ; for the log did not move any more ; and opening it they saw many fish. Then they built a fire, rubbing together pieces of wood, and they roasted fish. Then the Old Gods, looking below, said : ' Divine lord, what means that fire below ? Why do they thus smoke the heavens ? ' Straightway descended Tezcatlipoca and commenced to scold, saying : ' What is this fire doing here ? ' And seizing the fishes, he moulded their hinder-parts and changed their heads, and they were at once transformed into dogs."

A flood-myth which has for its hero one of the giants who were supposed to inhabit the earth in the first age, states that Xelhua, the giant in question, escaped the deluge by ascending the mountain of Tlaloc, and afterwards built the pyramid of Cholula. This he built in order that should a deluge come again he might escape to it. " When it had already reached a great height lightning from heaven fell and destroyed it. Those Indians who were under that chief who had escaped from the deluge made bricks from a mountain in Tlalmanalco, called Cocotle ; and from Tlalmanalco to Cholula ; Indians were placed to pass the bricks and cement from hand to hand ; and thus they built this tower that was called Tulan Cholula, which was so high that it appeared to reach heaven. And being content, since it seemed to them that they had a place to escape from the deluge if it should again happen, and from whence they might ascend into heaven," a precious stone fell from the sky and struck the ground. The pyramid of Cholula still remains.

A flood-myth of the Mixtecs, an ancient civilised people of south-western Mexico, has, for me, a very Atlantean complexion. It is to be found in the *Origin de los Indios* of Fray Gregorio Garcia, chap. 4, book iv. :—

" In the year and in the day of obscurity and darkness, when there were as yet no days nor years, the world was a chaos sunk in darkness, while the earth was covered with water on which slime and scum floated. One day the deer-god and goddess appeared. They had human form, and out of their magic they raised a *great mountain* out of the water and built on it beautiful palaces for their dwelling. These buildings stood in Upper Mixteca, close to the place Apoala (accumulation of water), and the mountain was called ' Place where the heavens stood.' " The gods had two little boys, who appear to have been twins. All were skilled in magic, and enjoyed the profoundest peace. They planted gardens with flowers and trees, and made a grass-grown level place for sacrifice to their ancestors. " The deer-gods had more sons and daughters, but there came a flood in which many of these perished. After the catastrophe was over the god, who is called ' the creator of all things,' formed the heavens and the earth and restored the human race."

CHAPTER IX

THE EVIDENCE FROM AMERICAN TRADITION—*contd.*

LET us glance at the descriptions of the Mexican gods of water, which seem to me to retain reminiscences of a period of cataclysmic deluge. The interpreter of the Codex Vaticanus A says, regarding the god Tlaloc : " On the 21st of December they celebrated the festival of this god, through whose instrumentality they say the earth became again visible after it had been covered with the waters of the deluge." According to Boturini, Tlaloc was the deity who raised the earth out of the waters of the flood and who counselled men by his divine messages written in the lightning and the thunderbolt to live wisely and morally. The Aztecs sacrificed children to him by drowning at the festival of Quaitleloa. He is the god of moisture and water *par excellence*, and possessed both beneficent and terrible aspects, and the learned priests of Mexico undoubtedly regarded him as the personification of the Tlequiauitl, or fire-rain, the disaster which closed one of the epochs of the ancient world. He wears Toltec dress, and this shows him to be the god of the oldest settled people in Mexico, whose history went back to a great antiquity.[1]

Chalchihuitlicue, his wife, is pictured in the Aubin tonalamatl, or calendar, as standing in water down which swirl away a jewel-box and armed man and a woman, the picture of a catastrophic flood taking place in a region of culture and civilisation.[2] Her myth in the Codex Telleriano-

[1] See my *Gods of Mexico*, section " Tlaloc," *passim*.
[2] This is explained in the Interpretative Codices as " loss of property, death in war, emblem of the *atocoa*," *i.e.* an expression meaning " all will be carried away by the water."

Remensis says that " Chalchihuitlicue was the woman who saved herself in the deluge. She is the woman who remained after the deluge." Everything seems to point to her as the goddess of change in human affairs, of speedy ruin, says Professor Seler.

It seems to me that if Quetzalcoatl can be equated with Atlas, Tlaloc and his wife Chalchihuitlicue can almost as readily be compared with Poseidon and Leucippe, the original figures in Plato's narrative. Tlaloc is god of water and the sea. That he is a sea-god whose worship was adapted to the needs of a landward people is plain. His mouth is furnished with immense tusks, and these, I believe, retain a memory of the walrus or some similar sea-form. Indeed his resemblance to the walrus in some of his pictures is not to be questioned. His shirt is known as the " mist " or " cloud-garment," and his sandals symbolise the foam of water. His abode was on a mountain on the road from Texcuco to Huetzotzinca, and here, it was thought, the drowned and dropsical—all those, in fact, who perished through the agency of water—went after death. Tlalocan, his paradise, is, in fact, of the same class as the Greek Elysian Fields or the Celtic Tir-nan-ogue.

The number of deities in the Mexican pantheon connected with fire seem also to point to the early influence of a volcanic area. The gods who are connected with fire are those of entirely Aztec origin, and as these were brought into Mexico by the Aztec people as late as the thirteenth century A.D., they could not have been of local origin, or influenced by local volcanic conditions. Xiuhtecuhtli, the Lord of Fire, was a god of exceedingly ancient origin. Although he undoubtedly appealed to the Mexican mind as the personification of fire, it was more as that element in its primeval and original form, its elemental shape. He is, indeed, the pre-solar fire which existed before the creation of the sun or moon ; and just as the gods of water ruled over moisture wherever

PLATE VII.

I

2

1. Tlaloc, God of Water.
2. Chalchihuitlicue, Goddess of Water and Floods.

Mexican Deities.

it was to be found, so was Xiuhtecutli imagined as holding sway over fire, whether it came from the heavens above or the earth beneath.   Thus we find him spoken of by Sahagun, the most trustworthy of the early Spanish writers on Mexican affairs, as dwelling in the navel of the earth, where the volcanic fires have their origin, and as having his place above, in what appears to be a species of cloud-castle, for the Mexican word for " embattlement " is derived from that for " cloud."   He is also called " He who entereth the blue stone pyramid," which is, of course, the sky.   He corresponds to the hour before sunrise, which makes it clear that his prehistoric precedence to the sun was insisted on in the priestly list of day-hours.   The texts dwell upon his antiquity, for he is indeed the " Old God," the god who existed before the foundations of the world, father and mother of the gods, the central volcanic, world-shaping, cataclysmic fire.

But these lesser myths pale into insignificance, regarded as evidence of Atlantean influence, when compared with those which deal with the extraordinary civilisation of the Toltecs and its founder Quetzalcoatl, one of whose aspects we have already briefly examined.   This myth, of primary importance to the study of Atlantean origins, has been so distorted by writers who had but a passing acquaintance with Mexican and Central American aboriginal literature, that it will be well to examine its sources with some care.

Quetzalcoatl, says Torquemada in his *Monarquia Indiana*, was the leader of a body of men who entered Mexico from the north by way of Panuco, dressed in long robes and black linen cut low at the neck, with short sleeves.   They came to Tollan, but finding the country there too thickly peopled, passed on to Cholula.   Quetzalcoatl was a man with ruddy complexion and long beard.   The Toltecs, his followers, were cunning handicraftsmen, builders, sculptors, and agriculturists.

Sahagun says that the arts had their inception with

Quetzalcoatl, whose houses were made of precious stones, silver, white, and red shells, and rich feathers. His folk were nimble and swift in passage from one place to another, and were known as " the swift ones who serrate the teeth." He had wealth and provision in plenty, and in his time maize was so large in the head that a man could not carry more than one stalk in his clasped arms. Cotton grew in all colours and did not require to be dyed. But sorcerers (the gods Tezcatlipoca and Uitzilopochtli) came against Quetzalcoatl, and gave him a draught which caused him to remember his ancient home with an intolerable longing. So he rose, and burned his beautiful mansion, turned all the coco-trees into mezquites, and dispatched the birds of brilliant plumage, so that they flew to another land. Betaking himself to the seashore with his followers, these nearly all perished through the cold of the mountains. When he reached the coast, he commanded that a raft of snakes should be constructed for him. In this he seated himself as in a canoe, put out to sea, and set out for the land of Tlapallan.

Where was this land of Tlapallan ? When Tezcatlipoca handed the magic draught to Quetzalcoatl he conjured him to go to Tlillan-Tlapallan, " where another old man awaits thee. He and you shall speak together, and on thy return thou shalt be as a youth, yea, as a boy." The interpreter of the Codex Vaticanus says : " Of Quetzalcoatl they relate that proceeding on his journey, he arrived at the Red Sea, which they named Tlapallan. . . . Quetzalcoatl was born on the sign One Cane ; and the year of the Spaniards' arrival commenced on the sign One Cane, according to their ancient computation ; whence the occasion arose of their believing that the Spaniards were their gods ; because they say that he had foretold that a bearded nation would arrive in those countries who would subject them."

In Central America a number of myths circled round the name of Quetzalcoatl. Nuñez de la Vega, Bishop of

Chuapas, tells us that he discovered a book among those Quiche manuscripts he had burned which purported to have been written by Votan, which, like Kukulkan and Gucumatz, is one of the Central American names for Quetzalcoatl. In this book Votan declared himself "a snake," a descendant of Imos of the line of Chan, of the race of Chivim. Proceeding to America by divine command, his mission being to lay the foundations of civilisation there, he departed from Valum Chivim (the Land of Chivim), and, passing the dwelling of the Thirteen Snakes, arrived in Valum Votan, whence, with some members of his family, he set out to form a settlement, ascending the Usumacinta River and ultimately founding the city of Palenque. By reason of their peculiar dress the Tzendal Indians called them Tzequitles, or " men with shirts," but consented to amalgamate with them. Ordoñez, who also drew from Votan's book, states that when Votan had established himself at Palenque, he made several visits to his original home. On one of these he came to a tower, which had been intended to reach the heavens, a project which had been brought to naught by the linguistic confusion of those who had conceived it. Finally, he was permitted to reach " the rock of heaven " by a subterranean passage. Returning to Palenque, he found that others of his race had arrived there. He built a temple by the Huehuetan River, known, from its subterranean chambers, as " the House of Darkness," and here he deposited the national records under the charge of certain old men and priestesses. " In the little history written in the Indian language," says Nuñez de la Vega, " all the provinces and cities in which he tarried are mentioned. . . . That he saw the great wall, namely the Tower of Babel, which was built from earth to heaven at the bidding of his grandfather Noah ; and that he tarried in Huehueta, which is a city in Soconusco, and that there he placed a tapir [*tlapiane*, a guardian] and a great treasure in a subterranean house. . . . This treasure consisted of jars, which were closed with covers of the same clay, and of a room in which the picture of the ancient heathens who are in the calendar are engraved in stone, together with jadeite and other superstitious images; and the chieftainess herself and the tlapianes, her guardians, surrendered all these things, *which were publicly burnt in the market-place of Huehueta when we inspected the aforesaid province in 1691.*"

Ixtlilxochitl has, naturally, much to say of the Toltecs, and gives two separate accounts of their early migrations. He describes Tlapallan as a region near the sea. The Toltecs, he says, did not set out to colonise distant lands from any impulse of their own, but were the victims of internecine dissension in the homeland. Thrust forth from their native soil, they reached Tlapallan in the year Itecpatl (A.D. 387). They arrived on the coast of Mexico 104 years after commencing their pilgrimage, stopping on the way at various stations. In another and later account of the Toltec migration, Ixtlilxochitl states that the chiefs of Tlapallan revolted against the royal power, and were banished from that region in A.D. 439. They then journeyed to Tlapallant-zinco, where they halted for three years before setting out on a prolonged pilgrimage which occupied over a century.

Founding the magnificent city of Tollan in A.D. 566, in the mountains north-west of the Mexican Valley, they enriched it with every species of artistic effort. The temple was a gem of architectural art and mural decoration. Its shrines were inlaid with gold, precious stones, and sea-shells, encrusted in bricks of silver. Some were formed of a brilliant red stone ornamented with shells. This scheme recalls the coloured masonry of Atlantis, with its white, red, and black stones.

The history of Tollan is strongly reminiscent of that of Atlantis. So profligate were kings and people, that the gods grew greatly displeased with them, and resolved to punish them. I am convinced that at the place where Plato's narrative breaks off he was about to tell us how Zeus first warned the Atlanteans, and later punished them. First a fierce frost visited the territory of the Toltecs, and this was followed by a summer of torrid heat. Then heavy rainstorms descended and terrible tempests swept through the land. Frogs, locusts, drought in turn plagued the disobedient Toltecs, and they were tormented by giants and demons. Finally the people, broken and ruined, fled to Guatemala and other parts of Central America.

There is now no question of the historical character of the Toltec civilisation of Tollan, Teotihuacan, and Cholula, that strange, pre-Aztec culture of which Quetzalcoatl is spoken of as the founder. The recent excavations of Señor Manuel Gamio and others have made it abundantly clear that this civilisation stretched into Central America, affecting that of Guatemala and Yucatan, to which it was allied. The myths concerning him insist upon the alien origin of Quetzalcoatl. He came, they say, from Tlillan-Tlapallan, that is " the Black and Red Land."

Now I am well aware that most Americanists regard this " Black and Red Land " as meaning " the Land of Writing," that is of picture-writing, because red and black ink is usually employed in the native manuscripts of the Nahua and the Central American Maya, and that they believe it to be the Huaxtec country on the east coast of Mexico, in the vicinity of Vera Cruz. But two salient facts are to be reckoned with in this regard. In the first place, the Huaxtec country, which possesses many ruins which hitherto have not received the attention they deserve from archæologists, has yielded, so far as I am aware, very few manuscripts or inscriptions of any sort, so that it can scarcely be identified as " the Land of Writing." Again, it is not reached by sea from Tollan. It seems to me that here, buried under the detritus of myth, we have a nucleus of historic fact, relating to a real personage, a culture-hero who came from a region situated " in the East," that is the Western Atlantic—in a word, from that Antilia of which the Antilles are the sole remaining vestiges.

That Quetzalcoatl was also regarded by the native Mexicans as the Trade Wind I am well aware. Indeed I was among the first to indicate his precise connection with the Trade Wind. But he represents that aerial current in a secondary and legendary sense only, just as the Scottish hero, William Wallace, is connected with one of the Eildon Hills, or as any other historical character comes in the course of generations to be associated with natural phenomena. The fact of Toltec culture remains. It is indissolubly associated with Quetzalcoatl, it had a speedy rise and a comparatively sudden downfall. Quetzalcoatl, the civiliser, the architect, the craftsman in jewellery and dyestuffs, the agriculturist, left behind him a very definite memory. A long line of priest-kings, and a longer line of priests, were called by his name. He introduced a religion totally at variance with the sanguinary faith of Mexico. The later Mexicans and Maya spoke of him as a priest quite as much as a god, and the Zapotecs and Cholulans reverenced priests said to be descended from him, and from these descent was assured in the most positive and careful manner.

I shall have much to say of Quetzalcoatl and his religion in the succeeding chapters, when I come to collate the less obvious evidences of an Atlantean past. At present I am dealing with the broader aspects of the question. We have seen that he is connected with myths of cataclysm and disaster, not as a destroyer, but as a reshaper of civilisation. His appearance, and that of his followers, are minutely described. They wore black, sleeveless tunics, and thus they are represented in the Mexican paintings. The manner in which they met and mingled with the natives in Central America is explicitly detailed. Voyages to and from the

Toltec homeland are recounted. On one occasion Quetzalcoatl beholds the building of a tower like that of Babel and
its fall. The Mexican myth makes it plain that he must
periodically return to Tlapallan for his magic draught, and
there speak with " another old man " if he would return
refreshed and reinvigorated. Does this refer entirely in
terms of allegory to the Trade Wind departing in early
summer to seek for the rains with which it will return in
the following spring ? In a mythical sense it certainly
does. But Sir James Fraser and others have shown us that
upon the personal strength of kings and rulers was thought
to depend the success of the community in agricultural
matters, and that agricultural failure formerly implied the
sacrifice of the aged and impotent monarch to the offended
gods, or his rejuvenation by a magical elixir. It would
seem to me, then, that the ancient ritual practice of
rejuvenation in the event of agricultural failure may have
obtained in Atlantis-Antilia, and that the myth of Quetzalcoatl, the Antilian culture-hero of Mexico and Central
America, arose in some such circumstances. We are told
that he searched for and discovered maize. I picture him
and his followers as partially isolated in the wild and barbarous land in which they have arrived as colonists, driven
thence by the dire necessities of disintegrating Antilia.
Twenty years pass, as the myth says, and he grows old.
The food-supply fails, a rainless season ruins the harvest.
Quetzalcoatl's personal powers as a king-magician are
impugned. Colonial opinion insists upon his return to
Tlapallan or Antilia, to receive from its king the magical
draught which will rejuvenate him, as it has been thought to
rejuvenate the kings of Egypt, and render him once more
fitted to preside over an agricultural community. He
sails back to Antilia. The idea arises, fostered, no doubt,
by colonial fear of its own inadequacy, that it is necessary
for him to return annually to the homeland, as only there

can he receive the benefit of the true and official magic. He does so, but on one occasion he does not return. And from the circumstances of his going and coming the beautiful allegory of the arrival and departure of the Trade Wind coming and going to Tlapallan is woven.

I do not think the justice of this reasoning will be questioned by those who have any acquaintance with the science of comparative religion. If a careful study of the circumstances of the myth be made it will be found to fit in with the whole hypothesis of king-sacrifice and monarchical rejuvenation by magical elixirs—the true genesis, indeed, of the search for the elixir of life. In one legend Quetzalcoatl is spoken of as immolating himself on a funeral pyre on the seashore, and we are told that his heart became the planet Venus. This merely substantiates the point of view stated above, which I will elaborate farther on.

I shall merely mention here the fact that Toltec and Maya civilisation did not originate on American soil, and shall retain the proofs of this for the chapter which deals with the evidence from American archæology. This civilisation first appears in America, like the Crô-Magnon in Europe, as full-blown, with a ready-made art, a high condition of ecclesiastical and social polity, and an advanced system of hieroglyphic writing. These have no roots in the soil. The language of the Maya of Central America has been associated by Professor Beuchat and others with the districts of the Antilles, and the vestiges of their early culture are to be found in these islands.

The Aztecs of Mexico were but late-comers to that country, arriving there about the eighth century of our era. Nor did they settle in the Plateau of Mexico till the thirteenth century. But they possessed many traditions of dwelling " on a great water " in a region they called Aztlan, or " the Land of Flamingoes." A legend of their migrations from that region, preserved in manuscript, tells us that

" this is the beginning of the record of the coming of the Mexicans from the place called Aztlan. It is by means of the water that they came this way, being four tribes, and in coming they rowed in boats." The accompanying picture shows the native Mexican idea of this homeland of Aztlan. It will be seen that it bears a certain resemblance to the description of Atlantis. When the Mexicans built Mexico, they did so on the model and plan of Aztlan, and that Mexico boasted a great pyramid-hill, rose from the centre of a lake, and was divided into zones of land and water, I shall show later in the chapter which deals with Atlantean topography.

Summarising the evidence from American tradition, we find :—

1. That it points to a later date for the Antilian than the Atlantean final cataclysm.

2. That many myths of flood and upheaval existed among the American races.

3. A number of these give prominence to a great hill resembling that on which the Atlantean temple of Poseidon was built.

4. There are reminiscences of the shaping of land and water into zones.

5. Stones are spoken of as being converted by gods or heroes into people, as in the Greek myth of Deucalion and Pyrrha, and by the same process.

6. American gods are described as holding the world on their heads, like Atlas, to whom the Mexican god Quetzal-coatl bears a strong resemblance.

7. Mexican myth speaks of a sequence of catastrophes to which dates are affixed. These were actually discussed at a meeting of native astrologers held within traditional memory.

8. The characteristics of the Mexican gods of fire and water exhibit marked signs of cataclysmic antecedents, and seem to show the early influence of a volcanic area.

9. The legends of Quetzalcoatl and the Toltecs are eloquent of the arrival in Mexico and Central America of a civilised people coming from an insular area in the east. The relics of their civilisation, their sacred books and treasures, were actually given up by their hereditary guardians to Bishop Nuñez de la Vega in 1691, and destroyed by him.

10. The history of Tollan is strongly reminiscent of that of Atlantis as told by Plato.

11. Tlapallan, the homeland of Quetzalcoatl and the Toltecs, was probably Antilia, the sister sub-continent or western fragment of Atlantis.

12. Probably the legend of Quetzalcoatl conserves the memory of an Antilian noble who, foreseeing the overthrow of his country by cataclysm, led one of several colonial expeditions to Mexico and Central America. The notion (prevalent in Egypt) that an aged king was unable to assist the growth of the crops magically was evidently an Antilian belief, and forced Quetzalcoatl to return to Antilia to receive rejuvenation by the medium of a magical elixir of life.

13. Toltec and Maya civilisation did not originate on American soil, but appeared there full blown. The language of the Maya has been classed as Antillean.

14. The Aztecs of Mexico possessed many traditions of dwelling " on a great water," in a region they called Aztlan. The native pictures of this resemble the Atlantean plan as seen in Carthage and elsewhere, and this model was carried out in the design of the native city of Mexico.

CHAPTER X

THE POPOL VUH AS AN ATLANTEAN RECORD

WHEN, at the instance of the late Mr Alfred Nutt, I took up the special study of the Popol Vuh some seventeen years ago, I was extremely doubtful of the American provenance of this extraordinary collection of Central American history and myth. It seemed to me that traditions of undoubted American origin had been overlaid or mingled with scriptural accounts and beliefs. I found that this view was adopted by other students who had made an intensive examination of the text, and thus felt myself justified in adhering to the opinion I had formed of its non-American character. There remained, however, a residuum of folk-lore and myth which I could not regard as being other than American, and by degrees I came to see that those tales and events which I had thought borrowed from Biblical or other sources, when collated with the narratives from which I believed them to be drawn, showed little or no actual similarity to them. That they were not European—that is, that they were not the result of contact with missionaries or other European agents of Western thought—I was convinced. Greatly puzzled, I asked myself, " Where did these legends, which seem neither of European nor American origin, have their place of origin ? "

The Popul Vuh was composed in the form in which we now possess it by a native of Guatemala in the seventeenth century, and translated from the Quiche language (a dialect of Maya) into Spanish by Francisco Ximenes, a father of the Church. The original text and translation were, however, lost between the beginning of the nineteenth century and the year 1854, when they were rediscovered by Dr C. Scherzer, an Austrian, in the library of the University of San Carlos in the city of Guatemala. The name Popol Vuh means " the Collection of Written Leaves," and this alone seems to prove that the work must have contained traditional matter reduced to writing at a very early period. Its contents deal with the mythology and history of the Quiche people of Central America, from the time of their origin to the period of the conquest of Central America by the Spaniards.

Space will not permit me to outline the entire contents of the work, and I must confine myself to those passages which seem to me to justify the thesis that it preserves for us a large measure of Atlantean-Antillean tradition—more especially Antillean—as America undoubtedly owed much more to the Western and more lately existing portion of old Atlantis than to the Eastern.

The narrative commences with an account of the creation of the world. First of all existed the Former, the Mother and Father of all living beings, the Cause of Existence, the Maker of everything worthy. At first there was nothing. No earth existed, only the silent sea, and the spaces of the heavens, only the Old Ones, the Serpents covered with Green Feathers and Blue Feathers—that is, the gods of sky and sea. These took counsel with Hurakan, the Heart of Heaven, the wind-god, the hurricane, and made the solid land, filling it with trees, plants, and animals. Then they made mannikins carved out of wood. But they were irreverent and angered the gods, who resolved to bring about their downfall. Then Hurakan caused the waters to be swollen, and a mighty flood came upon the mannikins accompanied by a thick, resinous rain. Great birds appeared and tore out their eyes and bit off their heads, their very domestic animals and household utensils jeered at them and made game of them. The unhappy mannikins ran hither and thither in their despair. They mounted upon the roofs of their houses, but these crumbled beneath their feet. They tried to climb to the tops of the trees, but the trees hurled them down. Even the caves closed before them. So were they almost utterly destroyed, and the remnant of them became monkeys, dwelling in the woods.

Now, I ask, is it possible for this legend to have arisen out of any other circumstances than those of cataclysm or volcanic catastrophe? Flood, the appearance of a tidal wave, the falling of fiery rain (a common phenomenon during a volcanic eruption), the crashing of houses, the falling of trees, the collapse of caverns, the last plight of the unhappy survivors reduced to the wild life of the forest? If this document is not a memory of terrestrial convulsion, I am at a loss to account for it otherwise.

Then let us glance briefly at the character of the supernatural beings who were the gods of the race so destroyed. At first there dwelt only in the upper sky, the Mother and the Father, who, we are informed later, were named Xpiyacoc and Xmucane, and who may be described as Father Earth and Mother Sky, male and female progenitors, such as we know the Atlanteans adored. The Gucumatz, the serpents covered with green and blue feathers, we are told, dwelt in the deep, and seem to have been the gods of subterranean disturbance. They are the same as Quetzalcoatl, their names have precisely the same meaning, and we know already that he was a god or hero who came from Tlapallan, a country situated in the Atlantic Ocean, to civilise Mexico. Another god, Hurakan, is, as his name shows, a god of tempest. It is from his name, indeed, that the word " hurricane " has come into use.

But, these gods notwithstanding, we find that the Quiche people who preserved the Popol Vuh had other deities of earthquake and terrestrial disturbance.

Ere the earth was quite recovered from the dreadful catastrophe which had descended upon it, there lived a proud and mischievous Titan named Vukub-Cakix (Seven Times-the-Colour-of-Fire) the Quiche name for the Great Macaw Bird. He shone with the brilliance of the sun and moon, and his teeth were of emerald. His boasting angered the gods, and they resolved to destroy him. His two sons Zipacna (Earth-heaper) and Cabrakan (Earthquake) cast the mountains about like toys and retarded the work of terrestrial reformation on which the gods had embarked. Two heroes were sent to earth to account for these disturbers. These were called Hun-Apu (Hunter with Blowpipe), and Xbalanque (Little Tiger). The former wounded Vukub-Cakix with a dart from his weapon, and the Father and Mother gods, masquerading as physicians, removed his teeth and eyes, so that he succumbed. Next they turned their attention to his sons, the maker of volcanoes and the destroyer of mountains, whom they also succeeded in accounting for.

But still other disturbing agencies remained—the subterranean gods of evil propensity, who dwelt in a gloomy realm named Xibalba, or Hades. The lords of this place, Hun-Came and Vukub-Came, challenged Hun-Apu and Xbalanque to a game of ball, and the brothers accepting this, journeyed to the infernal regions to meet them in tournament. Their adventures there, and those of their nephews and sons, show clearly that they had to undergo the tests of a secret society, and to this point I will return later, in the chapter on Egypt.

The third book of the Popol Vuh discovers the gods once more deliberating on the creation of man. Four men are created out of a paste of yellow and white maize, and four women are given them while they sleep. These were the ancestors of the Quiche people. At this time there was no sun, and comparative darkness lay upon the face of the earth.

The Quiche journeyed to a place called Tulan-Zuiva, or "The Seven Caves," where gods were given to them. This was a place of great misfortune to the Quiche, for here the race suffered alienation in its different branches through their speech being confounded, as at Babel. Separated from the main body, one band followed the god Tohil over lofty mountains, and on one occasion had to make a long detour across the bed of the ocean, the waters of which were miraculously divided to permit of their passage. At length they arrived at a mountain called Hacavitz, where it was foretold that they should see the sun. At last the luminary appeared. Shortly afterwards the first men, overcome by age, expired, or, rather, were translated to a higher sphere.

Now all this has little or no correspondence with the circumstances of other American myths. Indeed the entire atmosphere of the Popol Vuh seems to be American only in the secondary sense, in the sense that it has absorbed an American atmosphere, or been overlaid by American colouring.

As I have shown, the beginnings of the Popol Vuh are set in circumstances of catastrophe. The pantheon of gods it describes practically all have their origin in tempest or earthquake, some of them are even earthquake-makers, and the enemies of man; others are the leaders of a secret society, the ritual of which bears a strong resemblance to that of the Egyptian Book of the Dead. The remainder of the Quiche history is eloquent of migration in a world of darkness "where there was no sun," and of passage over a great sea, the waters of which were miraculously divided—probably a reference to the upheaval, temporary or otherwise, of a volcanic ridge raised above the sea, by which they passed from Antilia to America—for from Antilia I believe the ancestors of the Quiches and Maya to have come, as I shall proceed to show in the following chapter.

CHAPTER XI

THE EVIDENCE FROM CENTRAL AMERICAN ARCHÆOLOGY

IT is almost certainly from the strange culture of the Maya of Central America that we obtain a picture of what civilisation in ancient Antilia, the last sub-continental fragment of great Atlantis, was like. It is generally admitted that the culture of Central America bears a close general resemblance to that of Egypt. The school of Professor Elliot Smith accounts for the resemblance by postulating the slow spread of the Egyptian civilisation of the Pyramid epoch across the vast expanse of the Pacific. I will not endeavour within the comparatively brief limits of space at my disposal to combat this ingenious hypothesis in detail, but will only venture to remark that it appears to me highly improbable that the associated factors of culture which this school recognises as the evidences of the presence of " the Children of the Sun," the civilising race which originated in Egypt, could have held together through so many centuries as to have manifested themselves in times and places so widely apart as they are considered to have done. For example, the data regarding terrace-irrigation, pearl-fishing, metal-working, and the rest which we are told to regard as constant factors in the civilisation of the Children of the Sun, break down when applied to Mexico, where practically none of these obtained. It is clear, too, that the best authenticated myths of the civilised peoples of Central America speak of their culture as having arrived from the East and not from the West.

The civilised peoples of Central America occupied the tract of the North American continent from the Tropic of Cancer to Nicaragua. The beginnings of culture in this tract are to be found about the head-waters of the Usumacinta River and the Rio Grande in Guatemala, and that part of Chiapas which slopes down from the steep Cordilleras. This, by far the oldest district of Central American advancement, was probably colonised about a century before the commencement of the Christian era. The ruined sites of scores of cities, chief among which are the famous centres of Palenque, Piedras Negras, and Ocosingo, stretch eastward into Belize and southward to Honduras. The temples and palaces of this region, although the oldest examples of Maya architecture, bear the stamp of a dignity and a consciousness of metropolitan power not to be mistaken, so free and opulent is their ornamentation, so obvious the desire of their builders to surpass.

But some time in the sixth century of our era disaster overtook these communities. What the nature of it was we can only guess, and in this instance guessing will not avail us much. Whether because of pestilence or for religious reasons—invasion seems unlikely, to judge from the almost perfect condition of the buildings, which have not been subjected to the action of fire—the Maya of Guatemala and Chiapas journeyed southward into the inhospitable and almost waterless peninsula of Yucatan, where they once more commenced the task of raising settlements similar to those they had abandoned. Here we will not follow them for the present, as it is much more essential to our thesis to study them in their first American environment. Suffice it to say, that in Yucatan their art became less free and more conventional, and the political relations between the several city-states probably much more tumultuous than formerly.

Now the fact which most closely concerns us here is that when the Maya civilisation first manifests itself upon Central

American soil, it does so not in any simple or elementary manner, but as a full-blown culture, with a well-defined art, architecture, religion, and system of hieroglyphic writing. We find not a single trace of its evolution or development upon American ground. Thus early relics like the Tuxtla statuette and the Leiden Plate, which date respectively a century before and after the opening of the Christian era, display the same characteristics and the same script as objects which are known to belong to the century before the coming of the Spaniards—and nothing earlier has been discovered on Maya soil.

If we confine ourselves—as we must in view of considerations of space—to the discovery of Atlantean or Antillean resemblances in Maya civilisation, we shall find them sufficiently numerous. In the first place, Maya architecture, although it certainly has links and affinities with that of Egypt, preserves a striking character of its own which is eloquent of an art long segregated in an oceanic environment.

Maya architecture bears all the signs of a system of building evolved out of the most simple designs, but brought to a high state of complexity by centuries of slow evolution rather than by the introduction of novel ideas. It is clear that it owed nothing to any other and alien system, as, for example, Greek architecture did to that of Egypt and Babylonia. In the view of the writer it was developed from the idea of the oblong bamboo house. Many of the temples still exhibit signs of evolution from such a structure. Their walls are sculptured in the semblance of bamboo rods, just as the earliest Egyptian temples were carved in the likeness of wooden logs. This box-like structure was unrelieved by windows, and air and light entered it by the doorways only. If a second story was desired a similar " box " was built on the top of the original structure.

This applies only to such buildings as temples and palaces. The dwellings of the people were merely huts constructed of leaves and adobe—a certain sign that at one time the populace had been habituated to an environment in which earthquakes or volcanic disturbances had been frequent.

But one circumstance points very clearly to the fact that the Maya had been used to build their larger structures on plains surrounded by mountains—such a site, in short, as Plato describes as that of Atlantis. Practically all the principal sites in Guatemala and Chiapas are so situated. Palenque, for example, is built in the form of an amphitheatre, and nestles on the slopes of the Cordilleras. Standing on the central pyramid, the eye is met by a ring of palaces and temples raised upon artificial terraces. Why, it may be asked, were its structures so elevated ? It seems to me that this indicates a former architectural tradition which had in view occasional floodings. The Persian palaces of Persepolis, for example, are so raised because of seasonal floods. But there was no such risk in the situation in which Palenque was built. Again, it may be that the elevation was dictated by the tradition that similar buildings in an ancestral home had stood upon a sacred hill, such as is commonly alluded to in American legend, and which, we know, was the case in Atlantis.

Again, the Maya and Mexicans both believed that in building on the surface of the earth they were not constructing on any stable surface, but on the back of a great sea-monster, a cayman, alligator, or, as the *Book of the Kakchiquels* has it, " a whale with four feet," a leviathan which occasionally writhed and cast them into the ocean. Prudence thus dictated that their buildings should not rest entirely on the back of this monster, but should be founded on something more stable. Thus were they haunted by the notion or tradition of cataclysm. Probably their method of building construction was dictated by all of these beliefs.

And what do we find on the walls of these extraordinary structures ? With the question of Maya symbol and hieroglyphic writing we enter upon the consideration of a subject so vitally bound up with the thesis of the Atlantean-Antillean colonisation of Central America as to call for our most anxious inquiry. In the first place, we must absolutely cast behind us the wild and unscientific theories and alleged " discoveries " of Le Plongeon and his school. Regarding the true character of the hieroglyphic system of the Maya of Central America there is now no dubiety, but so that once and for all the absurd speculations to which it has given rise may be laid to rest, I am compelled at some length to outline the results by which serious students of the system have arrived at their present conclusions, and will later attempt to deduce from these the evidences of the Atlantean origin of this script, not by dint of mere asseveration but by aid of more logical means.

The strange system of writing anciently in use among the civilised peoples of Central America has not succeeded in attracting the same degree of popular interest in this country as the scripts of Egypt and Assyria, yet its claims upon the imagination are, perhaps, no less strong than those of hiero-glyphic or cuneiform. Our grandfathers waxed enthusiastic over the amateur explorations of Stephens among the crumbling cities of Yucatan and Chiapas, but although the governments of the United States, France, and Germany have freely encouraged research in American archæology, and its cultivation flourishes abroad, it still languishes among us. It is regrettable that British readers should remain unfamiliar with results so surprising and so creditable to human perseverance as those which have recently attended the discovery of the general purport of the Maya glyphic system. For the pursuit of this quest a far greater degree of effort and a higher ingenuity have been needful than for the unriddling of the ancient writings of Egypt or Sumeria. That the quaint symbols of the ancient Maya have so far met with only partial interpretation is, perhaps, one of the reasons why they fail to excite more general interest. But surely the privilege of watching the gradual revelation of these obscure glyphs is one on which our generation should place a higher value than it appears to think the opportunity merits.

The localities of Central America in which monuments bearing the involved nd fantastic characters of this script are most generally found are still inhabited by people of that Maya stock who once employed it. They embrace the remote peninsula of Yucatan, the uplands of Guatemala, and the districts of Tabasco, Chiapas, and even a portion of Honduras. But by far the greater number of inscriptions have been met with in the southern part of these provinces where the older branch of the Maya civilisation originally flourished. It is at such sites as Copan in Honduras, Quirigua and Tikal in Guatemala, and Piedras Negras and Palenque in Chiapas that important texts are found, rather than in Yucatan proper, although inscriptions of moment are not wanting at Uxmal, Chichen, Itza, and elsewhere in the northern spheres of Maya influence.

Just as the ancient writings of the Middle East are found inscribed on a variety of objects, so the Maya script is not only painted on paper or skin or carved on stone, but incised on wood, bone, shell, metal, and modelled on pottery. The mediums of stone and paper were the most popular among the Maya scribes, and all others may be dismissed from our consideration. The carven inscriptions usually occur upon the sides of monoliths, known as stele-shafts, which in shape, if not in their wealth of ornamental detail, recall the menhirs of Brittany. On altars, staircases, and frequently on the walls of temples and palaces, they are to be found nestling among the florid reliefs typical of Maya architecture. But the writing proper is confined to the few manuscripts or codices rescued from the pious attentions of the early Spanish ecclesiastical authorities and now in

European museums or libraries—the Dresden, Paris, and Madrid manuscripts.

The shape of the glyphs or symbols as they occur in the carven examples differs somewhat from that employed in the written characters, the former being adapted to the restrictions of the sculptor's chisel, the latter to the less limited technique of the scribe's brush. But the basic likeness between the forms is plainly apparent. At first sight the glyphs appear as a number of small squares rounded at the corners, representing human faces and other objects, highly conventionalised by generations of artistic usage. They have been described as " calculiform," or pebble-shaped, from the fact that the contour which encloses each of them resembles that of a small pebble. In this they are contained much as the hieroglyphs which make up the name of an Egyptian king are enclosed in a " cartouche " or oval contour. They are arranged in parallel columns, which are to be read two columns at a time, beginning with the uppermost glyph in the left-hand division. The reader must then work his way from left to right and top to bottom, ending with the lowest glyph in the second column. But should the glyphs be disposed in a horizontal band, the order of reading is from left to right in pairs.

The history of the prolonged endeavour to discover the hidden meaning of these characters so obstinately dumb, although one of continuous and patient effort, is not devoid of romantic quality and has, indeed, furnished more than one novelist with material for a tale of absorbing interest. In 1565 Landa, Bishop of Chiapas, who destroyed a large number of manuscripts on the plea that they were " the devil's picture-books," seems to have been smitten with a late compunction for his short-sighted policy, and addressed himself to the task of collecting all available information regarding the Maya writing from the native scribes who still practised it. He brought together a number of characters representing twenty-seven sounds, and the essay in which he preserved these was published by the enthusiastic but visionary Abbé Brasseur de Bourbourg at Paris in 1864, when French interest in Mexico was at its height. Landa's " alphabet " was at once hailed by Americanists as the key which would unlock the secrets of the Maya writing, the " Rosetta Stone " of America. But it was soon found that all attempts to decipher the glyphs by its agency were only partially successful, and it has been conjectured that the Indian scribes, who looked upon the bishop as the ruthless destroyer of their ancient records, purposely misled him. At the same time most of the names and symbols for the days and months as furnished by him are known to be correct, as is found by a comparison of them with the glyphs appearing in certain native books known as the Books of Chilan Balam, where they are shown with their phonetic equivalents in European letters.

In 1876 the French-Americanist, Leon de Rosny, published an alphabet of twenty-nine letters with numerous variants. But neither this, nor the attempt of another French savant, De Charency, can be taken seriously. Ten years later Dr Augustus le Plongeon published " An Ancient Mayan Hieratic Alphabet according to Mural Inscriptions." This, the most fantastic of the attempts to probe the mystery of the Maya symbols, compared and even identified them with those of Egypt, and did incalculable mischief in spreading the delusion that they had at last been deciphered, and were to be regarded as the prototypes of the Egyptian hieroglyphs. Most of Le Plongeon's " characters " are either symbolic details or bizarre inventions, unrepresented among the Maya glyphs.

The first student to throw any light on the manner in which the quest should be conducted, if final success were to be hoped for, was Professor Ernst Förstemann, of Dresden, who, about 1880, showed that the native records and inscriptions were chiefly concerned with the fixation of calendric festivals and the dating of monuments. He discovered and elucidated the elaborate and ingenious system of numeration in use among the peoples of ancient Central America, and showed how it was utilised to record astronomical and chronological facts. In short, his pioneer work made possible all subsequent progress in deciphering the texts. Curiously enough, an American student of the subject, Mr J. T. Goodman of Alameda, California, working independently, arrived at conclusions similar to those reached by Förstemann. Since that time the work has been carried on by the late Professor D. G. Brinton of the University of Pennsylvania, Professor Eduard Seler of Berlin, Mr S. G. Morley, and, notably, by Mr C. P. Bowditch of Boston, who, addressing himself to the task of placing the whole study on a systematic basis, has made it possible to survey the entire field of past endeavour, and has rendered further progress practicable.

Judging from the complete state of development at which the system had arrived at the date of the discovery of Central America by the Spaniards, there is every reason to refer its origin to a past of considerable antiquity. As Dr F. W. Hodges of the Bureau of American Ethnology remarked : " The earliest inscriptions now extant probably date from about the beginning of the Christian era, but such is the complexity of the glyphs and subject-matter, even at this early period, that in order to estimate the age of the system it is necessary to postulate a far greater antiquity for its origin. Indeed, all that can be safely accepted in this direction is that many centuries must have elapsed before the Maya hieroglyphic writing could have been developed to the highly complex stage where we first encounter it."

A brief examination of any Maya text reveals the presence of certain elements which occur repeatedly in the glyphs, but in varying combinations. Two or three small but separate signs frequently go to the making of each glyph. So numerous are the combinations and permutations of these, however, that the student might at first sight suppose that a great number of signs were employed in Maya writing. But closer observation will convince him that these elementary symbols are in reality few in number. His difficulty lies in identifying them and gaining experience of the different forms they take. In Egyptian texts the simple phonetic signs are unchanging under all circumstances of composition. Like the letters of our alphabet, they never vary, and may be recognised as unfailingly. But in the Maya texts the normal form of the element may be altered for reasons of space, individual peculiarities of style, or artistic symmetry. It has been ascertained, however, that each glyph holds one essential element, which was seldom altered, and that it is only in the case of accessory or supplementary elements that any great variation was permissible. But it is rare to find two glyphs which have the same meaning and the same elements precisely alike in drawing, contour, and general appearance. It is as if the letters of our alphabet were not standardised in form, but were subject to the caprice of each individual writer or printer. Such dissimilarities are often due to difference in the materials in which the glyphs are delineated, as well as to careless drawing and actual mistakes, for errors, and those not a few, have been encountered both in examples of the numeral system and the writing proper. These conditions render progress slow and results uncertain.

Sometimes the pebble-shaped outline or " cartouche " of a glyph is altered to a " head-shape " ; that is, the customary form is changed to the contour of a human head. The symbols usually confined to the outline are transferred to this " head-shape " ; or cunningly adapted to its physiognomy, in a manner which speaks volumes for the artistic ability of the Maya sculptors and scribes. These " head-variants," as they are called, are puzzling enough when the meaning of a glyph in its original form is already known. When it is unknown, they are baffling indeed.

The glyphs as a whole have been divided into two groups ; astronomical, calendric, and numerical signs (that is, glyphs used in counting time), and those having an explanatory function of some sort. The great majority of the symbols already deciphered belong to the first group. The second, which is much the smaller, in all probability relates the facts of Maya history.

As regards the question whether the system is phonetic or pictorial in character, much difference of opinion exists. Three principal theories have been advanced to account for the nature of the Maya writing. Some authorities believe the glyphs to be phonetic, each representing a fixed sound, and entirely dissociated from the presentation of any thought or idea. Others regard them as ideographic, each repre-senting in itself some complete idea or conception ; while a third school supposes them to partake of the nature of both types. It is obvious that the first theory cannot be accepted in its entirety. The glyphs unquestionably show traces of phoneticism, but all attempts to reduce them to a phonetic system or alphabet have signally failed.

The theory that they are ideographic has a larger follow-ing. But Brinton pointed out that a native writer was able to give Landa a written character for an unfamiliar sound (as, for example, that of a Spanish letter), and that the characters the Maya scribe employed for this purpose were certainly used in the native writings. These facts led Brinton to think that some sort of phonetic writing was not unknown to the Maya ; and, indeed, both the inscriptions and the manuscripts establish the soundness of this con-tention.

As we have seen, the phonetic sounds of certain glyphs

PLATE VIII.

The sign which means "sun."

The symbol for "moon."

The sign for " night " and "sky." The dots represent stars.

The sign for "beginning."

"The end."

"Tying together," "union."

"Division" is symbolised by a flint knife.

The serpent symbol for "water."

Sacrificial victim.

The sign for the year.

This symbol is read," Day of the new year in the month."

"Wind."

Maya Hieroglyphs.

relating to days and months are known from Landa's work, in which they are accompanied by their Maya names in European letters. In these, at least, he was not mistaken, as we glean from certain native manuscripts which record the names of the glyphs for the days and months in the same manner. One, for example, is known as *yax*, a picture of a tree-stump, which means " region " or " place." Another is *kin*, " sun," and when these symbols are combined they are known as *yaxkin*, " sun-region or warm region "— " the south." Similarly, the character representing the phonetic value *kin* is also found as an element for the words *likin*, " east," and *chikin*, " west," each of which has *kin* as its last syllable. These elements are thus manifestly phonetic. But this notwithstanding, the glyphs alluded to have meanings quite independent of their mere phonetic values. Primarily, their function is to convey the ideas of " sun " and " region," and they were used phonetically in a secondary manner only.

Such glyphs as are phonetic, it must be clear, rank not as letters, but as syllables. This kind of writing Brinton called ikonomatic, or rebus-writing—a script in which the characters do not indicate the meaning of the objects which they portray, but only the sounds of their names. Let us suppose, if the reader will pardon the homeliness of the illustration, that we draw pictures of a human eye, a can, a bear, a cobbler's awl, the numeral 4, and a ewe, and translate the rebus " I can bear all for you." In such a system the first picture is intended to recall not the idea " eye " but the sound of the word denoting the object, which is also that for the personal pronoun "I." Again, the picture of a bear does not represent the idea of that animal, but stands for the sound of its name. Such a method is occasionally employed in the Maya writing, especially, thinks Mr Bowditch, in the case of common nouns and abstract ideas. The writing in use among the Aztecs of Mexico was, indeed, entirely of this character, and it is believed that they drew inspiration from Maya sources at an early period.

The crux of the whole question, indeed, is : How far do phonetic elements enter into the composition of Maya glyphs? It seems probable that as the decipherment of Maya writing progresses an ever-increasing number of phonetic elements will be identified, though the idea of a glyph will always be found to overshadow its phonetic value. That is, in the consciousness of those who employed it, the system would, through generations of usage, come to possess a significance chiefly ideographic, and it would not necessitate any such effort of mental translation as a people unused to rebus-writing would have to make to comprehend it readily.

At an early stage in his researches Förstemann discovered the sign for zero or nought (a shell), which was derived from the symbol for " completeness," zero being regarded as the only complete or perfect number, incapable of division or multiplication. He was also able to show that the symbol for the moon (a cursive form of the head of the moon god), represented the Maya " month " of twenty days, the period in which the moon waxes and wanes, and therefore the number twenty. It was readily found that a dot stood for the numeral one, from the analogy of the Mexican manuscripts, in which the days of the month are numbered in their proper sequence by dots, and from the same source it was gleaned that a bar or dash represented five, a bar and a dot, six, two bars, ten, and so forth. But the manner in which the " higher mathematics " and system of dating of the Maya were elucidated is much too involved a process to be described in this place, and some account of the way in which a few of the more useful glyphs were identified will, doubtless, prove of greater interest to the reader.

Förstemann recognised from Landa's work that one of the signs for a certain day of the Maya month is called *akbal*, which means " night," and that the sign had the same significance and phonetic value as a glyph was suggested by the star-like dots which surround it. Now *akbal* is used as a day-sign because it also means " the beginning of the month," the Maya month commencing immediately after midnight. Therefore, when he found the sign *akbal* as an element of a glyph, and observed footsteps painted beneath it, Förstemann translated it as " beginning " or " forward movement." He found, too, that a glyph representing the number seven, which in Maya has the significance of " great " or " ultimate," means " the end." From the frequent contrast of these terms there can be little doubt that their significance is what he assumed it to be.

" Union " is denoted by the sting of a rattlesnake, the coils of that reptile appearing to the Maya as symbolical of " tying together." We have here the idea of representing the whole by the part, which is also to be remarked in the glyph for " dog," which is merely a drawing of the ear of that animal. In contrast to the sign of " union " is that for " division," or " cutting," which is represented by an obsidian knife. A half-closed hand means " to eat," derived from the action by which one raises food to the mouth. Added to the *kin* or " sun " sign it denotes *chikin*, " the west," probably from the circumstance that the Maya took their principal meal at the hour of sunset. *Likin*, " the east," is a combination of the sun-sign *kin* and the symbol for " king " (*ahau*), which is derived from a root meaning " to rise up," " to awake," so that the whole implies " the sun awakes," " the sun rises." *Xaman*, the north, is more directly symbolised by the face of the devouring earth-monster which was supposed to dwell in that region.

The figure denoting the spring equinox was traced because of its obvious representation of a cloud from which three streams of water are falling upon the earth. A square portion at the top represents the sky. The obsidian knife underneath denotes a division or period of time cut off, as it were, from other periods of the year. That the sign means " spring " is verified by its position among the other signs of the seasons.

Water is depicted by the figure of a serpent, which typifies the undulating nature of the element. The symbol known as " the sacrificial victim " is pictorially eloquent of its subject. Its first element is the vulture or death-bird, and the second shows a crouching and beaten captive, ready to be immolated to one of the terrible Maya deities whose horrid rites included human sacrifice.

The symbol signifying " the day of the new year," which occurred in the month Ceh, is composed of elements meaning " sun " or " day," " year," the sign for " division," and that for the month Ceh, the whole thus signifying " the day in which the year is separated in the month Ceh." The symbol for " wind " has also been determined from its accompaniment by a figure known to be a deity of the four cardinal points, whence all American tribes believed the wind to come.

Other glyphs identified relate to various colours, including red, yellow, white, and black, the names of certain deities and those of several planets, Venus and Mercury among them.

It is clear from what has been established that the texts are chiefly concerned with the fixation of religious festivals. But there is a residuum of matter which undoubtedly relates to historical occurrences of outstanding importance, to which the accompanying dates refer. What may these still obscure symbols not conceal ? So much can be said, that what they have to disclose will make terse reading, for the signs in which the precious information is latent are few. But so highly concentrated is the syllabic script of the ingenious Maya scribes, that such of it as remains dark to us may contain more of value than we suspect.

Having outlined the system of writing employed by the Maya, let us now look for any evidences we may be able to find of its Atlantean origin.

In the first place it was certainly not developed on American soil. There is not the slightest trace of its gradual evolution anywhere in Central America. When we are first able to trace it on the walls of the oldest temples in Guatemala and Chiapas we find its form and character very much the same as they were some twelve centuries later at the period of the arrival of the Spaniards.

Again, it was supposed to be the joint invention of Quetzalcoatl, the first Atlantean coloniser of Central America, and the old gods Cipactonal and Oxomoco, who may be equated with the " old, old ones," the " serpents covered with green and blue feathers," the oceanic deities, who dwelt in the depths of the sea, and who are alluded to in the Popol Vuh. Mendieta in his *Historia Ecclesiastica* relates a Mexican myth which tells us that the gods thought it well that the people should have some means of writing by which they might direct themselves, and Oxomoco and Cipactonal, who dwelt in a cave in Cuernavaca, especially considered the matter. Cipactonal thought that her descendant Quetzalcoatl should be consulted, and called him into council, and among them they undertook the arrangement of the calendar and its signs.

Thus it was those gods particularly associated with the Atlantic Ocean and the mysterious, ancient land which once existed there, whom the Mexicans and Maya regarded as the inventors or innovators of the art of writing, developed in Central America.

Some authorities are of the opinion that the name, Tlapallan, the traditional Atlantic home of Quetzalcoatl, should be translated " Land of Writing." As I have shown, it would seem to imply, " land of the black and red stones," still, it may have such a secondary meaning as the above. The inks used by the Maya scribes in their manuscripts were black and red in colour.

If we analyse the elements of the Maya hieroglyphs, we

shall assuredly find in them pictorial reminiscences of the environment whence their inventors came. What, then, does such an intensive examination of these forms disclose ?

One of the most frequently encountered signs is that representing the human ear. In Maya " ear " is *xicin*, which also means " shell." Although the resemblance is obvious, I do not think that it would have been likely to occur to other than a maritime people. " Shells had a peculiar sacredness in Maya symbolism," says Brinton, and oyster-shells occur again and again in the manuscripts, often in conjunction with fish, the whole meaning " the harvest of the sea." Sometimes they are associated with the cormorant, a maritime bird. The conch-shell is also frequently depicted.

The sign known as Ben-ik appeals to me as having a cataclysmic significance. Brinton alludes to it as " a worm-like figure," and Seler describes it as a symbol of " mother-earth." " It sometimes is drawn," says the first writer, " to have a fish-like appearance, and may symbolise the waters, the more so as it has occasionally as a superfix the ' cloud-balls.' " I take it to be a highly-conventionalised drawing of the earth-dragon which lies in the waters, and whose body is the earth, with buildings or cities on its back. Another version of it obviously represents a tower surrounded by the sea, a symbol for a city or fortress encompassed by a raging and agitated ocean. In Maya cosmology the earth was known as " the turreted castle," and, as we will see later, the entire architectural tradition of the Mediterranean-East Atlantic area in early times was connected with the turret or tower. Some authorities see in it the sign for " rain " or " flood," and it is probable that it embodied the idea of deluge.

We come now to a glyph which undoubtedly depicts the idea of deluge from above, accompanied by lightning. This is frequently associated with symbols representing dates or a time-count, and the whole seems to have reference to some such catastrophe as is alluded to in the Popol Vuh.

PLATE IX.

1

2

3

4

5

Maya Symbols.   (Taken from D. G. Brinton's *Maya Hieroglyphics*.)

1. The Heavenly Shield.   3. The Sign Ben-ik.
2. The Sign for " Deluge."   4. The Sign for the East.
            5. Humanity re-arising out of Deluge.

The design taken from the Paris Codex and reproduced in the accompanying plate, has, I think, an even deeper significance for us : I believe it to be an attempt to convey the idea of humanity arising out of a sunken land lost in a deluge of waters. The symbols at the base and on either side undoubtedly stand for Atlantis, as has already been pointed out by Mr M. A. Blackwell in his work on " The Swastika and Atlantis," published in *The Word*, and that the curving lines on which they appear represent engulfing waters is abundantly plain. The headless figure which rises out of the waves seems to represent mankind, unconquered and unconquerable, branching out east and west in new and glorious growth. This design is usually associated with Quetzalcoatl, the god of Tlapallan, the Land in the Ocean.

Equally interesting for us is the picture of the so-called heavenly shield. This appears to me to represent a city on the Atlantean plan, surrounded by zones of land and water, and having four roads leading to a central citadel, set between the powers of light and darkness. That the rather shapeless-looking masses between which it is situated are intended for mummy-bundles (the method in which the Maya disposed of their dead, mummified and bound up) no student of Central American antiquities will deny, and the fact that they are so represented shows them to be supernatural beings, gods, of the nature of " the majesty enveloped," as the mummy-bundle which contained the first four men alluded to in the Popul Vuh is called. Above are the signs of storm and deluge. Here, I venture to say, is a very real summary of the destruction of Atlantis, a veritable symbol of the final catastrophe.

The symbol for " east " in the Maya hieroglyphical system also commends itself to me as distinctively Atlantean. Here we see, as in the preceding symbol, the city or surrounded island, and the way to the sea, with the port gate and flanking towers. That this group should stand for

" east " seems to show that it was a reminiscence of an eastern locality.

It is manifestly impossible in a work of this scope to attempt the elucidation of the entire range of the Maya hieroglyphic system, which, indeed, would entail the reproduction of the manuscripts and carvings in which it appears on an extensive scale, but perhaps what has been said here will indicate to the student that Atlantean lore may be much enriched by a faithful study of these sources. The researches of Mr M. A. Blackwell, alluded to above, are significant and ingenious. Some of the symbols and signs which he reproduces from the works of Brasseur and Le Plongeon are not to be found in those of more authoritative writers on the subject, nor can I identify them on the monuments themselves.

The question now arises : Do we find in Maya art any evidence of an oceanic and Antilian connection ?

Let us examine some of the most frequently encountered motifs of Maya art. What has come to be known as the " plant and fish motif " is of common occurrence in many of the ruined cities, especially at Copan, Palenque, and Chichen Itza. The plant is described by Maudslay and Spinden as a water-plant, and resembles a water-lily, and in many cases a fish is shown, evidently feeding upon the petals. " The whole," says Spinden, " apparently carries the idea of water." It is attached as an ornamental detail to the bodies of animals and to the heads of divinities that are probably associated with water, as in the case of the god known as " the long-nosed god," probably Quetzalcoatl, who is shown in the Dresden manuscripts walking into the water and pulling up a water-plant. Fish and shells are shown in the water, the lower depths of which are coloured green, the shade of the tropical sea.

As I have already shown, what Spinden and others call " Atlantean " figures are quite commonly encountered at

PLATE X.

1   2

3

From Spinden's *Maya Art.*

1. Plant and Fish Symbol.   2. Quetzalcoatl wading in Water.
3. Two-headed Dragon.

Maya Symbolism.

Chichen Itza and elsewhere. These are usually bearded and have a close resemblance to European figures of the same class. There is, indeed, nothing American about these figures.

Costume, as represented in Maya art, was evidently the outcome of centuries of development in an atmosphere of high culture and mercantile advancement. Most of the figures represented are arrayed in robes of rich texture lavishly embroidered with silver and gold, the head-dresses are composed of rare and brilliant plumes, and the personages represented are loaded with jewellery, necklaces, belts, inlaid arm and leg-pieces, and earrings. That all this magnificence was evolved on American soil is simply unthinkable. It bespeaks centuries of patient endeavour in the weaving of textiles and the cutting of gems before such a height of excellence could have been arrived at. The statues and stelæ which meet the eye in the depths of the forests of Guatemala, and which have aroused the astonishment and admiration of all beholders, are not the work of a race newly sprung from barbarism. Indeed, they display all the marks of an ancient and almost decadent civilisation, a culture old and in its decline. Search for its beginnings as we may on American soil we shall not find them there. Those gorgeous temples and extraordinary statues, with all their bewildering detail of ornament and an art which has not its equal in the world for subtlety of expression or involved richness, must have had behind them not centuries but thousands of years of effort before such summits of achievement could possibly have been reached. To look on a Maya stele is to find oneself face to face with the result of countless ages of artistic endeavour and slow effort towards perfection. One has only to compare it with the art of races at the present time in a condition of barbarism to observe the profound gap that exists between them.

CHAPTER XII

THE EVIDENCE FROM CENTRAL AMERICAN ARCHÆOLOGY—*continued*

SEVERAL of the mythological figures portrayed in Maya sculpture and painting are unquestionably connected either with cataclysm or the ocean. That which Professor Maudslay calls the " Two-headed Dragon," as seen at Copan, for example, obviously typifies the earth in the form of a ravenous, devouring monster. We observe that the face on the left is disguised by a mask like the face of a beautiful woman held between the jaws of the leviathan, and this in my opinion is symbolic of the Maya idea that the earth was deceitful, beguiling, and most attractive when about to destroy. The opposite face gives the key to the true nature of this behemoth, cruel, savage, insatiable. " The lower jaw," says Spinden, " is represented as a bleached bone, and sometimes the nose has a cavity that likewise indicates death." On Stela M, at Copan, the monster's face bears the symbols of water and flood.

Sometimes, as at Quirigua and elsewhere, this dragon-form is merged in that of a great turtle. To several peoples, notably the Hindoos and Chinese, the belief was common that the earth rested on the carapace of a turtle. It is noticeable that at Quirigua this figure also occurs as an Atlantean or caryatid motif in low relief, therefore it must have been associated in the mind of the architect with the idea of Atlas, who, it has already been shown, is certainly portrayed on the Maya monuments.

The Maya manuscripts—as apart from the carvings and

sculptures — are only three in number : the Dresden, Paris, and Tro-Cortesianus. These are all obviously copies of much older MSS. They are, for the most part, of the nature of time-counts. At present I wish to examine them for any remnants of Antilian connection they may exhibit. The early writer Aguilar says that he learned from the native books themselves that they recorded no fewer than three cataclysms. The first was called Maya cimil, or " universal death," the second Oc na Kuchil, " the ravens enter the houses," an expression which explains itself, and the third, Hun yecil, or " universal deluge," a term which a Maya-Spanish dictionary explains by alluding to a tradition that the water at the flood was so high " that its surface was within the distance of one stalk of maguey from the sky." Another term for this catastrophe was bulcahal, haycahol or haycahil, or " universal earthquake and flood which destroyed the world."

" Destroyed the world ! " Not partially, but entirely— that is, the old world, the Antilia from which the Maya emigrated to Central America.

In the Codex Tro-Cortesianus we seem to have a picture with a decidedly Atlantean appearance. This picture, I take it, is a memory of the Atlantean story, much as told by Plato. We see a male and a female figure which possibly depicts the ancestral Atlantean gods known as Poseidon and Cleito, and these are surrounded by lines which may represent the zones of land and water mentioned in the myth. In the Tro-Cortesianus and also in the Dresden codices are many representations of Kukulkan or Quetzalcoatl, some of which show him seated in a boat coming from Tlapallan, but in all of which he is shown with the long proboscis of the tapir, which, we may recall, was the title (*Tlapianes*) given to the priests who guarded the remains of the Atlantean treasure and manuscripts found and destroyed by the Spanish priesthood.

But one of the most important mythological figures for us

is that of the serpent or water-goddess, which occurs in all three manuscripts. She is represented as an old woman with brown-stained body and claws in place of feet, and she wears on her head a knotted serpent. From a great inverted vase she pours down a flood of water upon the world. " Evidently we have here," says Förstemann, " a personification of water in its form of destroyer, a goddess of floods and cloud-bursts. . . . In the Dresden Codex, page 74, where something resembling a flood is represented, she wears the cross-bones of the death-god." " She was," says Brinton, " the personification of the thunderstorm. The vase she empties is the descending torrent of rain, the rattles she carries are the thunder-claps, her severe mien is the terror inspired by the din of the elements."

Now the important points here are that a hieroglyph which frequently accompanies her is that which is usually interpreted as the sign for " evil days," " disaster," and that her place is the east. That she is the same as the goddess whom I have already identified as the Atlantean mother-goddess there can be no doubt, as both possess the glyphs for thunder-clouds and water. Here, then, we have the goddess of an eastern oceanic locality, flood-making, thunder-sending, terrific, the dreaded deity of a people who lived in terror of the periodical cataclysms with which she visited them. If anything is clear in the religions of the Maya and Mexican peoples of Central America, it is that they believed themselves to be the creatures of heavenly sport, a remnant to be sacrificed at the pleasure of their divine masters. Tezcatlipoca (Hurakan, the storm-god in his Maya equivalent) is spoken of as " having his sport, his amusement with the people, terrifying them as he pleased," and the other gods seem to have been similarly disposed. " We are all the children of water," says a prayer of the inland Mexicans: " O Tlaloc, god of water, have mercy on us, slay us not ! " What are these things but recollections of an era of recurrent doom during which the behaviour of the elements reduced the race to a state of servile terror ?

We have, then, traced the Poseidon, Cleito, and Atlas of Plato's story, or deities strongly resembling them, in Central America. True, we can only infer that the old gods of Atlantis came to be regarded after the catastrophe as gods of destruction, but from the closing remarks of Plato's account it is safe to draw the inference that the Atlanteans had so offended Zeus that he intended to destroy them. It is not infrequently found that when a people is driven by elemental catastrophes to quit a locality that the deities of that region come to be regarded by them as malignant and destructive in their tendencies. We should note, too, that the Maya god of death and misfortune, Ah-puch, or Kun-hau, is associated with the East. He wears the symbol of the sea-snail, which is an invariable sign of a connection with the ocean in Maya symbolism, the ruff of the vulture, typical of death and disaster, and the symbol of the skull and cross-bones. He is accompanied by the moan-bird, a species of falcon, which, says Seler, typifies the thunder-cloud. This bird is the same as the Maya demon Cosla-huntox, " the thirteen layers of clouds," the terrific fiend of the thunderstorm.

Certain circumstances regarding the Maya sun-god seem to me of significance. Not only is he frequently represented as wearing a beard, but on the monuments, as at Copan, and on the pottery pipes of the Strebel collection, he is shown as having filed teeth. Now the filing or serration of the teeth was practised by the Toltecs, the followers of Quetzalcoatl, the god or culture-hero from the land of Tlapallan in the Atlantic. It is not an American practice, but is to be found in Africa and alsewhere. Therefore it would seem to have reached America and Africa from a common centre.

" But," says the sceptic, " if the Maya had a colonial connection with Atlantis or Antilia, how comes it that they had so entirely lost the art of seamanship ? They were not a maritime people, and that being so, it is highly improbable that they were ever acquainted with the seaman's art, or made long voyages."

A more absurd assumption could scarcely be imagined. That it has frequently been brought forward as a crushing reply to the hypothesis of a Maya connection with Atlantis, only proves a woeful lack of knowledge of Central American conditions on the part of those who advanced it. As a matter of fact the Maya were skilful sailors and made voyages of very considerable extent in ships of fair tonnage. One of them was sighted by Columbus during his third voyage. It was a good-sized vessel with masts and sails, and carried a crew of forty men, who assisted him in his sailing directions by signs. He speaks of houses, or cabins, fore and aft, in which women and children were accommodated, so that the voyages undertaken must have been of considerable extent.

When Cortes invaded Central America from Mexico, he found that a regular maritime commerce was being carried on by the Maya from the Laguna del Terminos. They supplied him with accurate charts of the coast and its inlets, which aided him in his endeavour. That the Mexicans had a very ancient memory of once having lived on the shores of a great sea has already been indicated, and that certain of the gods were worshipped in coastal areas because of their ability to supply an unlimited harvest of fish from the sea is clearly shown by one of their number being called " old fish-god of our flesh."

A certain goddess is shown suckling a fish. The fish is a constantly recurring factor in the ornamental designs on the Maya monuments. Another god, Opochtli, is spoken of as the inventor of the fishermen's net. The great importance of shells, both as an artistic motif and as charms and amulets, clearly indicates a former oceanic connection. Practically every god in the Mexican pantheon and many in that of the Maya is liberally adorned with sea-shells. Quetzalcoatl wore on his breast the " sliced shell of the seasnail," and the shell girdle was worn by most of the goddesses, while shells also hung from their skirts.

We now return to the question, posed at the commencement of this chapter and elsewhere : If the Maya civilisation did not develop on the soil where its remains are found to-day, where are the evidences of its early evolution to be met with ? So far I have given only a partial reply to this problem, merely mentioning in passing that the earlier developments of Maya art and culture as well as Maya linguistic affinities were to be found in the Antilles, the remnants of submerged Antilia.

Columbus, on his discovery of the Antilles, remarked upon the peaceable and civilised character of their inhabitants. The greater islands, Cuba, Haiti, Jamaica, and Porto Rico, were inhabited by people of the Arawak race, the lesser islands by Caribs. The Tainos, or Arawaks of Cuba, had founded a colony in Florida for the purpose of searching for the Fountain of Perpetual Youth. This, we may recall, was what Quetzalcoatl was advised to seek in the land of Tlapallan, that mystical country in the Atlantic, if he would return to Mexico " as a youth." The peoples of the Antilles were hardy sailors, who did not hesitate to attack the flotilla of Ponce de Leon when it appeared on their coasts, and who were quite capable of reaching the mainland in their large canoes with sails. Those of the Bahamas had a regular commerce with Havana. The Caribs who dwelt in the Lesser Antilles penetrated to the very heart of Brazil, and were, though given to cannibalism, like the Mexicans, the carriers of culture to that region, and, I strongly suspect, were the builders of the large ruined cities recently discovered there, regarding the origin of which there is not yet a sufficiency of data to speak with any degree of certainty.

The Caribs possessed two languages, one employed by the male and the other by the female portions of the population. This is, of course, clear evidence that they invaded the Lesser Antilles as pirates or refugees, that they brought no women of their own race with them, but slaughtered the men of the islands and took their women, who spoke Arawak. To enable them to make such a clean sweep of the males they must have arrived in very large numbers, and it seems to me that the expedition must have been of the nature of a definite invasion by a well-equipped army. But why did that army not return to its base ? The only inference is that it had no base to return to—that it had disappeared before the invaders came to the Lesser Antilles. The Caribs were not natives of any of the Antilles group, and certainly did not come originally from the American mainland, as Von den Steinen, who found remnants of them in the far interior of Brazil, says very definitely that they spoke the same language as the Caribs of the islands, " island Carib," as it is called, and not the Carib of the Guianas, the speech of those who later settled on the north-west mainland of South America.

But there was a still earlier race in the Antilles than either Carib or Arawak. These were the Guacanabibes, some of whom were still found surviving in the western part of Cuba by the invading Spaniards. Their remains have been discovered at Porto Rico by Mr J. W. Fewkes, and show them to have been distinct from the later comers. They lived in caves, and from the similarity in name and customs I take them to have been the same as the Guanches of the Canaries.

Many of these tribes, especially the Caribs, flattened the head, precisely as did the Maya of Guatemala, Chiapas, and Yucatan. They built large wooden houses. The zemies or gods of the Tainos of Cuba bore a strong resemblance, says Beuchat, to the naguals, or spiritual beast-guardians of the Maya. Their storm-goddess, Guabancex (who is, I think, the Sycorax of Shakespeare's *Tempest*, as Caliban is merely an older word for Carib, or cannibal)[1] was the same as the Maya goddess of flood and storm. Her ministers, Guatauva and Coatrischie, were supposed to gather the waters in the valleys between the mountains before the occurrence of one of the floods which occasionally devastated the islands.

The people of Hayti believed that the souls of the dead joined their ancestors in a mythical island called Coaibai, situated in the east. Like the Maya and Mexicans, they practised the art of embalming the dead.

A swarming population filled these islands. Their methods of government, costume, implements, art, and general mode of life show a strong resemblance to those of the Maya of Central America. But the likeness is such as is to be found between a people who have originally received a much larger measure of culture and a partially civilised community, for that the population of the Antilles were inferior in culture to the Maya there can be no reasonable doubt. I believe, then, that whereas the Maya were direct immigrants to Central America from the sunken land of Antilia, the peoples of the Antilles, with the exception of the Caribs, had always inhabited these islands and had received only a measure of the Antilian civilisation, which had filtered through to this archipelago through the agency of commerce, and that the Maya, on the final downfall of Antilia, had preferred, instead of settling in these comparatively barbarous portions of their domain, to push past them into the absolutely unknown but much more hospitable regions of Guatemala and Chiapas. The Caribs were, probably, bands of Antilians of the lower orders, sailors, it may be, who, finding themselves leaderless

[1] " My dam's god, Setebos," alluded to by Caliban, was in reality a god of the Patagonian Indians mentioned by Magellan.

and in extreme peril, seized upon shipping, and, sailing to the Lesser Antilles, settled there.   I do not, of course, mean to say that only one migration took place from slowly dis-integrating Antilia to Central America and the Antilles. This is, in fact, disproved by the terms of the myth of Quetzalcoatl, which informs us that more than one party of immigrants arrived on American soil.   And though Carib and Maya strongly resembled each other, there were yet such divergencies as can only be accounted for by a more or less prolonged isolation.

CHAPTER XIII

THE EVIDENCE FROM EGYPT

THE theory that Egyptian civilisation had an Atlantean origin has been hotly debated. I do not intend to enter into the welter of controversy, but to deal with the matter from a strictly practical point of view. In the present chapter I shall confine myself to those evidences which seem to me to link Egypt with Atlantis, and in that which follows shall point out the analogies between Egyptian and Central American civilisation in the hope of demonstrating their common origin.

In the chapters which deal with the anthropological evidence the very considerable amount of proof which exists that the dynastic population of Egypt was in large measure drawn from the Azilian-Tardenoisian stock—the Iberians of later times—has already been outlined. All authorities are agreed that a large proportion of the stock which went to make up the composite people known as the ancient Egyptians had a western origin—that is, that their elements were the same as those which first entered Spain about 10,000 B.C., and which are known as Azilian-Tardenoisian. That the race in question came from the disintegrating continent of Atlantis has already been proved or otherwise to the satisfaction of the reader according as he accepts or rejects the conclusions advanced in the chapters referred to, and here it is only necessary to bring evidence to bear that it continued its advance along the southern littoral of the Mediterranean, and entered Egypt, bringing with it a very considerable body of Atlantean culture.

No attempt will be made to deny that other and perhaps equally powerful colonies were planted in Egypt at subsequent periods from Asia and elsewhere. The evidence for these is not to be gainsaid. This is tantamount to saying that Egyptian dynastic culture was no more wholly Atlantean than was Maya culture. But it is maintained, nevertheless, that in the main the civilising influences which radiated from Atlantis were instrumental in colouring Egyptian culture more deeply than those which emanated from elsewhere.

The most satisfactory evidence which can be advanced to prove that Atlantean influences entered Egypt at an early period is that connected with the worship of Osiris. That it was not indigenous to the country is clear. The origins of the worship of Osiris are indeed obscure. It is impossible to glean from texts at what precise period in Egyptian history his cult first began to gain a footing in the Nile country, but that it is greatly more ancient than any text is certain. The first dynastic centres of his worship were Abydos and Mendes, and he may possibly be represented on a mace-head of Nar-mer found at Hieraconpolis, and on a wooden plaque of the reign of Udy-mu or Den (Hesepti), the fifth king of the First Dynasty, who is represented as dancing before him. This shows that a centre of Osirian worship existed at Abydos during the First Dynasty. But allusions in the Pyramid Texts make it clear that prior to this shrines to Osiris had been erected in various parts of Egypt. He is usually depicted as wrapped in mummy bandages and wearing the white, cone-shaped crown of the South, yet Dr Budge says of him: " His home and origin were possibly Libyan."

The work which affords us the truest insight into the character of Osiris is, of course, the so-called Book of the Dead, the Pert-em-hru, or " The Chapter of Coming Forth by Day," as it has been more literally translated, a subsidiary title of one of the recensions or versions of which may be rendered " The Chapter of Making Perfect the Khu " (or spirit), that is to say, " The Book of the Perfect Way." Certain parts of it are known to have been in use among the Egyptians at least four thousand years before our era, and its crude prototypes are to be found in the Pyramid Texts. With the introduction of mummification a more intricate system of ritual came into vogue, based on the belief that such ceremonies as it imposed would ensure the corpse against corruption, preserve it for ever, and bring it at last to a beatified existence with Osiris. Almost immediately prior to the dynastic era a great stimulus appears to have been given to the cult of Osiris throughout Egypt. He had now primarily become the god of the dead, and his dogma taught that from the preserved corpse would spring a beautified astral body, the future home of the spirit of the deceased.

But the greater number of the texts comprised in the Book of the Dead are in one form or another of much higher antiquity than the period of Mena, the first historical king of Egypt. Internal evidence shows that many of these were revised or edited long before the copies known to us were made. Even at as early a date as 3300 B.C. the professional writers who transcribed the ancient texts appear to have been so puzzled by their contents that they scarcely understood their purport. Dr Budge writes : " We are in any case justified in estimating the earliest form of the work to be contemporaneous with the foundation of the civilisation which we call ' Egyptian ' in the valley of the Nile."

So ancient was it, indeed, that it was certainly not " Egyptian." A hieratic inscription upon the sarcophagus of Queen Khnemnefert, wife of Mentu-hetep, a king of the Eleventh Dynasty (c. 2500 B.C.), states that a certain chapter of the Book of the Dead was discovered in the reign of Hesep-ti, the fifth king of the First Dynasty, who flourished about 4266 B.C. This sarcophagus affords us two copies of the said chapter. That as early as 2500 B.C. a chapter of the Book of the Dead should be referred to a date almost 2000 years before this period is astounding, and the mind reels at the idea of a tradition which during so many centuries could have preserved a religious formula almost unimpaired. Thus, forty-four centuries ago a chapter of this marvellous book was regarded as extremely ancient, mysterious, and difficult of comprehension. It is also to be noted that the inscription on the tomb of Queen Khnemnefert states that the chapter in question was " discovered " about 4266 B.C. If it was only discovered at that far-distant era, what periods of remoteness lie between that epoch and the time when it was first reduced to writing ? If it was merely discovered then, it was certainly not a thing Egyptian in its origin.

Whence did it come ? I am of opinion that the ritual described in the Book of the Dead, if not that of a mystical association or society, yet most strongly coloured the rituals of all later mystical societies. It has frequently been suggested that it constituted the ritual of a secret brotherhood, and that the various halls and passages mentioned in it symbolised the several stages of initiation through which the members had to pass. It seems to have powerfully influenced Greek mysteries, especially those of the Cabiri and Eleusis. This would seem to point to the probability that if the Book of the Dead did not contain an early type of initiatory ceremonial, it may have powerfully influenced the ceremonial of mysteries when they arose. On the other hand, it may be that it represents the ceremonial of an older mystery, which had been turned to other uses by the dynastic Egyptians, and members of modern mystical associations will readily recognise much of the ritual of these in its pages.

Now we have seen that the cult of Osiris was probably an importation from Libya to Egypt. Can we trace its beginnings still further westward? It was connected with the preservation of the body after death. We know that the amulets found on remains of the Aurignacian period in Spain are practically the prototypes of those encountered upon the various parts of the Egyptian mummy, and the universal use of the shell as the symbol of life among the early peoples of Spain is paralleled in Egypt. The pre-historic cave-paintings of the Pyrenees in some places seem to portray a ritual which resembles that of the Pyramid Texts with startling fidelity, and the primitive races of Spain have assuredly an ethnic connection with those of ancient Egypt.

The worship of Osiris, a cult of Libyan or Western origin, thus entered Egypt at an early period, achieved a high degree of popularity, and later merged with the cults of Ra and Amen, religions of Asiatic provenance. But so powerful was it that in due course the worship of Osiris triumphed over every other element in the Egyptian faith, until at last its chief god came to be recognised both at home and abroad as the deity of Egypt *par excellence.*

Now, to whatever part of Western Europe or North Africa we turn, we find reminiscences of this Osirian worship. That it arrived at its apogee in Egypt is not denied. There it came into contact with other cults, and borrowing and amalgamation unquestionably resulted therefrom, so that great complexity arose in the Osirian tradition. But in its simple and less complicated forms it is to be found in every country in Western Europe. The Scottish and Old English ballads of " John Barleycorn," for example, are nothing more nor less than the myth of Osiris, the life and death of the barley plant, in rural rhyme. Druidism is merely the cult of Osiris in another form, and the menhirs and dolmens of its architecture the rude parallels of the pyramid.

Recent investigators, among them Mr W. T. Perry of Manchester, have sought to show that all ancient culture arose in Egypt, from which it was disseminated during the Pyramid era. But this does not account for the entrance into Egypt at a much earlier date of the Osirian worship, a highly developed cult with ancient relationships in Spain and Northern Africa, where we find at a date at least 12,000 years B.C. what are undoubtedly the beginnings of the mummification of the human body, a practice inalienably associated with the Osirian worship, and with that alone.

The Crô-Magnons of the Biscay region, as we have seen, smeared the bodies of their dead with red oxide of iron. This was done to give them the colours of life. The blood was regarded as the true life-principle, and when the paleness of death supervened the body was painted in the hues of life, that when the soul once more awoke after its long spell of sleep, its earthly semblance would rise reinvigorated in all the glory of life. The process was one connected with sympathetic magic and the belief in resurrection and complete restoration of all the bodily powers, including the fluidity of the blood and the other bodily secretions. This idea evidently lay at the root of Crô-Magnon belief and practice, just as it lay at the root of the Osirian belief in bodily resurrection. Now precisely the same coloration of the corpse is found in the earliest specimens of Egyptian mummies. This, later, developed into the more artistic and realistic presentation of the body in the colours of life on the mummy-case, and we know that the Egyptians painted the statues of their gods " to make them healthy." But the earliest examples of this body-painting are encountered in Crô-Magnon graves and cave-tombs in Spain and France, and not in Egypt, thus proving conclusively that the custom was much older in Western Europe than in Egypt.

A Crô-Magnon burial in Wales, known as that of " the Red Lady of Paviland," although the remains seem to be those of a man, well illustrates such a burial, which must have occurred several thousands of years prior to any

interment of the kind in Egyptian soil. Says Dr Buckland,
who discovered the remains in 1823 : " They are all of them
stained superficially with a dark brick-red colour, and
enveloped by a coating of a kind of ruddle, composed of
red micaceous oxide of iron, which stained the earth, and
in some parts extended itself to the distance of about half
an inch around the surface of the bones. The body must
have been entirely surrounded or covered over at the time
of interment with this red substance."

That this and other cases of the same kind in Europe and
America, in which the practice still lingers, were the first
steps in the complicated development of the cult of
mummification seems clear. Equally clear, too, is the
proof that in the latter region charms and amulets, which
the dynastic Egyptians placed on the various organs of
the corpse to give them magical stability, were derived
from the numerous amulets discovered in Crô-Magnon
burials. The object of these was to protect and prolong
life in this world and the next. Shell necklaces, wild animals'
teeth, and ivory ornaments found in Crô-Magnon graves
were thought to contain the animating influence or " life-
substance " of certain deities. Professor Elliot Smith has
shown that the beginnings of the ideas underlying magical
and religious practice in this respect were connected with
shells, which were used by the peoples of Upper Palæolithic times in burial ceremonies, and these he connects
with later Egyptian and other amulets. These are found in
the Grimaldi caves at Mentone and elsewhere, in circumstances which greatly antedate any Egyptian interment of
the kind.

Thus the whole tendency of those early burial practices,
which later developed into the cult of mummification, clearly
had their known origin *in Western Europe* and not in Egypt,
and among the peoples who appear to have an Atlantean
connection, and spread from west to east. That we find them

in America in much the same form as in Egypt is proof
positive that they took similar shape in the western hemisphere, as will be shown in the following chapter.

To return to the Osirian connections of Druidism. Many
authors lay stress upon the " eastern " character of Druidism,
simply because of its similarity to oriental religions. It
does not seem to have occurred to them that it may have
had a western origin. As we advance from west to east
we find the manifestations of this widespread cult growing
more and more complex, until it culminates in the subtleties
of Egyptian religious practice. But surely the region in
which it is to be found in its most unalloyed simplicity is
more probably the place of its beginnings than is the centre
where we behold it mingling with Asiatic thought, and
presenting an appearance of culture-mixing, as it undoubtedly
does, in the Nile land.

What was Druidism ? Of recent years the most extraordinary efforts have been made to prove that it never had
any real existence. Notwithstanding the definite and clearly
expressed accounts of it which we have from Cæsar, Pliny,
Tacitus, and other classical authors of repute, modern
writers, suffering from " the credulity of incredulity,"
have actually essayed to build up a mass of evidence proving
that it never existed save in later popular imagination and
folk-belief. The attempt has signally failed. But it has
served one good purpose. The controversy which ensued
has greatly enlightened us upon the conditions and general
significance of this ancient faith.

In the first place, we are now justified in classing Druidism
as a religion of Iberian origin, having its European beginnings
in Spain, on which was later superimposed a mass of Celtic
belief. Siret, the distinguished Belgian archæologist, is of
opinion that it was brought to the shores of the Iberian
peninsula by certain " Easterners " from Egypt or Syria,
who introduced among the nations the worship of Egyptian

or Syrian deities and symbols, for example, the sacred palm-tree, and worshipped a goddess resembling the Egyptian Hathor, a form of Nut, the sky-goddess. Expelled from Spain, these adventurers settled in Gaul, Italy, and North Africa. The goddess Hathor or Nut was regarded as the cow of the heavenly regions, and was, therefore, associated with milk, and the milk-exuding fig of the sycamore. This lacteal fig, having no parallel in North-Western Europe, was replaced there by the milk-bearing hazel-nut and similar plants, which gave forth a like elixir symbolising the life-principle. The mistletoe berry was also regarded as a bearer of this magical milk. M. Siret has found evidence, too, that this cult was associated with the megalithic monuments usually regarded as Druidic. In a word, he has succeeded in showing that there was unquestionably a very ancient correspondence of belief between Egypt and Western Europe.

But these are by no means the only similarities between the religions alluded to. A study of the Welsh triads and such other Druidic documents as remain to us make it clear that further correspondences existed. Chief among them is the belief in metempsychosis or, as it is usually termed, "the doctrine of the transmigration of souls." This was not a Celtic, but an Iberian belief. It is alluded to by Diodorus Siculus, who flourished during the latter half of the first century A.D., as being prevalent in Gaul. The Welsh bard Taliessin is said to have inhabited the bodies of men and animals in turn, and even to have existed in plant form. Mongan, King of Ulster, underwent a similar experience. The ancient Britons refused to partake of the flesh of certain animals and birds, believing them to enshrine the souls of their ancestors. This idea is certainly found in Egypt, and is mentioned in the Book of the Dead where the soul is spoken of as taking various animal and floral forms. But it is remarkable that it is only in connection with the cult of Osiris, a cult certainly of western origin, that this idea obtains, and not in connection with those of the Asiatic gods of Egypt. Its appearance in India and elsewhere is infinitely later in historical time.

Now Osiris was the son of Nut, the divine cow, whose distorted worship M. Siret finds in Spain, Gaul, and Britain. We are then justified in looking in these regions for traces of her son. Are these to be found ?

Arthur—the King Arthur of a legend so widely diffused throughout Britain, France, and Spain—is, I believe, Asar, or Osiris.

At first sight this hypothesis may seem wildly improbable, but a prolonged consideration of the question has led me to believe in its substantial accuracy. I cannot elaborate it here any further than may serve to illustrate my main contention that the early elements of Osirian worship are to be found in Western Europe, and are to be referred to an Atlantean origin.

For generations the personality of Arthur was the subject of fierce controversy. Was he king or god, real or apochryphal ? We know that certain princes of Strathclyde, the ancient " Welsh " or Brythonic kingdom which stretched from Lothian in Scotland through Clydesdale to Wales, were called Arthur, and tradition in Britain associates him with that region. But there is also good evidence to show that if he were not at one time worshipped as a god, that later romance associated the actual man with some deity or other who had ceased to be worshipped, mingling the myths of that god with the history of the hero of reality. The process is one well known to students of mythology. Briefly, then, what Osirian elements do we find in the story of Arthur ?

Slain in his last battle with his treacherous nephew, Mordred, Arthur is carried off by his sisters in a barque to the mysterious Isle of Avallon, an oversea, or underworld, locality, " the Place of Apples," in the Western Sea. There he remains, neither dead nor alive, awaiting the fateful day when Britain shall require his aid once more.

Slain by his treacherous brother Set, the body of Osiris (as shown by Egyptian funerary practice and not by the Greek myth concerning him) is ferried in the sacred barque across the Nile, accompanied by his wailing sisters Isis and Nephthys to the region of Aalu, in the west, a place of plenteous fruits and grain. There Osiris rules as god of the not-dead—that is, the neither dead nor alive—awaiting a glorious resurrection.

The island paradise of Avallon to which Arthur was taken was undoubtedly associated with Druidism. We find it alluded to in such stories as that of Thomas the Rhymer, or True (*i.e.* " Druid ") Thomas, Ogier the Dane, and several old Breton tales. It is the same as the Anwynn of the Welsh myths, the Tir-nan-ogue of Celtic tradition—a place of rest and refreshment for the un-dead, " the Place of Heart's Desire." In some tales it is an island, in others a submarine locality. That it is one and the same as the Osirian Aalu can hardly be doubted.

It is to be noted that this island-paradise of the Celtic peoples was confounded with the " mythical " islands of the Middle Ages, Brazil (a Celtic name), St Brandan's Isle, and so forth. It is also to be observed that in more than one of the Irish myths it was located *at the bottom of the sea*.

The great body of mystical Celtic story known as the Grail Legend, with which Arthur is so closely associated, is undoubtedly connected with Osirian myth. The Fisher King who lies in the Grail Castle in a wounded condition has been identified with both Arthur and Osiris, and by German scholarship with Orpheus, with whom the celebrated Orphic mysteries were connected. The legend teems with Oriental references, and Miss Margaret Murray, Lecturer on Egyptian Language in University College,

London, has identified many of the place-names in the Grail story with actual localities in Egypt.

Horus, the son of Osiris, probably symbolises the resurrected form of that god. His myth strongly resembles that of Arthur. Both gather around them a large body of companions who devote themselves to the destruction of evil monsters. The symbol of Horus is the sun. So is that of Arthur, whose Round Table typifies the luminary of day. In combat he and his knights wax stronger as the sun rises to the zenith, and weaker as it nears its setting, and his final discomfiture takes place as the planet of day sinks beneath the horizon.

Most of Arthur's " knights " are merely old British Celtic gods disguised and distorted. King Loth of Lothian, his brother-in-law, is Llud or Nud, or Lug of the Long Arm, after whom Ludgate, the site of his ancient temple, is called. He resembles the Egyptian god Aten, whose worship was introduced into Egypt by King Akhen-aten, the father of Tut-ankh-amen. Both are described as having very long arms—the rays of the sun, ending in human hands. Sir Kay, the seneschal, is the British god Kai, who could walk under water with a torch in either hand like the Maya god Itzamna. Lancelot was brought up by the fairy Morgan le Fay in a submarine paradise. Morgan is the Irish goddess Morrigan, the raven, the same as the Roman fatæ, or fays. Merlin, says Rhys, is the god of Stonehenge. The legendary name of Britain in the Welsh triads is Plas Myrddin, " the enclosure of Merlin," who was evidently a deity of the first importance.

Arthur is thus clearly connected with the cult of Druidism, and that Druidism and the cult of Osiris had a common origin is equally plain. Druidism was not confined to Gaul and Britain, but spread eastwards to Galatia, where it constituted the religion of those " foolish Galatians " on whom St Paul visited his scorn, and both Druidism and the Osiris cult were connected with megalithic building and monumental architecture.

The adherents of Druidism and the Osirian religion both looked to an island paradise *in the west*. Both believed that a great monster lived in the ocean (apep in Egypt, addanc in Wales, etin in Scotland) which was combated daily by Horus, Arthur, or one of the latter's knights. This was, of course, the earth-devouring dragon of the waters, which caused them to overflow and drown the world in the cataclysm of Llyn-llion. The heroes of both myths reside in an island paradise awaiting return to the world of men. They are conveyed there in precisely the same manner. The worship of both cults is connected with the sky-cow, therefore with milk and milk-giving trees and plants. The serpent figures largely in both religions.

The founders of the Osirian religion who came from the west were Iberians. The founders of Druidism, according to Rhys and many other competent scholars, were also Iberians. The ancestors of those Iberians, as I have already shown, were the Azilian-Tardenoisians, who arrived in Spain about 10,000 years ago, bringing with them a culture the beginnings of which are not to be found in Europe. To me the chain of evidence appears as complete. The Druidic and Osirian cults, which resemble each other so strongly, had a common origin in Atlantean religion.

That religion, we may remember from the account of Plato, was connected with the bull. In Egypt the bull was worshipped under the form of Apis. Apis was merely a form of Osiris, the calf of the sky-goddess Nut, and to the bull which represented him other cattle were sacrificed. The cult of Serapis (Osiris-Apis) was of widespread distribution, and was brought by the Romans to Britain, where it flourished chiefly at York.

The bull was also sacred to the Druids, and was sacrificed at the ancient rite of Beltane (Bile's Fire), when cattle were driven into the flames. The rite, in a distorted form, is still celebrated in Scotland on May Day. As late as 1649 to 1678, according to the records of the Presbytery of Dingwall, bulls were sacrificed in the parish of Gairloch, in Ross-shire, and oblations of milk poured on the hills. The sacred bull is depicted on the Scottish Druidical standing-stones. In Northamptonshire, says Kelly in his *Folklore*, a calf was sacrificed by burning at Beltane. Bull-fighting, the popular sport of the Spaniards—the purest Iberian race,—is undoubtedly a survival from bull-sacrifice.

It would thus seem that the known similarities between the ancient religions of Western Europe and Egypt are capable of being referred to an Atlantean origin and root-religion, with which both had resemblances. When we further recall the many references which are found in Druidical legend to floods and submerged islands, and the fact that Osiris was, according to one myth, thought of as having been drowned in a flood, the circle of proof seems complete.

CHAPTER XIV

EGYPTIAN AND AMERICAN COMPARISONS IN THE LIGHT OF ATLANTEAN RESEARCH

RECENT research has made it abundantly clear that the civilisation of Egypt and America sprang from one common source. The intimate resemblance between the two cultures has led to the formation of an hypothesis on the part of the school of Professor G. Elliot Smith that the Egyptian influence of the Pyramid era circled the world by way of the Pacific and thus reached America.

It seems much more likely, to my way of thinking, that, if Egyptian civilisation reached America, it did so by a more direct route than *via* Asia. It is unlikely, too, that, as this school holds, the Egyptian ideas to be observed in America should have presented an appearance and spirit so purely Egyptian had they come through an Asiatic filter. That is, the hypothesis of their entrance by way of Asia supposes a duration of time for their passage thence which altogether precludes the possibility that they could have reached American soil without much greater fundamental alteration than they exhibit. This is not to say that Chinese or Cambodian or Polynesian influences did not impinge upon American civilisation. I am convinced that they did; but I am just as certain that the evidences of Egyptian culture in Central America were as untouched by Asiatic influences in their passage to the New World as was later European culture on its way thence.

There is, says Brasseur de Bourbourg, a river Nil or Nile in Guatemala which harbours many crocodiles, and on the banks of which are to be seen the ruins of pyramids. I cannot believe that such an association of ideas came together in Guatemala after a filtration of thousands of years through Asia and across the Pacific. Nor is the alleged route clearly marked. Again, the pantheon of Mexican mythology is the shadow of that of Egypt. Quetzalcoatl is Thoth, or Osiris, Ciuacoatl is Isis, Piltzintecutli is Horus, Xochipilli is Bes. The list might be extended *ad infinitum*. Such resemblances, if they are to be found in India, are certainly not encountered in China, and the surrogates of the Central American gods in Japan are demonstrably of later origin. Actual mummification is to be found in Mexico and Peru : only its memory in China.

All this seems to go to prove that direct contact was at one time achieved between Egypt and America. Egyptian records speak of prolonged voyages. A people who could round the Cape of Good Hope, as did the Egyptians in the reign of Necho, were surely capable of making almost any sea passage. Direct contact, I feel convinced, between Egypt and America took place by way of Atlantis, the shorter and more feasible route, rather than by the deserts and boundless wastes of Asia, or *via* the Pacific, or more probably Atlantis was responsible for the civilisation of both.

Perhaps the outstanding similarity between the two cultures is the manner in which they disposed of the dead. Mummification in America was evidently as much a system which had been introduced as was the case in Egypt. The native custom of disposing of the dead in Mexico and among the Maya was by fire or burial. A compromise was arrived at by which the embalmed bodies of chiefs and kings were consumed by the flames of a funerary pyre. The mummy thus disposed of was prepared in various ways according to the traditions of the province where the rite took place. In Michoacan and elsewhere it bore a striking resemblance to the Egyptian mummy, swathed as it was in numerous wrappings. But on the Mexican plateau and in the south, the corpse was bound up in a squatting posture and placed in what is known as a " mummy-bundle " of stout cloth, secured by a network of rope. To this a false head was affixed, and the whole was elaborately decorated with religious symbols.

Our knowledge of the Mexican mummy is gleaned chiefly from fugitive descriptions in native and colonial literature, and from its pictured representation in the native paintings or codices. In the Popol Vuh, the sacred book of the Quiches of Guatemala, we are informed that on the death of the first men their bodies were found to have been miraculously placed in a bundle known as " the majesty enveloped." The region in which this occurrence was supposed to have taken place boasted a culture greatly more ancient than the Mexican proper, that of the Maya, who practised several kinds of sepulture, but buried the bodies of persons of importance in elaborate tombs. In more than one of these have been found large vessels closely resembling the canopic jars placed round the tombs of the Egyptian kings and priests and having, like them, lids representing the heads of the supporters or gods of the four points of the compass. Certain colours were allotted by the Egyptians, through the process of mummification, to the various organs of the body as well as to the cardinal points : the north (red) to the lungs, the south (white) to the liver, the east (yellow) to the stomach, and the west (black) to the intestines ; so that it is indeed startling to find that the colours and organs associated by the Maya with these points are nearly identical with those allotted to them by the Egyptians : north (white) lungs, south (yellow) belly, east (red) larger intestines, west (black) intestines. Thus the colours and organs for the west agree absolutely, and the north agrees as to the organ allotted. But more important still is the point that the " Canopic jars, which went out of fashion in Egypt, were

continued in use by the Maya and placed under the protec-
tion of the Bacabs, their gods of the four coloured cardinal
points. Apparently the Egyptian system of mummification
which reached America was accompanied by the Egyptian
doctrines in less modified form than one might be led to
expect, especially when one considers how varied were the
cultural influences to which these doctrines must have been
subjected during the process of gradual transmission from
Egypt to the Far East, and across the Pacific to America "
(D. A. Mackenzie, in *Folklore*, June 1923). Nor does the
similarity end here, for these receptacles were intended for
the preservation of the eviscerated organs of the deceased.
Such a striking analogy, it has been argued, can scarcely be
due to fortuitous circumstances.

One of the most enlightening of the pictures of Mexican
mummies in the native paintings is that on sheet 60 of
the Codex Magliabecchiano, preserved in the Biblioteca
Nazionale in Florence. It represents the mummy-bundle
of a dead warrior. The swathed figure appears to stand
upright, in a manner reminiscent of the embalmed form of
the dead Osiris. It wears the insignia of the dead, the head-
band with a plate of torquoise-mosaic, blue ear and nose-
plugs, and the shoulder-band of paper. On its head is a
large drooping panache of feathers, and the banner of
Uitzilopochtli, the patron god of warriors. Its hair is
decorated with cotton-balls, the emblem of the deities of
the Underworld, to whom it is to be consigned, and beside
it is the blue hairless dog which preceded it to the Mexican
Hades, and which was sacrificed on the death of its master.
In front of it lie the gifts which it must present to Mictlan-
tecutli, Lord of the Dead, and these are accompanied by a
symbol bearing an extraordinary resemblance to the tat
sign which was buried with Egyptian mummies, and which
was thought to provide the deceased on his resurrection
with a new backbone.

Above this iš seen a severed hand, which had belonged to a wizard or a woman who had died in childbed, and this was supposed to give light to the dead man in the Underworld. It is, in fact, the same as " the hand of glory," the hand of a dead person, a symbol which was in use not so very long ago among Irish burglars, in the belief that the weird light which shone from it would paralyse the energies of those whom they sought to rob. The mummy's face-painting is that of the god Uitzilopochtli, and represents the starry sky of night.

The same codex provides us with yet another similar painting. This shows us a mummy-bundle packed in white cotton cloth and secured with stout ropes. Its occupant wears the mantle of the dead, and is evidently that of a telpochtli or young warrior who had not yet achieved membership in one of the orders of knighthood. The banner of the war-god springs from the back, and the head is surmounted by the cotton-ball symbols. In front is the sign resembling the tat, which is considered by some Americanists to represent another mummy-bundle. Bundles of this kind were certainly found in Mexico. The myth of the creation of the sun and moon states that the gods who killed themselves in terror at sight of the first sun left their raiment to their personal servants, and that each retainer made a bundle of this, wrapping his master's clothing round a stick, placing a chalchihuitl or jadeite stone inside to serve as a heart, and naming the whole after the god to whom it had belonged. The Franciscan priest Olmos found such a relic in Tlalmanco, which showed evidences of very considerable age. Obviously these sacred bundles are in the same category with the " medicine-bundle " of the North American Indian tribes, and it would seem that from such a form certain of the Mexican gods were developed, notably the deity of the planet Venus, who, like the Egyptian Osiris, is represented as a mummy and wears the insignia of the warriors who died by sacrifice. For the Mexicans, the recurring periods of the planet Venus were connected with the return of the souls of the dead. At such times they held a festival which somewhat resembled the " Feast of All Souls," at which the people took hands and danced round a sham mummy-bundle hoisted on the top of a pole. A picture of the ceremony is given on sheet 28 of the Codex Borbonicus, and another, in which the priests are seen manufacturing the mock mummy, is to be found in the Sahagun MS. housed in the Biblioteca del Palacio at Madrid. Some carry the bundle with its false head daubed in the crude likeness of life, others place it in position on the top of the pole, and are seen in the act of affixing to it the paper ornaments, banners, and other insignia with which it was decorated.

Mention has already been made of the resemblance of the mummies of Michoacan to those of the Egyptians. In a Spanish manuscript of the sixteenth century known as the " Relacion de las ceremonios y ritos de Michoacan," considerable information is given regarding the funerary methods of the inhabitants of this region. The pictures it contains exhibit the whole process of funerary custom. In the first of the series we see the dead chief lying on his couch covered with a blanket; in the next, priests blow on conch-shells and beat drums to assemble the people to the funeral. The third depicts the cortège *en route* to the funeral pyre. The mummy, swathed in numerous rolls of cotton, is carried on the heads of four bearers towards the blazing fire to which it is about to be committed, priests and mourners gather around it, and the disconsolate widow, her body blackened in sign of mourning, grovels before the pyre.

Both in Mexico and Peru, as in Egypt, the pyramidal erections were utilised for the burial of the distinguished dead. Some years ago a tunnelling of the teocalli or great pyramid of the Sacred City of Cholula, in Mexico, disclosed remains, probably royal, which had been buried there at a comparatively early date. If somewhat exceptional in the isthmian region, such a disposition of the dead was quite common in the Yunca districts of Peru, where the mummy (*malqui*) was frequently deposited in small pyramidical structures known as huacas. At Miraflores, Charrillos, and elsewhere, tumuli of this description are found, built of adobe or mud-brick, and in formation like a small stepped pyramid, hollow in the centre, in which the mummy with its funerary furniture was deposited. Many of these chambers are found to contain layer upon layer of mummified bodies, separated from each other by deposits of osier-reeds. Some of these huaca-pyramids are not more than 10 or 12 feet in height, but others range from 40 to 60 metres, and have foundations of cut stone. In the Quichua or Inca districts of Peru the mummy was usually deposited in caves, which are of such frequent occurrence in that mountainous region as to render the building of huacas unnecessary.

The Peruvian process of mummification more closely resembled the Egyptian than that employed by the Mexicans. The body was carefully embalmed, and I am informed by an expert anatomist who has examined many specimens, both of Egyptian and Peruvian origin, that the process in both cases was very nearly the same. The house of the deceased was set apart for his mummy, a staff of servants was appointed for it, and it was endowed with lands, so that offerings might be constantly provided for it. There is evidence that in earlier times friends and dependents immolated themselves at the funeral ceremony, but later a llama, which was called by the name of the supposititious human victim, was accepted as a substitute. The ancient Temple of the Sun at Cuzco was found by the followers of Pizarro to contain the mummies of thirteen deceased Incas, seated round the altar of the Sun, the corresponding Temple of the Moon containing the embalmed remains of their consorts.

Pola de Ondegardo, a relentless hunter of treasure, ferreted out practically every one of the royal mummies which had been hidden by the faithful Peruvians, with one exception, and these, like the embalmed corpses of the nobility, which were buried in double-chambered caves (one for the mummy and his ghost, and the other for his property), were stripped of their jewellery by the insatiable conquistadors. The heights overlooking the valley of the river Yucay are honeycombed with these burial caves, all of which have long since been ransacked in the search for treasure.

In some cases the mummies of Mexico and Peru show resemblances which would seem to point to an ancient cultural connection between the two methods. Peruvian mummies are found wrapped up in bundles, much in the same manner as those found in Mexican tombs. We do not find that the intestines were removed in the Peruvian examples, as was the case in Mexico and among the Maya ; and it is noticeable that as we proceed from Mexico to the Maya country it is only in the border regions, where the cultures of these countries mingle, that the Canopic jars are first encountered in tombs. This would seem to show that the inception of the practice in America was due to the Maya, the older race. But that the practice of preserving the dead had a wide distribution throughout America, and particularly its northern part, is proved by the present-day customs of many North American Indian tribes who practise canoe and tree-burial. In Kentucky, for example, the body was dried and filled with sand, then wrapped in skins or matting, and placed in a cave or hut. In the Darien peninsula, the viscera were removed and the trunk was filled with resin, after which the corpse was smoked and preserved in the house. The Aleutians embalmed the bodies of their chiefs by similar methods, and the Virginian Indians removed the entire skin, afterwards fitting it to the skeleton again.

In my view, closely as the funerary customs of Egypt, Mexico, and Peru resemble each other, they do so not because one was copied from the other, but because all sprang from one common source—Atlantis. I have already shown that the origins of Egyptian mummification were laid, centuries before the civilising race entered Egypt, in Western Europe. I have also made it clear that the race which practised mummification in Central America was not indigenous to that country, but came from an oceanic locality in the East. On both hands, then, there seem to be good grounds for believing that the originators of human mummification both in Egypt and America came from an oceanic centre in the Atlantic. In the case of America, tradition expressly states this to be the fact, and in that of Egypt an irrefragable chain of evidence proves it to be so.

But was mummification practised in Atlantis? The process commenced there. When the Crô-Magnons and Azilian-Tardenoisians quitted the sinking continent, they carried the germ of the idea with them, as is proved by their funerary remains in France, Spain, and elsewhere. At the period when they arrived in Europe the custom of mummification in Atlantis was probably in a stage of early development, such as we see it in the cave-burials of Western Europe where as yet the actual process of preservation was only in an embryonic condition, though the placing of amulets on the corpse, much as in the later Egyptian mummy, had been in use probably for ages. But the best proof exists that the whole process was slowly evolving in the remains of Atlantis itself, and was finally introduced in a more advanced form into America.

The Guanches of the Canary Islands, the last remnant of the Atlantean population, embalmed their dead. The sandals upon the feet of the statue of the so-called Chac-mool discovered at Chichen-Itza in Yucatan are " exact representations of those found on the feet of the Guanches, the early inhabitants of the Canary Islands, whose mummies are occasionally discovered in the caves of Teneriffe."

These Guanche mummies, many of which have been discovered in the Barranco de Fataga in Grand Canary, bear a close resemblance to both those of Egypt and America. They usually have a profusion of red hair, and are buried or placed on the left side. The body is often in an advanced state of dessication, wrapped in goatskin, with the hands crossed over the breast in the manner of some of the Peruvian mummies. They are, generally speaking, discovered in caverns in the rock-face, in a crouching or sitting position, like that of the mummies of Mexico or Peru and the earlier interments in Egypt, rather than stretched out in the late Egyptian manner. That the method of their embalmment and the general manner of preserving them was fundamentally the same in origin as obtained both in Egypt and America no observer of experience can doubt.

I believe that further confirmation of the ancient connection between America and Egypt by way of Atlantis is to be found by a comparison of the sacred mysteries of these countries. As has already been stated, the Egyptian Book of the Dead is undoubtedly connected with certain ancient mysteries, and is, indeed, the fount and source of all mystical practice, ancient and modern. The Mexican Codex Vaticanus A presents a close parallel to the Egyptian work, so much so, in fact, that it has been called by Edward James Payne, an Americanist of experience, " the Mexican Book of the Dead." In its pages the corpse is depicted as dressed for burial, the soul, like the Egyptian Ba, escaping from the mouth. The spirit is ushered into the presence of the god Tezcatlipoca, just as the Egyptian ghost is brought before Osiris, by a priest dressed in an ocelot-skin (the Egyptian high priest is dressed in a leopard-skin), and stands naked with a wooden yoke round his neck to receive sentence. He is then given over to the tests which precede entrance to the abode of the dead precisely as was the Egyptian defunct.

As I have already indicated, certain passages in the Popol Vuh assuredly describe initiatory tests into a secret society, much after the manner of those which had to be undergone by the Egyptian soul. When Hunhun-Apu and Vukub-Hunapu descended into the gloomy region of Xibalba, the Place of the Dead, at the invitation of its lords, they found that every preparation had been made to " hocus " them, just as is frequently done even to-day in the primary rites of certain mystical or pseudo-mystical societies, such, for example, as " The Horsemen," a body composed of agricultural labourers in the North of Scotland which subjects its members to much rough usage and horseplay before they are initiated and entrusted with the " Horseman's Word." On their entrance to the gloomy realm the brothers beheld two seated figures whom they mistook for the Lords of Xibalba, only to find that they were made of wood. Next they were asked to sit on the seat of honour, which, to their dismay, was a red-hot stone. Their sons and nephews underwent a similar experience, but succeeded in outwitting the Xibalbans. But they had first to face the ordeals of the House of Lances, the House of Cold, the House of Pumas, the House of Fire, and the House of Bats. These several " houses " forcibly recall the several halls through which the Egyptian spirit had to pass.

Moreover, the deities who dwelt in this grim monarchy had an agricultural connection, like Osiris and Isis in Egypt and Demeter and Kore in Greece. Xquiq, the daughter of one of the Lords of Xibalba, is probably the same as Kore or Persephone. She was able to gather a basket of maize where no maize grew. Plutonic deities are universally gods of fruitfulness.

We find, too, that the North American Indians, Australian Blackfellows, and other backward races, celebrate the self-same type of mystery as is connected with the worship of Osiris and that of the Greek Demeter. Whence did this likeness spring? These mysteries resemble each other too closely not to have had a common origin. They have been perpetuated to a certain extent in modern Freemasonry. Where must we look for the region in which they had their beginnings?

We have already seen that the Osirian cult had its origin in Western Europe or North-West Africa. Sanchoniathon, the Carthaginian, tells us that the mysterious cult of the Cabiri, which was of Carthaginian origin, was connected with Osiris. The Cabiri, he says, set down their records of the past by command of the god Thoth, " and they delivered them to their successors and to foreigners, of whom one was Isiris (Osiris), the inventor of the three letters, the brother of Chua, who is called the first Phœnician." Phœnician myth had it that the Titans (Rephaim), that is Atlas and his kin, were their ancestors. The worship of the Cabiri seems to have been brought from the Phœnician settlements in North-Western Africa to Greece. It has been maintained that it was of Egyptian origin, but we have seen that the myth records its delegation to Osiris. The Cabiri were, indeed, regarded by the nations of antiquity as the most ancient of all gods of whose worship there was any record. The mysteries of Eleusis and Bacchus were regarded as things of yesterday compared with these antique rites, the beginnings of which were lost in the mists of time. The Cabiri were represented to the profane in the guise of powerful deities armed with darts, lances, or hammers, sometimes as pygmies or dwarfs, and were distinguished by wearing the apron of the smith or mason. They were connected with the elements, particularly with fire and water, and with Vulcan, the god of fire and metallurgy. They were two in number, and were later reflected in the Dioscuri, Castor and Pollux, the heavenly twins, who resemble the

Atlantean offspring of Poseidon. Poseidon, indeed, was worshipped along with the Cabiri at Berytus. The mysteries connected with the Cabiri appear to have closely resembled those of Osiris, Demeter, Orpheus, and the other mystic rites of antiquity.

Now we encounter deities closely resembling the Cabiri in Mexico—the twin brothers Uitzilopochtli and Tezcatlipoca, who seem to be the same as the hero-twins of the Popol Vuh. Like the Cabiri, they are armed with the spear and are connected with the stars of the two hemispheres of which they are the respective chiefs. In later times it would seem that the images of the Cabiri grew in number, and were placed outside their temples. We may recollect that in Plato's account of Atlantis ten golden statues of the Atlantean gods or kings are spoken of as standing in front of the Temple of Poseidon. This practice bears a close resemblance to the ten images of the Tzitzimine or elemental deities whose images were placed round the idol of Uitzilopochtli in his temple at Mexico.

Just as the Dioscuri, Castor and Pollux, the later representations of the Cabiri, presided over war, so did the Mexican gods alluded to above. Uitzilopochtli was the chief oracle of Mexico, and strange rites and mysteries were enacted in connection with the worship of Tezcatlipoca, the patron of Mexican witchcraft and sorcery.

But these are by no means the only gods of the Old and New World who closely resemble each other. Many of the gods of Mexico bear a strong likeness to those of Egypt, and this can scarcely have been due to mere chance.

Thus the Mexican Quetzalcoatl bears a close resemblance to the Egyptian Thoth. Both are represented as having the heads of birds with long beaks, both are the inventors of writing, and are connected with the moon. In one of his forms Thoth is represented as the dog-headed ape, Cynocephalus, whilst Quetzalcoatl takes the guise of a dog supposed to bring lightning from the sky. Both were also deities of rain and wind, masters of magic and medicine.

The dog-headed Anubis had also his counterpart in Mexico in the dog-like god Xolotl, who is also represented with a dog's head in the Codex Borbonicus (sheet 16) and the Codex Vaticanus B. The dog in Mexico, like the dog in Egypt, was supposed to accompany his master to the place of the dead, and both of these gods appear to have originated from this belief.

The Egyptian god, Bes, seems to be almost reflected in the Mexican deity, Xochipilli. Bes is depicted as a huge dwarf, with enormous stomach, bow-legs, thick lips, and protruding tongue. His nose is flat, his eyebrows shaggy. He wears a tiara of feathers, and a panther-skin with the tail hanging behind. He was thought of as provider of amusements to the gods, as a grotesque dancer, and harp-player, and came to be regarded as god of the dance, of music, and joviality.

Like Bes, Xochipilli or Macuil Xochitl wears a panache of brightly-coloured feathers, and a dress with an appendage like that of Bes. Sahagun calls him " the god of those who served for the amusement or pastime of the great." He is, indeed, the god of merriment, of dance and sport, the jester or buffoon, the palace slave or entertainer.

The Egyptian Set and the Mexican Tezcatlipoca are also extraordinarily akin in their attributes. Set is the deity of night and darkness. He is represented with the head of an animal which has been likened to that of the camel or the okapi, but which seems to belong to neither. Storms, earthquakes, and eclipses, were attributed to his agency. He is identified with the constellation of the Great Bear, the region of cold, darkness, and death. He is the mortal enemy of Osiris and Horus, the sun-gods, even although he is the blood-brother of the former. His hieroglyph is

PLATE XI.

Thoth.

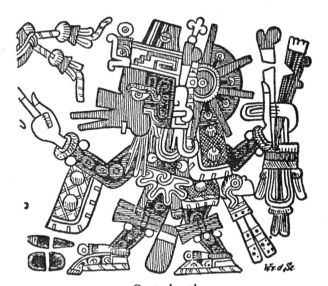

Quetzalcoatl.

Thoth and Quetzalcoatl compared.

a stone which seems to symbolise the stony or desert country on either side of the Nile.

Now practically every one of these associations is reflected in the figure of Tezcatlipoca. He, too, presides over darkness and the night, and is symbolised in certain of the Mexican manuscripts by the head of an animal *unknown in Mexico*, and seemingly also unknown in Egypt, which is identical with that which represents Set. He was the deity of storm, earthquake, and eclipse, and, like Set, we find him identified in the *Historia de las Mexicanos* with the Great Bear, from whence no good thing might come. He typifies coldness, sereness, and sin. Although he is the brother of the sun-god Uitzilopochtli, he is also his mortal enemy. His names Yaotl and Yaomitl, indeed, signify "Enemy" and "Dreaded Enemy." He, too, is represented by a stone, the tepochtli or "wizard stone," from which tempests were believed to arise. He is the terrifying god, the horror by night. Like Set, he is painted black.

It would, indeed, be difficult to find two mythological figures which resemble each other more closely in the majority of their attributes. This resemblance cannot be fortuitous. It must have behind it a common original, whence both of these figures arose.

Compare, too, Isis with the Mexican goddess Ciuacoatl. Isis is usually represented in her statues as carrying the child Horus. As she seeks through the length and breadth of Egypt for Osiris she grieves pitifully, moaning and crying aloud in her woe. A pottery figure of Ciuacoatl in the Uhde Collection in Berlin bears a close resemblance to Isis. She wears a head-dress strikingly reminiscent of that of Isis in her shape of Hathor, and carries an infant. Like Isis, she wanders about crying and moaning.

These by no means exhaust the resemblances between the Egyptian and Mexican pantheons, but space forbids their more exhaustive comparison. Striking similarities also present themselves between the mythical beliefs of the two countries. One of such must suffice. The symbol of the bird and serpent is common to both. Herodotus informs us that the Egyptians believed that the sacred ibis destroyed the serpent. With the Mexicans, as one of their most famous myths alleges, that which relates to the founding of the city of Mexico, the eagle performed a similar office. The cult of the serpent was equally venerated by the Egyptians, Druids, and Mexicans. In a Mexican manuscript the gods are seen dragging the serpent of darkness through the universe precisely as the genii of light towed the serpent Ankh-neteru. But a comparison of Egyptian and American serpent-cults would occupy a volume greatly exceeding this in bulk.

Nor were the similarities between the art and architecture of Mexico and Egypt any less remarkable. The likeness of the Mexican teocalli to the Egyptian pyramid has frequently been commented on. For long these teocallis or " houses of the gods " were believed to have been " high-places " or exaggerated altars only. But recent research has made it clear that many of them were also designed, like the Egyptian pyramids, as the last resting-places of kings. In the district of the Totonacs, to the north of Vera Cruz, many architectural remains of a highly interesting character are encountered. Here the teocalli or pyramidal type of building is frequently crowned by a covered-in temple with a massive roof. The most striking examples found in Mexico are the remains of Teotihuacan and Xochicalco. The former was the religious Mecca of the Nahua or Mexican races, and in its neighbourhood are still to be seen the teocallis of the Sun and Moon, surrounded by extensive burying-grounds where devout Mexicans were laid in the hope that if interred there they would find entrance to the paradise of the Sun. The pyramid of the Moon has a base covering 426 feet, and a height of 137 feet. That of the Sun is of still greater dimensions, with a base of 735 feet, and a height of 203 feet. The base of the pyramid of Cholula, 45 acres, is considerably greater than that of any of the Egyptian pyramids.

Let us compare the Egyptian and Mexican pyramidal structures briefly. The Mexican pyramids, like those of Egypt, had the same (inaccurate) orientation towards the points of the compass, the line through the centres of the structures is roughly that of the astronomical meridian; both were built in grades or " steps," the difference in the case of the Egyptian being that the steps were filled in and the sides rendered smooth, although this was also frequently effected in Mexico and Central America. Both were used as places of sepulture, and their interior arrangements are analogous. Waldeck found near Palenque two pyramids in a perfect state of preservation, square at the base, pointed at the top, their sides forming equilateral triangles. The pyramid of Teotihuacan has an opening 69 feet from its base entering upon a gallery along which egress is only to be had by crawling on hands and knees. This extends inwards on an incline for a distance of 25 feet, and terminates in two sepulchral chambers, each 5 feet square. Lowenstein describing this gallery states that it is " 157 feet long, increasing in height to over 6½ feet as it penetrates the pyramid, the well is over 6 feet square, extending apparently to the base and up to the summit. Other cross-galleries are blocked by debris." This arrangement is almost precisely similar to that of the interior of the Egyptian pyramid of Cheops.

Near Tezcuco is Xochicalco, the Hill of Flowers, a teocalli which one writer at least believes to be a facsimile of the temple hill of Atlantis. The porphyry quarries from which its stones were taken—great blocks some 12 feet in length —are many miles distant. The extraordinarily beautiful

sculpture which adorns its sides has excited universal admiration, but unfortunately it is now a ruin, mere fragments of
its massive stones remaining.

The question now arises, is it possible to associate these
structures with direct Egyptian influence? Assuredly it
is not. They possess a character of their own which makes
it very certain that they were not the result of Egyptian
influence at first-hand. Moreover, it is clear that pyramid
building in Egypt was not originally a thing Egyptian.
Until the reign of King Zoser in the Third Dynasty the tombs
of the Egyptian kings were built of sun-dried bricks which
lined pits in the ground or sand. The stone or granite
pyramid was undoubtedly introduced by a stone-using
people from the West—the people who built cairns and
tumuli, menhirs and dolmens in Spain, France, and Britain.
Professor Elliot Smith shows clearly enough that the dolmen,
a large stone upheld by three other great stones and covered
with an earthen mound, was a burial chamber, and he
believes it to have been a degenerate form of the pyramid.
But if the theory of evolutionary processes is worth anything, it is evidently the earliest form of the pyramid. The
early Egyptians were not a stone-using people to any great
extent, but confined themselves to brick. It was only when
the Iberians, descendants of the Atlanteans, entered Egypt
that stone-building had its rise in that country.

We see, then, that, like most resemblances between
Egyptian and Mexican civilisation, we must look to a common
centre for the origin of the pyramids of both countries
rather than to Egypt as the place of its genesis.

No one can compare Mexican and Egyptian architecture,
art, and social customs without being greatly struck by their
inherent similarities. But these are similarities arising not
from direct influence or immigration. That is, indeed, obvious, not only because of the great lapse of time which
divides these cultures, but from the circumstance that both

were the heirs of a much more ancient culture. The fact that these related civilisations entered their respective spheres one from the east and the other from the west is itself sufficient to make it plain that the common centre which was the parent of both must have had its rise either in North-Western Africa, Western Europe, or in some Atlantic continental area or related areas connected by land-bridge with Europe or Africa, and now submerged. The first hypotheses do not allow for the introduction of the especial type of culture which we have been considering to the American continent. Their only alternative is the Atlantean hypothesis, and when one alternative only remains it must, according to reason, contain the answer to any given problem. We do not know whether the Atlanteans built pyramids or what their art was like. But if analogy—on which the whole basis of archæology rests—is of any avail in the reconstruction of vanished civilisations we can regard their architecture and art as the prototypes of those of Mexico and Egypt.

CHAPTER XV

THE EVIDENCE FROM OLD PERU

SCATTERED over the western slope of the Peruvian Andean range are the architectural remains of a civilisation which must be regarded as one of the most remarkable produced by the aboriginal American race. For many centuries mankind had gradually been advancing in this area to the condition in which it was discovered by the invading Spaniards in 1534, and many of the architectural remains which still exist in Peru are of an antiquity far greater than the foundation of the Incan dynasty which flourished at the coming of Pizarro. Ruined edifices, built of gigantic blocks of stone, and often described as " Cyclopean," must undoubtedly be referred to a period in Peruvian development of which we have not even any legendary knowledge. These are met with throughout the length and breadth of the country, and are known as the remains of the megalithic or Andean period.

Legends relate that when the founders of Peruvian civilisation left the island of Titicaca, the sun-god delivered into their keeping a golden branch which would take root in the earth at the spot where they were destined to dwell and found a centre of enlightenment for the human race. This marvel occurred at Cuzco, afterwards the capital of the Incan dominions. Situated at an altitude of over eleven thousand feet above the level of the sea, the ancient city rose imposingly upon a series of artificial terraces, constructed of immense masses of earth held together by Cyclopean walls, built of extremely hard rocks of great size carried by main force from the quarries of Anduhaylillas, twenty-two miles distant. The Peruvians possessed no draught animals, except the llama, and the blocks must have been dragged from the quarry to the plateau of Cuzco by gangs of labourers. Authorities are agreed that all modern masonry is inferior when compared with that seen in the edifices of Cuzco. The great blocks were first carefully squared, and then joined together by means of a mortise about 1 foot deep by $1\frac{1}{2}$ in diameter, into which a tenon of nearly the same size, hewn out of the upper block, fitted securely. The walls required no mortar to keep them together, for their weight was so great that specific gravity took the place of cement.

Over all towered the mighty Sacsahuaman, or fortress, built on an airy rock which cleaves the meeting rivers of Huatenay and Rodadero. From the town side one might not ascend it, and the sole mode of access was a little path cut in the living rock which overhangs the banks of the Rodadero. The total length of the walls which enclose it is one thousand eight hundred feet, disposed in three great circles, and its bastions and angles of projection and re-entrance resemble those of a modern fortress. It was absolutely impregnable to a force not provided with artillery, and the early Spaniards implicitly believed that the Peruvians had been assisted in its construction by the Father of Evil.

Three entrances gave access to the outer enclosure, and immense blocks of stone were held ever ready to close these up at the first hint of danger. In a round tower in the centre of the citadel were placed the treasures of the Incas, and it was from this that the last descendant of that ill-fated line hurled himself upon the failure of the last native insurrection against the cavaliers of Spain, in which Juan Pizarro lost his life. The hill near this gigantic fortress, the interior works of which are now a heap of ruins, is covered with richly carved blocks of granite which evidently served the purpose of seats, and long galleries ornamented with descending terraces and broken by sculptured niches run round its slopes.

The Temple of the Sun, now converted into a Dominican convent, was situated on a hill 80 feet above the river Huatenay, and was reached by a series of enchanting garden-terraces, filled with the most marvellous designs wrought in solid silver and gold. The very garden implements—hoes, spades, and mattocks—were of solid silver. These facts are vouched for by numerous eye-witnesses, among them Pedro Pizarro himself, and subsequent historians have seen no reason to regard their descriptions as in any way untrustworthy. Models of animals and insects of gold and silver adorned the spacious grounds, and such was the splendour of the surroundings that the entire quarter was known as Coricancha, or the City of Gold. The temple occupies one side of a vast court, called Intipampa, or Field of the Sun. The inner and outer walls, it is said, were covered with sheets of gold, and as evidence of this Squier states that he himself saw in various houses in Cuzco sheets of gold which had been stripped from the gleaming walls of the Temple of the Sun. These, he says, were of the thickness of paper.

The exterior of this famous temple gave an impression of massiveness rather than of grace, and the immense pylons or monoliths which supported the doorway remind one of the Egyptian type of masonry. The interior was profusely ornamented with plates of gold, and in a suitably exalted position was placed a huge plaque of the same precious metal upon which were depicted the features of the deity to whom the fane was dedicated. This was so placed that the beams of the rising sun fell upon it and bathed it in a flood of radiant light. The scintillation of the hundreds of precious stones with which its surface was enriched, according to an eye-witness, made its brilliance almost insupportable, and the atmosphere of mysterious splendour was heightened by the presence of the magnificently attired mummies of the dead Incas which were grouped around this dazzling object. The roof was made from choice woods, but was covered only by a thatching of maize straw.

The utensils in this temple were all of the most precious metals. Twelve large vases of silver held the sacred grain, and even the pipes which conducted the water-supply through the earth were of silver. The splendid altar-piece representing the sun-god fell as booty to one Mancio Serra de Leguicano, a reckless gambler, who lost it on a single throw of the dice. The walls of the Aclahuasi, or House of the Virgins of the Sun, are still standing close at hand for a length of 750 feet. Here the daughters of the Incas were subjected for many years to a rigorous discipline.

Throughout the city of Cuzco extend long reaches of walls of stone cut with a nicety and fitting together with a precision unequalled in any of the ancient structures of Europe or Asia. Many of these have been used as quarries from which to erect more modern buildings, but a large number form the bases upon which later dwellings have arisen, and it is no uncommon thing to see a mansion, the lower courses of which are composed of the original Incan stone walls on which has been superimposed the rubble walls faced with stucco of the modern Peruvian abode. The centre of the aboriginal city was the Huacapata, or great square, now occupied in part by the modern plaza, from which most of the principal streets radiated. Cuzco, like Rome, was built on a series of hills, so that the early architects were obliged to level the declivities, and to form terraces upon which their buildings might rest. These terraces were confined by walls of the " Cyclopean " type—that is, built of stones of irregular sizes, but all fitting into one another with the greatest nicety. To relieve the monotony of these long stretches of masonry the Peruvian builders introduced niches at regular intervals, not unlike the Egyptian pylon doorway in shape—that is, narrower at the top than at the base.   The precision with which these stones are fitted is beyond all praise.   Those which bear up the terrace of the palace of Rocca weigh, many of them, several tons each, and are as hard as granite.   Yet so finely are they fitted that it is said a penknife-blade cannot be introduced between them.   One of them, the famous " Stone of Twelve Angles," is met on each of its dozen sides by another stone, into all of which this fits exactly.   In all of these massive walls there is absolutely no cement, the stones holding together by reason of the marvellous accuracy with which their superficies meet one another.   Some authorities give it as their opinion that the Peruvian masonry is unequalled on the face of the globe for finish, and that the finest needle could not be introduced between the stones which compose some of the walls at Cuzco.

The general design of the ancient Peruvian building was that of a block built round a court, upon which most of the apartments opened.   Many of these were large, and a native historian describes some, of which the remains exist to bear out his statements, as being capable of containing 60 horsemen with room enough to exercise with their lances.   The Huacapata, or great square, was surrounded on three sides by great public buildings for the shelter of the inhabitants in bad weather, each of which was capable of containing several thousand people.

The Aclahuasi, or Convent of the Virgins of the Sun, still exists in the convent of Santa Catalina.   In this edifice dwelt those maidens who were set apart for the service of the sun god, and from whose ranks the brides of the Incas were taken.   If any of them were detected in a love-affair, death instantly followed, and the youth who had rashly disturbed the sanctity of the convent was also doomed to the dreadful doom of being cast from the beetling crags of the

" Gate of Death " at Ollantay-Tampu. Nor did priestly vengeance cease here, for the very village whence the Lothario originated was levelled with the ground as being a nest whence similar vipers might emanate. This conventual establishment is now 750 feet long by from 20 to 25 feet high, and its masonic and architectural finish closely resembles that of the Temple of the Sun. The existing walls show no entrance or opening.

A very fine remnant of Inca architecture is the wall looking on to the square called Pampa Maroni. It has been pierced here and there by modern doorways in its length of 380 feet, and its joints are so smooth that if the faces of the stones were dressed down flat they could hardly be seen at all. In the street of San Agustin a portion of this wall runs for a length of 800 feet, but it is broken at intervals by modern structures. It formed the north-east side of the palaces of the Yupanqui Incas.

Near the remains of the palace of the Inca Rocca were the Yachahuasi, or schools, founded by that ruler. They were plain, unadorned seminaries, and led down to the terraces of the little river Rodadero. Here the amautes, or wise men, taught the infant mind how to read the language of quipus, or knotted cords, the tales of gods and heroes, music, and native engineering, and astrology.

In the vicinity of Cuzco, and especially in that of the Rodadero Hill, an eminence more than half a mile in circumference, and at least 80 feet high, several notable terraces exist. Here is to be seen the immense Piedra Causada, or Tired Stone, of which the native historian Garcilasso speaks as having required 20,000 men to move it, and which, rolling over, killed 300 workmen. This statement is of a piece with much else in the chronicler's rather mendacious " history." The stone weighs probably over 1000 tons, and was certainly never moved by human power. Its upper surface is cut into seats, water reservoirs, niches, and staircases, the object of elaborating which will always remain a mystery. The Rodadero Hill itself was shored up into terraces, and its grooved centre, or sunk pathway, was a favourite resort of the Incan youth, who chased each other through the depression on high days and holidays. Most of the stones which faced this eminence have, however, been carried to the town for modern building purposes. But on the summit of this hill are a number of broad stone-seats cut into the rock, and rising one above the other with the precision of the benches in a Roman amphitheatre. These are known as the Seat of the Inca, and tradition recounts that the three Incas in whose reigns the mighty fortress of Sacsahuaman was constructed came to these thrones carved in the rocky hillside and from that point of vantage were enabled to watch and superintend the construction of the great work of fortification which was gradually rising up on the mountain-side beyond.

The rocks all over the plateau which stretches beyond the fortress of Sacsahuaman are carved into a myriad shapes. Seats and couches — veritable divans some of these—in stone niches, flights of steps, basins for catching rain-water, cut with the precision and accuracy of a sculptor, abound. It would seem as if these Cyclopean masons, their vigour unabated upon the completion of the great mountain citadel, had rioted in their art, and had revelled in the execution of countless tasks which might have appalled an army of skilled European artificers equipped with the best and most modern tools. There are traces of many small shrines on this expanse, which probably served as oracles.

The great Incan fortress of Ollantay-Tampu, situated some forty-five miles north of Cuzco, was built to defend the Valley of the Yucay from the inroads of the ferocious Chinchos Indians, who dwelt in the impenetrable forests watered by the Amazon and its tributaries. The immensity of the walls, which are built for the most part of red porphyry and average 25 feet in height, render this ancient fortress comparable to the mightiest structures of antiquity in the Old World. Squier compared Ollantay-Tampu to the castles of the Rhine. The comparison holds good only inasmuch as the Peruvian fortress, like the more graceful strongholds of Germany, is perched upon a dizzy height, which on one side overhangs a deep and rapid river. Stupendous walls zigzag from point to point, from angle to angle, of a huge cliff, and seem more like the work of some modern master of the art of fortification than the Cyclopean labour of the countless throngs of dark-skinned toilers who reared it long ago at the behest of their celestial ruler, the Inca. The fortress proper is a long, low building of two stories in height, loopholed and turreted. Above this tower the walls of another fortress, or rather outwork, and at points above, below, at every possible elevation, are placed round towers of stone of varying sizes, all of which are provided with many port-holes, so that a heavy flight of arrows might be brought to bear upon an approaching enemy. This salient outwork embraces a series of terraces, which, because of their peculiar and gigantic structure, are world-famous. The road to these leads through an ancient gateway grooved for a portcullis. The terraces are ascended on one side by steps, and on the other by an inclined plane over half a mile in length, over which the gigantic stones of which the fortress is composed were dragged by sweating bands of conquered provincials. Many of the immense stones used in the construction of the fortress still remain upon this road, abandoned, perhaps, by reason of flaws or other unfitness. This plane is guarded at intervals by square stone buildings, like block-houses, and is supported by an embankment of stone inclining inwards and more than 60 feet high.

The first line of defence climbs the mountain-side, zigzagging from point to point, until it meets a precipice with a sheer fall of 1000 feet. This wall, about 25 feet in height, is built of unfaced stone, cemented on each side, and provided with an inner shelf upon which the defenders might stand. Within this wall is a concretion of huddled buildings, doorways, isolated blocks of porphyry, terraces of vast design, and several fine stairways, the stone for all of which was quarried some seven miles away, in a spot upwards of 3000 feet above the valley, and dragged up the steep slopes of Ollantay by sheer human force. A number of the stones which lie scattered about are hewn into shape, and ready to be fitted, and many are mortised and clamped to permit them to be joined to others. Some of these blocks approach 20 feet in length, by 5 feet broad and 4 feet deep, and are perfectly squared and admirably polished, and the joints where they meet one another are scarcely perceptible. Six of these mighty blocks, which seem as if quarried by Titans, support a terrace placed at an inclination against it. The faces of these are imperfectly polished, and some are not even properly hewn, showing that the work of facing them was never completed, and probably hurriedly abandoned. But the greatest of the monolithic marvels which Ollantay has to show are the " Tired Stones," enormous blocks, lying on the inclined plane leading to the fortress, as if abandoned by the masons, who found it impossible to drag such monstrous burdens up the face of the hill. One of them is 21 feet 5 inches long, by 15 feet broad, and is partially embedded in the soil, into which it must have sunk by reason of its own weight.

I have described these remains of Peruvian grandeur at some length, because in my estimation they preserve the atmosphere of what I believe Atlantis to have resembled better perhaps than any other remains, American, European, or Asiatic. These ruins are frequently of " Cyclopean " character, especially those of the plateau of Lake Titicaca, built, say archæologists, by the prehistoric " Andeans," who developed their civilisation long before the days of the

Incan dynasties. On this plateau was situated the " city " of Tiahuanaco, on the southern side of the lake, built at a level 13,000 feet above the sea, occupying nearly half an acre in extent, and constructed of enormous megalithic blocks of trachytic rock. The great doorway, carved out of a single block of rock, is 7 feet in height, by 13½ feet wide, and 1½ feet thick. The upper part of this massive portal is carved with symbolic figures. In the centre is a figure in high relief, the head surrounded by solar rays, and in each hand a sceptre, the end of which terminates in the head of a condor. This figure is flanked on either side by three tiers of kneeling suppliants, each of whom is winged, and bears a similar sceptre. Elsewhere are mighty blocks of stone, some 36 feet long, remains of enormous walls, standing monoliths, and in earlier times colossal statues were seen on the site. When the Spanish conquerors arrived no tradition remained regarding the founders of these structures, and their origin still remains a mystery, but that they represent the remains of some mighty prehistoric kingdom is practically admitted.

The greatest mystery of all regarding the ruins at Tiahuanaco is the selection of the site. For what reason did the prehistoric Andeans build here ? The surroundings are totally unsuited to the raising of such edifices, and the tableland upon which they are placed is at once desolate and difficult of access. The snow-line is contiguous, vegetation will not grow, and breathing at such a height is no easy matter. There is, however, reason to believe that the plateau has risen considerably since it was occupied by the Andeans.

Now whence did the megalithic people who built Tiahuanaco come ? Brinton, Squier, and Markham believed them to be indigenous, but modern archæology will not countenance a hypothesis so narrow and unlikely. Some traditions state that they came from the south—that is, from the direction of Bolivia : others say that they came from the

north by sea. Probably both are correct. The present
Republic of Argentina was at a remote period covered by a
vast, partially land-locked sea, and beside the shores of this
the ancestors of the later Peruvians, the Quichua-Aymara,
probably dwelt as fishers or fowlers. But the earlier stock,
the Andeans, almost certainly arrived, after the fall of
Antilia, on the shores of Brazil, and working their way by
degrees up the Amazon, arrived at last in Peru. But has
Peru any " Atlantean " legends ?

Like other races, the Peruvians had their own version
of the Flood. A certain man took his llama to a good
feeding-place, but the beast moaned and would not eat, and
on its master questioning it, assured him that in five days the
sea would rise and engulf the earth. The man, alarmed,
asked if there was no way of escape, and the animal advised
him to climb to the top of a high mountain, taking with
him food sufficient for five days. The Flood came as pre-
dicted, and after another five days the water fell, leaving only
this one man alive.

This cataclysm was followed by a peculiar incident.
On a high mountain-top appeared five eggs, from one of
which a demi-god Paricaca emerged. Now, as all students
of symbolism know, the egg is the same as the fertility pot,
which in turn is the equivalent of the Ark in which the
universal Noah embarks during the season of world-flood.
I believe these Peruvian " eggs " to symbolise the great
arks or ships of the Atlanteans washed up by the Flood
upon some mountain-top in Peru. From the ark of the
Flood humanity is, as it were, rehatched and born anew.
All races appear to have regarded the Flood as a re-
birth, as we shall see in the chapter which deals with that
phenomenon.

Now, as we saw in the chapter dealing with the geological
evidence, a theory exists which has for its basis the statement that the Peruvians were Iberians who entered Peru

from North Africa by way of a still existing land-bridge. It is, however, much more probable that their resemblance to the Iberian peoples results from the common origin of both from the Atlantean race. This is not to say that the Peruvian people as a whole were Atlantean or Iberian any more than were the races of Central America or Mexico. But that the ruling class was Iberian or Atlantean in origin admits of little question. The Quichuas, tradition tells us, were originally " fair," that is, they were not so dark as the native races, and had blue eyes, and sometimes auburn hair. Even to-day their descendants are considerably lighter in hue than the surrounding stocks. Moreover their architecture, as described above, bears the closest possible resemblance to that of ancient Libya and Egypt. The pylon doorways, the polygonal masonry observed in certain examples, the entire form and structure of their mighty megalithic monuments approximate so closely to the earlier architecture of the Old World, to that of Crete and Carthage as well as that of North Africa, as to leave no possibility of doubt regarding the original relationship of their forms with the structures of Peru.

Let us see how far Peruvian myth reveals an Atlantean connection. We find that, as in the case of the story of Deucalion and Pyrrha, the Greek Noah and his wife, stones in Peru were capable of becoming men. We are told that when Cuzco was attacked by the Chancas Indians, one of its defenders erected stones to which he attached shields and weapons so that they should appear to represent so many warriors. The hero Pachacutic, hard pressed for aid, cried to them with such vehemence to come to his assistance that they became men and rushed to help him.

The Peruvians had at least one tale referring to a sunken island. The water-goddess, who presided over Lake Titicaca, became angry with Huaina Ccapac, the eleventh Inca, who had determined to build on an island in the lake a shrine to the god Yatiri or Pachacamac. He accordingly raised a temple on the island of Titicaca itself. But the deity in whose honour it had been built refused to vouchsafe any reply to his worshippers or priests. Huaina then commanded that the shrine should be transferred to the island of Apiuguela. But still there was no response. He then inaugurated a temple on the island of Paopiti, and lavished upon it many sacrifices. But the offended tutelary goddess of the lake, irritated beyond endurance by this continued invasion of her domain, lashed the waters into such a frenzy of storm that the island and the shrine which covered it disappeared beneath the waves, and were never thereafter beheld by mortal eye.

The Peruvian god Pariacaca was a deity of cataclysm. He formed the lake called after him in three days and nights by hurling rain and hail at one of the local gods. Another myth of the Peruvians speaks of twin-gods, Apocatequil and Piguerão, the former of whom was said to have brought the Peruvian race " out of darkness into the light of day." He also was a deity of thunder. The statue of Apocatequil, along with those of his mother and brother, were erected on a mountain. Always we find in these myths the mountain or hill, and the holy place on which statues are raised, as in Plato's story of Atlantis. Indeed there seems to be no escape from it in America.

But the worship of the Peruvians shows very clearly that at one time they must have dwelt in an oceanic area. It is significant that the inland tribes looked upon the sea as a menacing deity, whilst the people of the coast reverenced it as a benevolent spirit, calling it Mama-cocha or " Mother-sea," since it yielded them a prolific harvest of fish. They worshipped the whale, fairly common on that coast, and even the lesser fish were adored by them. It was believed that the prototype of each species of fish dwelt in the upper world and sent his servants into the deep for the use of man.

In the legends of Viracocha, a great culture-hero and rain-god, who is similar to the Mexican Quetzalcoatl, we read that again and again he sent terrible storms and cataclysms upon mankind, for their sins against him. He finally forgave them, and taught them the arts of life, and in the end disappeared into the ocean, like Quetzalcoatl, and, like him, was thought of as coming from the region of the dawn.

The Canaris Indians of Canaribamba in Quito, had a myth of deluge and destruction closely resembling those of Central America and Mexico. They told how, when a great flood evertook them, twin brothers fled to a very high mountain called Huacaquan, and as the waters rose the hill ascended simultaneously, so that they escaped drowning. When the flood had abated, they built a small house in a valley and lived on herbs. Eventually they married " bird-women "—that is, women dressed in the plumage of birds.

Thonapa, a divine personage, was so badly treated by the people of Yamquisapa in the province of Alla-suyu, that he laid a curse upon them, and caused a lake to appear where their town stood. The people of this locality worshipped an idol in the form of a woman on the top of a high hill Cachapucara. This idol Thonapa detested, so he burnt it and destroyed the hill on which it stood. He changed an entire concourse of Indians into stones because they refused to hearken to his preaching. The people of Tuja-manacu were so bent upon pleasure that he treated them in a similar fashion. Like Quetzalcoatl he disappeared into the sea.

Pariacaca, the demi-god who had emerged from one of the eggs or " arks," as related above, came, like Poseidon, to a hill-country, where he was insulted by the people. In wrath he sent a flood upon them so that their village was destroyed. In the neighbourhood he met a very beautiful girl, Choque Suso (the Cleito of Plato ?) weeping bitterly.

He inquired of her why she wept, and she told him that the maize-crop was dying for lack of water. He fell in love with her, and assured her that if she would return his passion he would provide the much needed water. She consented to his suit, and he irrigated the whole land, as did Poseidon in Atlantis. Pariacaca eventually turned his wife into a statue.

This myth agrees almost in every detail with that of Plato. We have in both cases the hill, the finding of the beautiful girl, the making of an irrigation zone, and finally the appearance of the loved one as a stone image or idol. Could the resemblance be closer? Note, too, that the cataclysms alluded to in these myths are invariably brought about by the wickedness or careless love of pleasure of the human race.

A fish-god, Pachacamac, had a great temple built to him on the right bank of the River Lurin, on the coast of the Chinca country. Here a great mound of stone and adobe rises to a height of 200 feet. This temple is built on three wide terraces with a platform on the summit. Here the god spoke oracularly to the people, who came from great distances to consult him. Miguel Astete, one of the Spanish conquerors, says that in 1533 an idol of wood was found here in a large, well-painted building, and was summarily destroyed. As we shall see in the next chapter, this building was undoubtedly of the Atlantean type.

CHAPTER XVI

THE GEOGRAPHY AND TOPOGRAPHY OF ATLANTIS

IN my remarks with reference to the plan of the city of Carthage in Chapter II and its resemblance to that of Atlantis as described by Plato, I have already alluded to the circumstance that the design of the Atlantean capital appears to have been copied far and wide. It is a fact well known to archæologists that the plan and outline of the great cities of antiquity were very frequently carried out in their colonial settlements, and that the tendency was to model them as closely as possible upon the mother-city. Thus more than one of the cities of Southern Yucatan were modelled upon the older cities of Guatemala; the cities of southern Egypt bore a close resemblance to those of the Delta; Rome is said to have been modelled upon Troy, Corcyra upon Corinth, and so forth. It seems, then, not at all improbable that many sites may have been erected according to the plan of the Atlantean metropolis.

We may recollect that Atlantis was encircled by several zones of land and water. Now one of the most common plans of the early settlements in those Atlantic regions, which were probably in touch with Atlantis in early times, is that of the settlement located on an island within an island— or when, owing to the situation, that was impossible, a site enclosed by several zones of land and water. Hanno, the Carthaginian voyager, when speaking of certain ape-like people whom he encountered upon the west coast of Africa during his famous voyage, states that they dwelt in a village situated " on an island within an island," showing that this type of zone-surrounded site characterised an early African community-plan.

Recent researches in connection with the ancient forts of the Aran Islands, six miles from the coast of Galway, are illuminating in an Atlantean connection. In the ancient traditions of the people of the mainland they figure as the home of giants and workers in magic, and in later legend they are identified with the enchanted western isles of Hy Brasil and Tir-nan-Og. Many ancient customs are preserved in the islands, the inhabitants still using the coracle boat described by Himilco, another Carthaginian traveller, 2400 years ago.

The salient thing regarding these island fortifications so far as they concern us is that they were undoubtedly built upon the Atlantean plan. One of them, Dun Aengusa or the Fort of Angus, on the island of Inismor, stands on the edge of a cliff 300 feet above the Atlantic. Outward from the centre the ruins consist of a strong oval enclosure or citadel, measuring internally 150 by 130 feet, and two concentric outer walls, which never formed a complete circle, but ended on the edge of the cliff. On the tops of these walls are terraces reached by flights of steps. The fort is built of large blocks of local limestone from 3 to 7 feet long.

Another similar structure, Dubh Cathan or the Black Fort, also in Inismor, is situated on a promontory 400 feet above the sea.

The most recent investigators are inclined to assign these erections to the Bronze Age. Tradition states that they were inhabited by the Firbolgs, who, after being expelled by the Milesians, wandered in Scotland for many years, eventually returning to Ireland. Now the Firbolgs were the pre-Gaelic people of Ireland, the Iberians, that is the same race as the Azilian-Tardenoisians who seem to have come from Atlantis.

PLATE XII.

The Citadel of Dun Ængusa, Aran Islands.

(Photo by Dr G. Fogerty, R.N.)

The buildings in question are almost certainly debased examples of the Atlantean style of architecture. This is amply demonstrated by the two outer walls, the central tower, and the height on which the whole is perched. Atlantean town-planning appears to have insisted upon three things—a citadel upon a lofty eminence, ring upon ring of defending walls, and, lastly, alternate zones of land and water. But it must be manifest that in the case of such forts as those of the Aran Isles, standing as they did at a great height above the wild Atlantic waste, the latter disposition was unnecessary. Or perhaps in the upheaval of society which followed the break-up of Atlantis the engineering knowledge essential to the making of great canals or moats was lost, and only the recollection of the general plan remained in the consciousness of the race.

In any event the frequency with which buildings on this plan occur in the Atlantic area renders it impossible that the design could have been of purely fortuitous occurrence there. Says Mr E. W. Lynam of the British Museum: " The Aran forts form the western end of that long chain of forts which has its other end in Thessaly and Mycenæ." Quite so: or rather I should regard their eastern and northern examples as two arms of development radiating from lost Atlantis.

Similar to these structures, indeed in many cases one and the same with them, are the brochs of Scotland and the nuraghe of Sardinia. Describing the latter, Mr T. Eric Peet, the author of *Rough Stone Monuments*, writes: " All the nuraghi stand in commanding situations overlooking large tracts of country, and the more important a position is from a strategical point of view, the stronger will be the nuraghe which defends it." " In the Balearic Isles," says Mr Donald A. Mackenzie, " are towers called talayots which ' resemble rather closely,' in Peet's opinion, the nuraghi of Sardinia. The architecture of the talayots, the nuraghi, and the brochs resemble that of the beehive tombs of Mycenæ."

Once more we must stress the racial origin of the people who built these structures. The men who raised the nuraghi and talayots were certainly Iberians, the " Mediterranean race " of Sergi. So were the Picts who built the Scottish brochs. These latter are capacious, round towers, and are usually erected on promontories jutting into the sea. Many of them have or had surrounding walls. All are of the debased type of Atlantean architecture.

Starting, then, from a knowledge of the Atlantean design as described in Plato, we find that is reflected not only in that of Carthage, but in numerous other ancient sites scattered over the length and breadth of those areas where we might expect to find architectural remains approximating to the Atlantean model—on the one hand along the entire stretch of the Mediterranean, and on the other along the sea-coasts of the Western Atlantic, to Britain and Ireland. It will not serve to regard them as arising in historical succession from east to west. The Iberians, the builders of these venerable monuments, did not originate in the eastern region of the Mediterannean, so that it is impossible to regard that sphere as the starting-point of their architectural history.

Nor is it contended that all of these structures approximate with exactitude to the original Atlantean model. In certain cases only some of its tendencies appear, but, as in the case of tradition, we can fill up the gaps by analogical methods. For example, we find fragments of the legend of Godiva in India which piece in so accurately with the English version of the story that we know they must at one time have belonged to it. The inference is that both versions of the tale owe their origin to an older and more complete version. So it is with the architectural model of old Atlantis : we find its fragments and memories scattered

PLATE XIII.

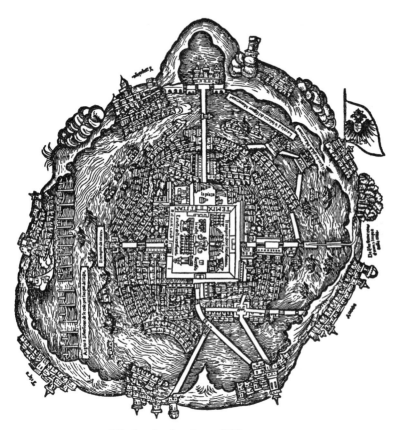

Mexico in the time of Montezuma.

over the coasts of the Mediterranean and the Atlantic for thousands of miles. What one fragment lacks in certain details the other exhibits, and the resemblance of all as well as the fitting together of the broken pieces of the puzzle carry us back with unerring precision to the original prototype as described by Plato.

The question now arises: Do we find in America any trace of this Atlantean style of architecture? Assuredly we do. The plan of Mexico-Tenochtitlan, the Aztec prototype of Mexico City which illustrates the *Letters of Cortes* to the Emperor Charles V, bears a startling resemblance to Plato's description of Atlantis. Mexico was built in the midst of a lake. Here we see the zones of land and water, represented by the mainland, the causeways which cross and recross the lake, and the numerous canals which flow round the great central pyramid of Uitzilopochtli, the high-place, analogous to the Temple of Poseidon. The locality, too, whence the Aztecs were believed to have come, and known as Aztlan, " Place of the Flamingo People," was, as depicted in the maps of the Aztecs, a place of similar character, situated in a lake and surrounded by walls.

The description in the preceding chapter of the Cyclopean structures of Peru undoubtedly assists the belief in the Atlantean character of Incan architecture, with the use of vast blocks of stone, its huge fortresses like those of Sacsahuaman and Ollantay, perched upon the almost inaccessible crags of steep declivities. Moreover, these latter are built of a red stone similar in character to that employed by the Atlanteans. The plan of the Peruvian fortresses is undoubtedly based on the Atlantean model. Here we have the circular or semi-circular walls, the central citadel, with the high or holy place in the midst. Add to this the description of such sites in numerous American myths and legends, and little more evidence is required to assure us of the precision of this view.

Again we have at least one instance of a Peruvian shrine being built upon an island in the midst of a lake—that referred to in the legend of Lake Titicaca.

In Mexico and Central America we also find traces of this particular type of architecture. The great generality of the Kus or pyramid-temples found so frequently in the latter region are built on artificial mounds of considerable height. In Mexico certain hills and mountains were sacred to the maize-goddess, Coatlicue, and that such a mountain actually existed in the vicinity of Tollan, the city of the Toltecs, is proved by the statement of Sahagun. The figure of the goddess was placed on this height, and her son Uitzilopochtli, who is in some of the manuscripts depicted as a species of Atlas upholding one of the world-directions, was also worshipped there. The situation is reminiscent of the Atlantean tale regarding Cleito—to which the name Coatlicue bears a suspicious resemblance—and Atlas, to whose name the first portion of Uitzilopochtli's name also bears a similarity. Here we find Coatlicue = Cleito, and Uitzil = Atlas. The degree and nature of the corruption is what might be expected from those who spoke the Mexican tongue. Once more we encounter the combination of the goddess, the sacred mountain, and the sun. The mountain was with the less civilised races of Mexico the natural pyramid, and the farther north we penetrate in the American continent the more universally does it take the place of the Maya stone pyramid, until, when we enter the region of the less sophisticated North American tribes in the comparatively level Mississippi area, we find them making up for the lack of natural eminences by raising pyramids of earth unfaced with stone.

Was the pyramid in Egypt, Central America, and Mexico, then, but a later reminiscence of the original Atlantean sacred hill ? Everything seems to point to this. It may be objected that in some parts of Mexico and Egypt it was

PLATE XIV.

Aztlan, the Original Home of the Aztecs.

(From a Mexican MS.)

Ruins in MacElmo's Cañon, Colorado.

unaccompanied by the zones of land and water characteristic of the Atlantean model. But this objection is readily overcome when we recollect the waterless and arid conditions which obtain in the countries in question, where the environment rendered a faithful adherence to the Atlantean design out of the question.

Pyramid, broch, and nuraghe, then, appear to be but diverse manifestations of the one original model of the Atlantean central height on which stood the Temple of Poseidon. But it is to be remarked that wherever these are found they are either erected on a natural height or else such an acclivity is artificially provided. The pyramid is, indeed, the sacred hill of Atlantis. That it is not surmounted by a temple in Egypt is explained by the circumstance that though in Central America we find shrines on the summits of pyramids, in Mexico and Peru we find them replaced by mere flimsy erections of timber. There is also proof that on the earliest pyramids in Egypt such shrines were superposed, but the comparative ease with which they were reached by robbers occasioned their incorporation at a later stage in the pyramid itself. Alternatively the broch or nuraghe is merely a development of the Atlantean shrine frequently situated on a natural height, which thus took the place of the pyramid. We see, then, how in different regions and under different conditions the Atlantean hill and shrine evolved into two quite separate but distinctly traceable forms.

We may now pass on to the consideration of the latitude of the continent of Atlantis. M. Termier says that we " must not even consider " this problem. Doubtless he is right, but little harm can be done if we debate its former whereabouts in a spirit of such free controversy as is not in any way hampered by dogmatic assertion.

I believe the main continental mass of Atlantis to have occupied substantially the position claimed for the Eocene continent by Mr J. Starke Gardner in *Popular Science* of July 1878. This location is still marked on maps and charts, which show deep-sea soundings as "Dolphin's Ridge," after the findings of the U.S. ship *Dolphin*, which took soundings in that locality.

This ridge, the last remaining portion of which is the Azores group, is connected on its southern side by a longer submarine spit or peninsula with South America, and this may account for the presence of the Andean and Incan civilisations there, and for their differentiation from those of Mexico and Central America. From this submarine spit, almost at the point of its connection with the South American mass, there branches off another ridge connecting with the West African island of St Paul's. Between Dolphin's Ridge and Madeira there is no very vast distance, and the probability is that both were linked up at no very distant date, geologically speaking, by a land-bridge, or by islands, with Spain and Africa.

An American warship doing useful peace work has recently made a journey from Newport, Rhode Island, to Gibraltar, and as it passed over the sea it took soundings of the depths, and was able to make an accurate chart of 3200 miles of the bed of the Atlantic.

This was done by means of a new sounding device known as the tonic depth-finder, invented by Mr Harvey Hayes of the United States Navy. It is a marvellous instrument, and will in four minutes make a more accurate sounding than has hitherto been possible in three hours.

A sound impulse is sent out from a steel disc in the bottom of the vessel, and this sound-wave is echoed back from the bottom of the sea. By timing the journey of the wave and its echo the depth can be exactly determined; and when a continuous series of soundings is taken as the vessel passes across the sea, a chart of the ocean-bed can be drawn, showing with minute accuracy its heights and depths.

PLATE XV.

A Peruvian Pyramid or Huaca.

El Castillo, Chichen-Itza, a Central American Pyramid.

American Pyramids.

So convinced was the American Government of the value of the tonic depth-finder that they equipped the destroyer *Stewart* with it, and sent it on a trial journey across the Atlantic. The apparatus, says an official report, worked perfectly throughout the trip. About 900 soundings were taken for depths varying between 9 and 3200 fathoms, the greatest depth being nearly four miles. The expedition revealed that directly off the Atlantic coast from Newport the ocean bed dips practically straight down to a depth of 2750 fathoms, or over 3 miles, and at that depth it undulates like a great plateau almost as far as the Azores.

Recent volcanic disturbances in the bed of the Atlantic ocean have also given scientists food for furious thought. The result of quite recent soundings taken by the Western Telegraph Company have sent a thrill of surprise throughout the civilised world. A vessel belonging to this company was searching (August 1923) for a lost telegraph cable which had been laid twenty-five years before, and the officers of the company found to their astonishment in taking soundings at the exact spot where it had been laid down that *the surface of the ocean-bed there had risen during that time by nearly two and a quarter miles* ! In view of a fact so striking the scoffer may perhaps find it necessary calmly to review his repeated assertion that no movement has taken place in the bed of the Atlantic Ocean, and it seems to me that this late evidence fully upholds the contention of those eminent geologists who have stated that the ocean-bed of the Atlantic has risen and sunk not once but many times in the course of geological history.

I will refrain from forcing or straining the natural conclusion. Such facts as I have laid before the reader are far more eloquent than any halting advocacy of mine.

Dolphin's Ridge, then, I accept as the site of lost Atlantis. But, as I have said before, I also believe that it was connected by an insular chain with Antilia, a mass similar in size, the remains of which are the Antilles group, where an analogous civilisation flourished until a much later period.

The shape of Dolphin's Ridge on the chart is a long oval, having a considerable bulge on its north-western side. The Azores are situated on its extreme eastern " coast." Plato tells us that " the whole country was very lofty and precipitous on the side of the sea, but the country immediately about, and surrounding the city, was a level plain, itself surrounded by mountains which descended toward the sea." I agree with Donnelly that " one has but to look at the profile of the Dolphin's Ridge " as revealed by the deep-sea soundings of the *Challenger* . . . to see that this is a faithful description of that precipitous elevation. " The surrounding mountains " which sheltered the plain from the north are represented in the present peaks of the Azores.

On 14th February 1909 a communication appeared in *The Times,* pointing out that both in outline and detail the prehistoric civilisation of Crete corresponded to Atlantis as described by Plato. " The disappearance of the island corresponds to what archæology tells us of the utter collapse of the empire of Knossos, followed by the replacement even of Cretan sailors by Phœnician at Egyptian ports," says Mr F. K. Hoare, writing in the *Westminster Gazette* of 11th October 1919. " After all, in nine hundred years in an unhistorical age a collapse so sensational might well have been taken rather too literally."

The facts of Cretan history, however, do not at all agree with Plato's story. In the first place, the downfall of Cretan civilisation took place about 1200 B.C., or about the period of the Twentieth Dynasty in Egypt, so that it is unlikely that only 600 years later Egyptian priests should have assured a Greek traveller that the epoch of the disappearance of Atlantis (if Crete were Atlantis) went back nine thousand years.

I rather tend to a conclusion which otherwise explains

the resemblances between Crete and Atlantis as set forth by the writer in *The Times*. This conclusion is almost the converse of his argument that Crete was the "fabled" Atlantis, with the story of which it had become mythologically confused. It is that Cretan civilisation was modelled upon that of Atlantis. The resemblances are strong. The palace of Knossos stands like the city of Atlantis upon a level plain, surrounded by mountains, but there are no "zones of land and water" in this instance, although the vast and ingenious system of drainage unearthed at Knossos might possibly approximate to these. The bull seems to have been sacred as in Atlantis, and the large arena at Knossos was almost certainly used for bull-fights. There was no race-course as in Atlantis, the horse being unknown in ancient Crete until near the conclusion of its existence. But there is no doubt that after the downfall of their civilisation the Cretans, augmented by other racial elements, invaded the mainland of Greece, and this may have given rise to the idea in the Greek mind that Greece was invaded by Atlanteans.

The theory that Crete was a colony of Atlantis is greatly assisted by the circumstance that the Cretans were largely of that Iberian race which undoubtedly emanated from Atlantis. Here we find isolated in the Mediterranean a civilisation which passed away at least four hundred years before Hellenic culture awakened. It had trading relations with Egypt, to which, however, it owed only small cultural debts. Its people were of a race which, we have seen, was partly Iberian. They worshipped a goddess who was connected with the serpent, like the Mexican Coatlicue, whom she markedly resembles in details of costume. Like Coatlicue, too, she was closely connected with sea-shells, many of which were offered up to her as votive objects. Pottery figurines were made of both goddesses, and these objects have a general likeness. Vast tanks were found in the vicinity of the palace. Lastly, in the celebrated labyrinth the rites of some secret religion like that of Osiris, or the Cabiri, probably took place.

If we admit that Atlantean influence survived in the building of Carthage, and in the much earlier Egyptian forms of architecture, it is not surprising that we should also find reminiscences of it in the remains of Cretan culture.

The more likely hypothesis, then, would seem to be that Crete was colonised by a people of Iberian stock deeply imbued with Atlantean reminiscences. Early Minoan civilisation dates roughly from about 3400 B.C. We have no Minoan legends to afford us a horizon as to where this people had dwelt in the interval between the submergence of the Atlantean continent and the date given above. They were isolated, a civilised island contiguous to semi-savage coasts. Egypt was the nearest cultured community. They did not come thence. Whence they did come I am not prepared to say ; nor in the present condition of archæological knowledge can any man venture an opinion. But we know that the Iberian stock which colonised Crete, bringing with it civilising influences, found there a race approximating to the Hellenic Greeks, among which fair and rufous types predominated. An ordinary female type was that of a woman with dark reddish hair and sharp, fine features, such as is often seen to-day in the north of Scotland. The clothes worn by the Cretan ladies resembled very closely those in fashion in Europe some years ago—a many-flounced, bell-shaped skirt and a sort of jacquette. Over the upper part of the skirt was worn on ceremonial occasions a short apron like that used by Freemasons, on which similar designs were sewn. The entire Cretan civilisation was obviously a thing introduced from elsewhere, the fag-end of an old and almost decadent culture. Can it be that a last spur or island of the Atlantean continent survived until about 3500 B.C., and that its inhabitants, sailing from catastrophe (ships had then been ploughing the Mediterranean for 1500 years) and undesirous of settling on the savage and inhospitable coasts of Spain or Italy, held eastward until they came upon the island of Crete, only partially occupied by a people amenable to culture, where they could be safe to carry on the civilisation of their ancestors without fear of intrusion or invasion ?

Moreover, tradition, stronger than a thousand generations, has given its unanimous verdict in the legends of a score of nations that the ancient land of Atlantis was, as its very name implies, situated without the Pillars of Hercules, and not within these mythical boundaries. This alone disposes of the belief that Crete came in a later day to be regarded as the Atlantis of Plato. Nor could the alleged dimensions of the island-continent as described by him have been in any way connected with a legend based on such a belief. In my opinion Atlantis was credited with such vast dimensions because of a confused folk-memory that the insular chain which connected it with Antilia stretched for thousands of miles across the Atlantic Ocean.

I would suggest that no city or civilised state of Atlantis existed at the period alluded to by Plato—9600 B.C. But I do believe that the comparatively rude colonists who reached Europe at that date, and which were represented by the Azilian-Tardenoisians, were reinforced from the ancient island-continent whence they came, so that when at last the city of Atlantis did arise, the news of its foundation was spread far and wide through uncivilised Europe. There were certainly cities in Egypt in pre-dynastic times about 6000 B.C., and if we allow a thousand years for the spread of the Atlantean civilisation to the Nile-land, no great stretching of the probabilities is required to date the founding of Atlantis at not later than 7000 B.C.

This of course does not mean that there did not previously exist on the same site a large settlement of Azilian-Tardenoisian character by no means of a backward or barbarian character, so that the city of Atlantis may well have had a background of antiquity extending into the past for another two thousand years or more.

The memory of such a city as Atlantis may grow dim in the human mind, but that our race could quite lose all recollection of the earliest civic community in its history is to ask too much from common intelligence. The tale of its pyramids and palaces must for thousands of years have been handed down from generation to generation of the rude peoples of Europe until it became at last a glowing and golden legend, stimulating the imagination of thousands, and remaining as a deathless if unwritten Iliad. Troy vanished, and men in after ages thought it had never been, until the vision and enthusiasm of a Schliemann brought it to light once again. And let it be remembered that the man who justified his dreams of Troy to the confusion of a thousand scoffers entertained as firm a belief in the existence of a submerged Atlantis. Did Britain sink beneath the waves, did London vanish in cataclysm, would not the recollection of such a world-throe persist for untold ages after the perishable records of the present day had long been unavailable to men ? Who can doubt it ? Who can question that the saga of London's passing would give rise to as great a future controversy as that which still rages around the memory of Atlantis, that earliest metropolis of the world ?

CHAPTER XVII

THE FLOOD

IT has more than once been argued that the Biblical and pagan accounts of the Deluge retain a memory of the great cataclysm by which Atlantis perished. Before we venture any opinion as to the probability of this, let us first briefly examine the more important accounts which deal with what is popularly known as " the Flood " with a view to finding therein such evidence as would seem to connect them in any way with the Atlantean catastrophe.

The account of the Deluge given in chapters vi to viii of Genesis is too widely known to require description. It tells us that the degeneracy and corruptness of the first civilised race had so grieved the Creator that He had resolved upon its total destruction by the agency of a deluge. That the divine or heavenly race had become degenerate through intermarriage with the earthly denizens of the world—that " the sons of God (supernatural beings) saw the daughters of men that they were fair ; and they took them wives of all which they chose," precisely as did Poseidon and his sons, and that " there were giants (Titans) in the earth in those days "—all circumstances absolutely paralleled in the Atlantis legend.

Now it has been abundantly proved by Assyriologists of experience that the Deluge story as given in Genesis has a very intimate connection with that set forth at considerable length in the Babylonian myth of Gilgamesh, deciphered from the cuneiform text inscribed on tablets of clay found in the palace library of Assurbanipal at Nineveh. Gilgamesh, a hero who resembles Hercules in his attributes, is smitten by a fell disease, and is induced to seek his ancestor, Ut-napishtim, the Babylonian Noah, in a distant and semi-supernatural country with a view to being relieved of his affliction. In the course of conversation the patriarch acquaints him with the story of the Deluge. He tells Gilgamesh how he constructed an ark at the behest of the god Ea, the Lord of Waters, god of the primeval deep, the founder of Babylonian culture, a figure almost identical with Poseidon. A terrible account of the Flood follows, and the work of the gods of thunder and storm is picturesquely related. Even the divinities themselves are alarmed. But the ark with its cargo of human beings and animals survives the fury of the elements. Mountain and plain were devastated, the archangels of the abyss wrought destruction, the surface of the earth was broken up. Here we do not find a mere flooding of the earth as in Genesis, but—and the Babylonian is by far the older account—the total destruction of a large portion of it. " Humanity was returned to the mud," " like to the race of fishes, men are filling the sea "; " water-spouts descend with frightful violence from the heavens," " *no continent appeared on the waste of waters* " ; such are the phrases we encounter. At last the ark stranded on the mountain of Nizir. Ut-napishtim then loosed a dove, which returned ; then a swallow, which also came back ; and, lastly, a raven, which did not. In the end the god Bel released Ut-napishtim and his family from the ark, and told him that he would " reside afar at the mouth of the river."

This account tells us that Gilgamesh was ruler of Erech in Babylonia and that other human beings were resident there, so it is clear that the tale was not intended by the Babylonian priests to apply to the destruction of the whole earth, or to Babylonia, but to some distant portion of the world. In order to reach the home of Ut-napishtim Gilgamesh has to undertake a long and arduous journey. In the first place he has a nine days' march to the sea, then he takes ship and sails for fifteen days until he at last reaches the home of Ut-napishtim.

There exists, however, another version of the Flood story which has come down to us from Babylonian sources. This is the account of the Chaldean priest Berosus, who says of the hero Sisuthrus : " The deity Cronus appeared to him in a vision, and warned him that upon the fifteenth day of the month Dæsius there would be a flood, which would destroy mankind. He therefore enjoined him to write a history of the beginning, procedure, and conclusion of all things, and to bury it in the City of the Sun at Sippara ; to build a vessel, and take with him into it his friends and relatives, and convey on board everything necessary to sustain life, together with all the different quadrupeds and birds, and trust himself fearlessly to the deep. Having asked the deity whither he was to sail, he was answered, ' To the gods ! ' upon which he offered a prayer for the good of mankind. He then obeyed the divine admonition, and built a vessel five stadia in length and two in breadth, into which he put everything he had prepared, and, last of all, his wife, children, and friends. After the Flood had abated, Sisuthrus sent out birds from the vessel, which, not finding any food nor any place whereupon they might alight, returned to him again. After an interval of some days he sent them forth a second time, and they now returned with their feet tinged with mud. He made a third trial with these birds, but they returned to him no more, from which he judged that the surface of the earth had appeared above the waters. He therefore made an opening in the vessel, and on looking out he found that it was stranded upon the side of a mountain, upon which he immediately quitted it with his wife, his daughter, and the pilot. Sisuthrus then paid his adoration

to the earth, and having constructed an altar, offered
sacrifices to the gods, after which he and those who were
with him instantly disappeared. Those who remained
within, finding that their companions did not return,
quitted the vessel with many lamentations, and continually
called on Sisuthrus by name. Him they saw no more, but
they could distinguish his voice in the air, and could hear
him admonishing them to pay a due regard to religion, and
informing them that he and his friends, on account of their
piety, were translated to live with the gods. The vessel was
stranded in Armenia. Some parts of it still remain on the
Corcyrean mountains, and the people scrape off the bitumen
with which it was outwardly coated and use it for amulets
and bracelets."

There is little doubt that both of these Babylonian accounts
are of much older origin than at first sight would appear
probable. Indeed their provenance would seem to be
Sumerian, the gift of an older civilisation to the less cultured
Babylonians. A fragmentary version of the Flood story discovered by American excavators at Nippur is couched in the
non-Semitic tongue of this ancient people, and was written,
it is estimated, about 2100 B.C. But by this epoch the
Sumerian tongue was practically a dead language, the sacred
or hieratic speech of Babylonia, so that the story it enshrined
was bound to be much more venerable than the date alluded
to would lead us to suppose. There is every reason to
believe that it is merely a copy from a much older tablet.
The presumption is strong that the Deluge legend dates
from a time anterior to the occupation of the country by
the Semites. The German Oriental Society in excavating
the site of Shurippak on the Euphrates discovered Sumerian
tablets believed to have been written not later than 3400 B.C.
It was at Shurippak that the Deluge was thought of as
originating, and there are traces there which seem to imply
that the site was once destroyed by flooding. But the

story must have been even more ancient than the date mentioned above, perhaps not much later than the epoch of the submergence of Atlantis. It bears every sign of a hoary antiquity, and its circumstances were probably confounded at a later era with the local deluge at Shurippak.

It may be profitable to examine briefly such later traces of the cataclysm story as remain to us in the traditions of the more modern Semitic races. " These," says Parker in his *Legends and Traditions of the Old Testament,* " tell us some curious stories relative to the fate of those old and exterminated tribes, the origin of which is easily distinguished. The tribe of Ad, descended from Ad, the son of Uz, the great-grandson of Noah, after the confusion of tongues at the Dispersion of Mankind, settled in the province of Hadramaut, in Arabia, in a district called Al Akkaf, or the Winding Sands. The first king of this tribe was Shedad, the son of Ad, of whom it is said that he finished a magnificent city his father had begun, and built a fine palace in it, adorned with delightful gardens, for which he spared neither cost nor labour, because he wished to inculcate in his tribe a superstitious veneration of himself as a deity. This garden or paradise was called the Garden of Irem, and is specially mentioned by Mohammed in the eighty-ninth chapter of the Koran, entitled The Daybreak, revealed, as he pretends, at Mecca. The city, with its gardens, the Arabian writers inform us, is still standing in the deserts of Eden, and is preserved as a monument of Divine justice, but never visible except to those few who are the especial favourites of the Prophet. It happened that a person named Colabah, who was searching for a lost camel, found himself suddenly at the gates of this city, and, finding no inhabitants in it, he speedily retreated in terror. His adventures reached the ears of a certain caliph, who sent for him and examined him on the subject. The honest owner of the lost camel could tell the caliph no more than the above, but as a proof that he had seen the city he produced some fine stones which he had picked up during his short stay.

" The legend assigns the cause of the desolation of this city in the manner stated by the Moslem apostle himself. The Adites, it appears, gradually became gross idolaters; God sent a prophet named Hud [1] to reclaim them, but they refused to listen to him, and therefore they were punished by a hot and suffocating wind, which blew seven nights and eight days without intermission, accompanied by a terrible earthquake, which overthrew their idols and destroyed the tribe, with the exception of a few who believed in the announcements of Hud and returned with him to another place. The traditionary legend states, that before the Adites were thus punished they were afflicted by a severe drought, which lasted for four years, and all their cattle perished. They deputed a personage called Lokman to proceed to Mecca with sixty attendants to beg rain, which not being granted, the said Lokman, with some of his company, remained at Mecca, and thereby escaped destruction. These were the ancestors of a tribe called the Lesser Ad, who were afterwards changed into monkeys! The Prophet Hud, we are told, returned into Hadramaut, and was buried near a place called Hesec, where, it seems, a small town still standing is designated Kahr Hud, or the 'Sepulchre of Hud.'"

The strong resemblance of this legend to that given in the Central American Popol Vuh will at once occur to the reader. Here we find the hot fiery winds, the earthquake, and the metamorphosis of men into monkeys. Yet the races who preserved their respective stories were separated by more than half the circumference of the globe! Is it not indulging the " credulity of incredulity " to assert that these so strongly similar traditions are of independent

[1] Otherwise Heber, whom the Jews acknowledge to have been a prophet.

origin, and that they did not spring from one common source ? Is it not, indeed, quite obvious that they did so ?

But an even more extraordinary justification of the underlying truth of the circumstances of the Atlantean tradition is to be encountered in the Oriental legends connected with Enoch, the descendant of Adam in the fifth generation. Eusebius maintains that he was acknowledged by the Babylonians as the inventor of astrology, and *that he is the Atlas of the Greeks*. Several of the Christian Fathers connect him with the " angels," or supernatural race who wed with the daughters of men.

Several Greek legends relating to the Flood have already been alluded to, but these may well be added to for the sake of comparison. " I have heard in Greece," says Lucian, " what the Greeks say of Deucalion. The present race of men, they allege, is not the first, for they totally perished, but a second generation, who, being descended from Deucalion, increased to a great multitude. Of those former men they thus speak—they were insolent, and addicted to unjust actions ; they neither regarded oaths, nor were they hospitable to strangers, nor listened to suppliants ; and this complicated wickedness was the cause of their destruction. On a sudden the earth poured forth a vast quantity of water, great rains fell, the rivers overflowed, and the sea rose to a prodigious height ; all things became water, and all men were destroyed ; only Deucalion was left for a second race of men, on account of his prudence and piety. He was saved in this manner : He went into a large ark or chest, and when he was within, there entered swine, horses, lions, serpents, and all other creatures which live on earth, by pairs. He received them all, and they did him no hurt, for the gods created a friendship among them, so that they all sailed in one chest whilst the waters prevailed."

That the Romans were conversant with the story of the Deluge is plain from the passage in Ovid's *Metamorphoses*, which so vividly describes it.   That we have here a Roman echo of the Hellenic legend of Atlantis who can doubt ? The men of the Iron Age were so impious and degraded that Jupiter resolved to destroy them at a blow. What followed is given below as translated by the vivid pen of Dryden :—

" Thus ended he ; the greater gods assent,
 By clamours urging his severe intent ;
 The less fill up the cry of punishment.
 Yet still with pity they remember man,
 And mourn as much as heavenly spirits can.
        —But Jove
 Concludes to pour a watery deluge down,
 And what he durst not burn resolves to drown.
 The Northern breath that freezes blood he binds
 With all the race of cloud-dispelling winds.
 The South he loosed, who night and horror brings
 And fogs are shaken from his flaggy wings.
 With rain his robe and heaving mantle flow,
 And lazy mists are lowering on his brow.
 The skies from pole to pole with peals resound,
 And showers enlarged come pouring on the ground.
 Nor from his patrimonial heaven alone
 Is Jove content to pour his vengeance down,
 But from his brother of the seas he craves
 To help him with auxiliary waves.
 The watery tyrant calls his brooks and floods,
 Who roll from mossy caves—their choice abodes—
 The floods, by nature enemies to land,
 And proudly swelling with their new command,
 Remove the living stones that stopp'd their way
 And gushing from their source augment the sea.
 Then with his mace their monarch struck the ground,
 With inward trembling Earth received the wound,
 And rising streams a ready passage found.
 Th' expanded waters gather on the plain,
 They float the fields, and overtop the grain,

Then rushing onwards with a sweeping sway
Bear flocks, and folds, and labouring hinds away.
Nor safe their dwellings were, for, sapp'd by floods,
Their houses fell upon their household gods.
The solid piles, too strongly built to fall,
High o'er their heads behold a watery wall.
Now seas and earth were in confusion lost,
A world of waters, and without a coast.
The most of mortals perish in the flood,
The small remainder die for want of food.
   A mountain of stupendous height there stands
Betwixt the Athenian and Bœotian lands.
Parnassus is its name, whose forky rise
Mounts through the clouds and mates the lofty skies.
High on the summit of this dubious cliff,
Deucalion, wafting, moor'd his little skiff.
He with his wife were only left behind
Of perish'd man ; they two were human kind.
The mountain Nymphs and Thetis they adore,
And from her oracles relief implore.
The most upright of mortal men was he,
The most sincere and holy woman she.
   When Jupiter, surveying earth from high,
Beheld it in a lake of water lie—
That where so many million lately lived,
But two, the best of either sex, survived,
He loos'd the Northern wind ; fierce Boreas flies
To puff away the clouds, and purge the skies.
Serenely, while he blows, the vapours driven,
Discover Heaven to Earth, and Earth to Heaven."

The scene is completed by the deliverance of Deucalion
and Pyrrha from the shallop in which they had been tossed
to and fro over the tempestuous waste of waters.

The legend of Dardanus, whom the Flood overtook in
Samothrace, has a close resemblance in certain of its passages
to that of Atlantis. The natives of Samothrace, according
to Diodorus Siculus, averred that the sea rose and covered

a great part of the level country in their island, and that the survivors fled to the high mountainous land beyond. As a memorial of their salvation from the Deluge they raised landmarks all round the island and built altars on which they continued to sacrifice to the gods for many succeeding generations. Centuries later, fishermen drew up in their nets the stone capitals of pillars, the eloquent witnesses of cities deep drowned in the surrounding sea.

It has generally been assumed that no vestige of Egyptian tradition clings to the legend of the Flood. This is scarcely correct, for Plutarch, Plato, and Diodorus Siculus all speak of Osiris as connected in some manner with the idea of deluge. Plutarch in his description of Osiris entering the fatal chest at the behest of his treacherous brother Set, places the date of that occurrence as in the very month and the same day of the month as that on which Noah was understood to enter the ark—the 17th of November, the second month after the autumnal equinox, when the sun passes through Scorpio.

The Hindus possess a similar flood legend to that found in the Scriptures. "The demon Hayagiwa," says Sir William Jones in his translation, " having purloined the Vedas or sacred books from the custody of Brahma while he was reposing, the whole race of men became corrupt, except the seven Rishis and Satyavrata, who then reigned in Dravira, a maritime region to the south of Carnata. This prince was performing his ablutions in the river Critimala when Vishnu appeared to him in the shape of a small fish, and after several augmentations of bulk in different waters, Satyavrata was placed in the ocean, and was thus addressed by the mysterious stranger : ' In seven days all creatures who have offended me shall be destroyed by a deluge, but thou shalt be preserved in a spacious vessel miraculously formed. Take, therefore, all kinds of medicinal herbs and grain for food, and, together with the seven holy men, your respective wives, and pairs of all animals, enter the Ark without fear. There thou shalt know God face to face, and all thy questions shall be answered.' Saying this he disappeared, and after seven days the ocean began to overflow the coast, and the earth to be flooded by constant showers, when Satyavrata, meditating on the deity, saw a large vessel moving on the waters. It approached towards him, and he entered it, in all respects conforming to the instructions of Vishnu, who, in the form of a vast fish, suffered the vessel to be tied with a great sea-serpent, as with a cable, to his measureless horn. When the deluge ceased Vishnu slew the demon and recovered the Vedas, instructed Satyavrata in divine knowledge, and appointed him the seventh Menu by the name of Vawaswata." This old tradition of the Deluge is also alluded to in an ode by a Hindu poet named Jayadeva: "Thou recoverest the Veda in the waters of the ocean of destruction, placing it joyfully in the bosom of the ark fabricated by thee, O Cesava, assuming the body of a fish. Be victorious, O Heri, Lord of the Universe."

Several European myths of cataclysm have already been alluded to, but in order that the evidence for the widespread character of the Flood legend may be more complete, we may, perhaps, briefly mention others. Perhaps the most celebrated European Flood legend is that of the sunken city of Ys, in Brittany. This picturesque legend tells us that in the early days of the Christian epoch the city of Ys, or Ker-is, was ruled by a prince called Gradlon, surnamed Meur, which in Celtic means "the Great." Gradlon was a saintly and pious man, and acted as patron to Gwennole, founder and first abbé of the first monastery built in Armorica. But besides being a religious man, Gradlon was a prudent prince, and defended his capital of Ys from the invasions of the sea by constructing an immense basin to receive the overflow of the water at high tide. This basin had a secret gate, of which the king alone possessed the key, and which he opened and closed at the necessary times.

Gradlon, as is so often the case with pious men, had a wayward child, the princess Dahut, who, on one occasion, while her father was sleeping, gave a secret banquet to her lover, in which the pair, excited with wine, committed folly after folly, until at last it occurred to the frivolous girl to open the sluice-gate. Stealing noiselessly into her sleeping father's chamber she detached from his girdle the key he guarded so jealously, and opened the gate. The water immediately rushed in and submerged the entire city.

But, as usual, there is more than one version of this interesting legend. The city of Ys, says another account, was a place rich in commerce and the arts, but so given over to luxury as to arouse the ire of St Gwennole, who, in the manner of Jeremiah, foretold its ruin. It was situated where now a piece of water, the Étang de Laval, washes the desolate shores of the Bay of Trespasses—though another version of the tale has it that it stood in the vast basin which now forms the Bay of Douarnenez. A strong dike protected it from the ocean, the sluices only admitting sufficient water for the needs of the town. Gradlon constantly bore round his neck a silver key which opened at the same time the vast sluices and the city gates. He lived in great state in a palace of marble, cedar, and gold, and his only grief was the conduct of his daughter Dahut, who, it is said, " had made a crown of her vices and taken for her pages the seven capital sins." But retribution was at hand, and the wicked city met with sudden destruction, for one night Dahut stole the silver key for the purpose of opening the city gates to admit her lover, and in the darkness by mistake opened the sluices. King Gradlon was awakened by St Gwennole, who commanded him to flee, as the torrent was reaching the palace. He mounted his horse, and, taking his worthless daughter behind him, set off at a gallop, the incoming flood seething and boiling at his steed's fetlocks. The torrent was about to overtake and submerge him when a voice from behind called out : " Throw the demon thou carriest into the sea if thou dost not desire to perish." Dahut at that moment fell from the horse's back into the water and the torrent immediately stopped its course. Gradlon reached Quimper safe and sound, but nothing is said as to his subsequent career.

An ancient ballad on the subject, which, however, bears marks of having been tampered with, states, on the other hand, that Gradlon led his people into extravagances of every kind, and that Dahut received the key from him, the misuse of which precipitated the catastrophe. Dahut, the ballad continues, became a mermaid and haunted the waters which roll over the site of the city where she loved and feasted. " Fisherman," ends the ballad, " have you seen the daughter of the sea combing her golden hair in the midday sun at the fringes of the beach ? " " Yes," replies the fisherman, " I have seen the white daughter of the sea, and I have heard her sing, and her songs were plaintive as the sound of the waves."

The legend of Ys, of the town swallowed up by the sea, is common to the several branches of the Celtic race. In Wales the site of the submerged city is in Cardigan Bay, and in Ireland it is Lough Neagh, as Tom Moore says :—

> " On Lough Neagh's bank as the fisherman strays,
>   When the clear, cold eve's declining,
> He sees the round towers of other days
>   In the wave beneath him shining."

This legend had its rise in an extraordinary story which was given currency to by Giraldus Cambrensis in his *Topography of Ireland*, to the effect that a certain extremely wicked tribe were punished for their sins by the inundation of their territory.

" Now there was a common proverb," says Gerald, " in the mouths of the tribe, that whenever the well-spring of that country was left uncovered (for out of reverence shown to it, from a barbarous superstition, the spring was kept covered and sealed), it would immediately overflow and inundate the whole province, drowning and destroying the whole population. It happened, however, on some occasion that a young woman, who had come to the spring to draw water, after filling her pitcher, but before she had closed the well, ran in great haste to her little boy, whom she heard crying at a spot not far from the spring where she had left him. But the voice of the people is the voice of God ; and on her way back she met such a flood of water from the spring that it swept off her and the boy, and the inundation was so violent that they both, and the whole tribe, with their cattle, were drowned in an hour in this partial and local deluge. The waters, having covered the whole surface of that fertile district, were converted into a permanent lake. A not improbable confirmation of this occurrence is found in the fact that the fishermen in that lake see distinctly under the water, in calm weather, ecclesiastical towers, which, according to the custom of the country, are slender and lofty, and, moreover, round ; and they frequently point them out to strangers travelling through these parts, who wonder what could have caused such a catastrophe."

In the Welsh version of this fascinating legend it is the bard Gwyddno, of the twelfth century, who tells of the downfall of the submerged city, and two of the strophes which occur in his poem are also found in the Breton poem. The Welsh bard may have received the story from Breton sources, or the converse may be the case.

The legend that Cardigan Bay contains a submerged territory is widely known, and strangely enough seems to be corroborated by the shape of the coast-line, the contour of which suggests the subsidence of a large body of land. Like their brothers of Ireland, the fishermen of Wales assert that at low tide they can see the ruins of ancient edifices far down beneath the clear waters of the bay.

Before the days of the French Revolution there was still to be seen at Quimper, between the two towers of the cathedral, a figure of King Gradlon mounted on his faithful courser, but in the stormy year 1793 the name of king was in bad odour and the ignorant populace deprived the statue of its head. However, in 1859, it was restored. Legend attributes the introduction of the vine into Brittany to King Gradlon, and on St Cecilia's Day a regular ritual was gone through in Quimper in connection with his counterfeit presentment. A company of singers mounted on a platform. While they sang a hymn in praise of King Gradlon, one of the choristers, provided with a flagon of wine, a napkin, and a golden hanap (or cup), mounted on the crupper of the king's horse, poured out a cup of wine, which he offered ceremoniously to the lips of the statue and then drank himself, carefully wiped with his napkin the moustache of the king, placed a branch of laurel in his hand, and then threw down the hanap in the midst of the crowd below, in honour of the first planter of the grape in Brittany. To whoever caught the cup before it fell, and presented it uninjured to the chapter, was adjudged a prize of two hundred crowns.

Now it seems to me that about these ceremonial acts there is a distinct savour of traditional practice, that, indeed, a strong background of legend might be discovered behind these practices. Between the cathedral towers of Quimper was placed what seems to have been nothing more or less than an idol of Gradlon Meur, who introduced the vine into Brittany. That Gradlon Meur is the name of a god I have no doubt. The title Meur, Mheur, or Mhor, " great," is attached to several Celtic deities, especially in their later and more modern significance, as, for example, the Cailleach Mheur, or " old-wife," goddess of the Scottish Highlands.

15

And this Gradlon was obviously a deity of deluge, whose strange rites linger in Brittany even to the present day. Note the description of his palace. Does it not recall that of Atlantis in some of its circumstances ? We are told that " a strong dike protected it from the ocean," " an immense basin " was formed " to receive the overflow of the water at high tide," there were gates which opened and closed on the sea-way, as in Atlantis and Carthage, and the palace of Gradlon was of cedar, silver, and gold. The inhabitants of the city were wicked, and retribution followed upon their vices. If the legend of Ys is not a variant of that of Atlantis I am greatly mistaken.

It is, then, pretty obvious from the terms of the legends which have been summarised above, no less than from those of America and elsewhere which were described in an earlier chapter, that practically all of them are more or less distantly connected with one and the same tradition, that, indeed, all can be referred back to a common origin. Time, environment, and other circumstances, have conspired to alter their several details, but not their general tendency; but it is remarkable that out of the whole mass of tradition thus presented can be pieced together practically every single detail as found in the accounts of Plato. This, as Gomme and others have pointed out, is one of the true tests of myth, and is known as " the test of recurrence." Do we find in a number of myths dealing with one especial theme all the elements of a more perfectly expressed story which we possess in a literary form ? If so we are justified in regarding the literary form as approximating to the original myth, as a tradition crystallised in writing, and these portions of the other legends which partially approximate to its circumstances as " broken lights " of the original, which through the chances of time and environment have become altered to chime in with local topography or religious prejudice.

CHAPTER XVIII

CONCLUSION

IT may seem merely impertinent in the present fragmentary condition of our knowledge to make any attempt to reconstruct the conditions of life in Atlantis. But what has been set down in these pages affords us more than a mere misty vision of the island-continent, indeed the assemblage of the proof it contains would seem to go far to provide us with an outline and summary of Atlantean life.

And first as regards the race itself. This appears to have been composite, as was only natural in the case of peoples spread over a broad oceanic belt. Thus the Aurignacians or Crô-Magnons, the first Atlantean wave in Europe, were exceptionally tall, sons of the gods indeed, the male height averaging from 6 ft. 1 in. to 6 ft. 7 in., although the women were small, the proof of a mixed race. They were fair or brunette in pigmentation, and probably had blue or brown eyes, like the Guanches of the Canaries. The second immigrant race, the Azilian-Tardenoisians, were shorter in stature, and darker in colouring, and I venture to deduce from their maritime habits that they were originally an insular people, possibly inhabiting some of the larger islands to the west of Atlantis, from which Celtic tradition would seem to make them come. I allude, of course, to the Fomorians, who are spoken of in Irish legend as arriving in Erin from " the West."

It seems clear from the state of culture of these races when they first arrived in the Biscay region that Atlantis, at the date of their departure, was as yet in the Stone Age.

But this by no means implies that the civilisation they had was of a low degree. The cultures of ancient Mexico and Central America were still in the Stone Age when discovered by Europeans, but, nevertheless, displayed to their conquerors a condition of life quite as advanced, as complex, and as colourful as was that of China a generation ago. They possessed a social system which was obviously the result of ages of civilised usage, and a well-digested legal code equal to any human emergency, with well-developed arts and crafts.

We may, indeed, regard the Atlantis of the period antedating the final catastrophe as enjoying a civilisation closely akin to that of ancient Central America. Its architecture we can envisage as of a type likely to hold in embryo the architectural tendencies of both Egypt and Mexico—the pyramid based on the conception of the sacred hill, and crowned by a shrine or temple. Probably these structures were of earth faced with stone, and not of stone alone, as in Egypt, where the pyramid was obviously a memory of the sacred hill, and earth was unprocurable. We must also regard the Babylonian or Sumerian Ziggurat, or temple, as evolved from the idea of the hill crowned by the shrine, as all Assyriologists admit. Atlantean dwelling-houses would probably resemble those common in both Egypt and Mexico; that is, they would in all likelihood be constructed from brick or adobe sun-dried from mud.

The religion of the Atlanteans must have approximated to those of Egypt and Mexico—not that it was likely to partake of the gloomy horrors of the latter, which were of relatively late introduction. The spirit underlying both Mexican and Egyptian religion was the same—the worship of nature and natural forces—as evinced in wind, water, and growth. Doubtless the gods of Atlantis resembled those of the other two countries alluded to, and their system of religious polity or theology was probably the prototype of those ancient mysteries which are found both in the East and in America, and have so powerfully influenced the practice of all mystical societies even to the present day. We may regard the Osirian religion in Egypt and that described in the Quiche Popol Vuh of Guatemala as approximating to that of ancient Atlantis—that is a faith of which the idea of resurrection after death was the very core of belief, and which was in some manner connected with the growth of the crops as symbolic of bodily resurrection. There must also have been associated with it that cult of the twin which is so widespread, and which has examples in Asiatic, European, and American faiths.

The government of Atlantis appears to have been monarchical, yet this monarchy was limited so far as its dependence upon the heavenly powers was concerned. It was, in fact, a theocracy, precisely as were the Mexican and Egyptian types of government. No measure of real national importance could be initiated without first receiving full sanction for it from the gods. So it was in Egypt, where the gods were consulted on every possible occasion as regards matters of government, and the same holds good of Mexico, whose tlatoani, or king, was merely the mouthpiece of the holy oracles.

It must be clear, then, to anyone of disciplined imagination, if not to the pedant, that from some such centre as Atlantis the seeds of civilisation were spread broadcast over Europe and North Africa. It is plain from what has gone before, as from the admission of men of science, that the culture-bed of the world's civilisation is " officially " unknown. In some nucleus irretrievably lost so far as its material manifestations are concerned, and untraceable by ordinary means, the knowledge of the arts and the refinements which differentiate man from the lower races which preceded him had their first inception. The races who found refuge in European soil from the wreck and catastrophe of this lost continent have been proved by the labours of archæologists to have been of a physical type superior to any at present existing, to have possessed that greater cranial capacity which is the undoubted mark of distinguished mental ability. A consensus of opinion also exists among anthropologists that the first wave of the Atlantean race, the Crô-Magnons, were instrumental in bringing to European soil the seeds of its present civilisation, and, as has been shown, this culture progressed not from East to West, as has been asserted so frequently and with such blind and positive dogmatism, but from West to East. A soil more congenial to the immediate incubation and flowering of Atlantean genius may at first have been encountered by it in Egypt and the East, where conditions probably approximated more closely to those of the old island home. But in the event the renaissance of the Crô-Magnon spirit as evinced in the rise of the several British races in later times, once it had been acclimatised to these regions, far outstripped Oriental advancement. If a patriotic Scotsman may be pardoned the boast, I may say that I devoutly believe that Scotland's admitted superiority in the mental and spiritual spheres springs almost entirely from the preponderant degree of Crô-Magnon blood which certainly runs in the veins of her people, whose height and cranial capacity, as well as other physical signs, show them to be mostly of Crô-Magnon race. England, too, undoubtedly draws much of her sanity, her physical prowess and marked superiority in the things of the mind from the same source, and if much of her blood be Iberian, is not that too Atlantean, and has that admixture not pre-eminently endowed her with the greatest poets who ever touched the harp? To an admixture of Crô-Magnon and Iberian blood we owe the genius of Shakespeare and Burns, Massinger and Ben Jonson. Milton, Scott, and, to come to our own times, Mr H. G. Wells and Mr Galsworthy are almost purely Crô-Magnon—indeed our literary types strongly resemble the carefully designed bust of a Crô-Magnon man executed under scientific supervision by a distinguished Belgian sculptor.

The general inadequacy and tentative nature of this essay will have made it plain to the discriminating reader that we are only on the threshold of the great quest for the bones of drowned Atlantis. Nothing is to be gained by dogmatic assertion. In these pages enthusiasm has doubtless frequently outstripped caution and even probability, but if errors and false hypotheses are to be encountered therein, I must plead that these are due to a spirit of experiment. and archæological enterprise, and that in any case they should not be taken as stultifying future effort in the unravelling of a great human problem, with which more incisive minds will assuredly busy themselves in the near future. My desire has been to clear the ground, to provide a basis and outline in virtue of which other students may proceed to a more worthy elaboration and excogitation of what appears to me a vital chapter in human origins and advancement. Perhaps many of the points I have tried to make are worthless and merit the condemnation which I doubt not they will receive. But I would plead that the case I have so weakly endeavoured to set forth should not be judged by the shortcomings of its advocate. Many more worthy causes have found protagonists who were moved to plead on their behalf by a feeling of inward certainty to justify which they could bring only inadequate proof and expression, and among these I may be numbered. But however poor my testimony, the intuition which inspired it remains powerful and irrefragable, indestructible, indeed, as the world-memory of that ancient and original culture I have attempted to unveil.

Yes, there is more, much more, than mere material proof to be considered in relation to such questions as that which we have been discussing. Atlantis sleeps beneath the seas.

But not reason alone, nor the apparatus of scholarship, will, in the end, serve to probe her ancient mysteries. Men of insight have written of strange visions, and of stranger supernatural communications they have been vouchsafed regarding her pristine life. In many quarters these have been received with scorn. In some cases their content and testimony appear to me as highly improbable, having regard to the proven facts of science. But for my own part I would hasten to say that I am too ignorant of the powers of the human soul to weigh the evidence they present with justice and impartiality. Imagination, vision, if rightly interpreted and utilised, is one of the most powerful aids to historical and archæological understanding; and the ability to cast an eagle glance down the avenues of the ages is, it seems to me, but one of the first steps in psychic progress.